£14.99

CU00647819

CATHOLIC
STAFFORDSHIRE
1500–1850

Ad Maiorem Dei Gloriam

CATHOLIC STAFFORDSHIRE 1500–1850

Michael Greenslade

GRACEWING

First published in 2006

Gracewing
2 Southern Avenue
Leominster
Herefordshire HR6 0QF

UK ISBN 0 85244 655 1
978 0 85244 655 3

Typeset by Action Publishing Technology Ltd,
Gloucester GL1 5SR
Printed by
Biddles Ltd, King's Lynn PE30 4LS

CONTENTS

ABBREVIATIONS

Anstruther, *Seminary Priests*	G. Anstruther, *The Seminary Priests* i (St Edmund's College, Ware, and Ushaw College, Durham, no date; foreword dated 1968); ii (Great Wakering, 1975); iii (Great Wakering, 1976); iv (Great Wakering, 1977)
B.A.A.	Birmingham Archdiocesan Archives, Cathedral House, St Chad's Queensway, Birmingham
C.R.S.	*Catholic Record Society*
Cal. S.P. Dom.	*Calendar of State Papers, Domestic Series*
Complete Peerage	G. E. C[okayne], *The Complete Peerage*
Foley, *English Province S.J.*	H. Foley, *Records of the English Province of the Society of Jesus*
L.R.O.	Lichfield Record Office

Mid. Cath. Hist.	*Midland Catholic History* (the Journal of the Midland Catholic History Society)
Oxford D.N.B.	*Oxford Dictionary of National Biography* (2004)
S.H.C.	*Collections for a History of Staffordshire* (Staffordshire Record Society, formerly William Salt Archaeological Society)
v (2)	H. S. Grazebrook, *The Heraldic Visitations of Staffordshire made by Sir Richard St George, Norroy, in 1614 and by Sir William Dugdale, Norroy, in the years 1663 and 1664* (1885)
new series, v	G. Wrottesley, 'The Giffards' (1902)
1915	W. N. Landor, *Staffordshire Incumbents and Parochial Records (1530–1680)* (1916)
4th series, ix	A. G. Petti (ed.), *Roman Catholicism in Elizabethan and Jacobean Staffordshire: Documents from the Bagot Papers* (1979)
S.R.O.	Staffordshire Record Office
Shaw, *Staffs.*	S. Shaw, *The History and Antiquities of Staffordshire*, i (1798); ii (1801)

Staffs. Cath. Hist.	*Staffordshire Catholic History* (the Journal of the Staffordshire Catholic History Society)
iii, pp. 1–23	F. Roberts, 'The Society of Jesus in Staffordshire' (1963)
xiv	'Catholic Chapels in Staffordshire', from *The Catholic Magazine and Review*, v (1834) and vi (1835) – (1974)
xvii	M. W. Greenslade, 'The 1767 Return of Staffordshire Papists' (1977)
xx, pp. 1–25	'Historical Sketches of Catholic Missions', from *The Official Catholic Directory of the Province of Birmingham* (1981)
V.C.H. Staffs.	*Victoria County History of Staffordshire*
iii, pp. 99–115	M. W. Greenslade, 'Roman Catholicism'
W.S.L.	William Salt Library, Stafford

ILLUSTRATIONS

Note: Staffordshire Views and S1905 (bound volumes of printed portraits) are collections in the William Salt Library, Stafford, and are reproduced, along with other items from the Library, by permission of the Trustees. Items from St Mary's College, Oscott, are reproduced by permission of the College.

Masters of the Guild of SS. Mary and John the Baptist, Lichfield, John Jennens and Richard Watwode. From the guild book. *Pages 4 and 5*.

St Peter's, Wolverhampton. Lithograph (1838) by C. Burton (from a drawing by R. Noyes) in Staffordshire Views, xii. 90b. *Page 8*.

St John's Hospital, Lichfield. Drawing by J. Buckler, 1833, in Staffordshire Views, v. 248. *Page 10*.

St James's, Barton-under-Needwood. Drawing by J. Buckler, 1839, in Staffordshire Views, i. 133. *Page 11*.

Croxden Abbey. remains of the east range of the cloister and of the south transept of the church. Watercolour drawing by J. Buckler, 1839, in Staffordshire Views, iii. 174. *Page 14*.

Trentham Church and Hall. R. Plot, *The Natural History of*

Staffordshire (Oxford, 1686), plate XXIII (between pp. 266–7). *Page 18.*

Canon Arthur Dudley removing some of St Chad's bones from Lichfield Cathedral in 1538. A window designed by Donald Taunton of John Hardman & Co. in 1932, one of a series telling the story of the relics of St Chad in St Edward's Chapel, St Chad's Cathedral, Birmingham. Photograph by Fr Peter Dennison, reproduced by permission of the Dean of the Cathedral. *Page 20.*

Stourton Castle. S. Shaw, *The History and Antiquities of Staffordshire*, ii (1801), facing p. 267. *Page 26.*

Orphreys on the vestments at St Mary's, Cresswell. Reproduced by permission of Fr Jan Nowotnik. *Pages 29–31.*

Hamstall Ridware Church and Manor House. S. Shaw, *The History and Antiquities of Staffordshire*, i (1798), facing p. 157. *Page 42.*

Chillington Hall in the early eighteenth century. Detail from Staffordshire Record Office, D590/363b. Reproduced by permission of the Record Office. *Page 46.*

Sandon Hall. R. Plot, *The Natural History of Staffordshire* (Oxford, 1686), plate IV (between pp. 60–1). *Page 47.*

Tutbury Castle about the time of the imprisonment there of Mary, Queen of Scots. Engraving (1733) in Staffordshire Views, xi. 74, based on a late sixteenth-century drawing in the National Archives (Public Record Office), MR1/17. *Page 54.*

A pane from a window formerly at Hall Hill, Abbots Bromley, and now in the William Salt Library. *Page 58.*

St Edmund Gennings, with depictions of his arrest and his hanging, drawing and quartering. John Gennings, *The Life*

Bonaventure Giffard, Vicar Apostolic of the Midland District 1688–1703 and of the London District 1703–1734. Painting by R. van Bleeck at Archbishop's House, Westminster, reproduced by permission of the Cardinal Archbishop of Westminster. *Page 150.*

The Deanery, Wolverhampton. Drawing by J. Buckler, 1837, in Staffordshire Views, xii. 88b. *Page 152.*

George Witham, Vicar Apostolic of the Midland District 1703–16 and of the Northern District 1716–25: J. Gillow, *St. Thomas's Priory* (no date, mid to later 1890s), facing p. 82. *Page 162.*

Longbirch. Drawing by T. P. Wood, 1838, in Staffordshire Views, ii.136a. *Page 164.*

Giffard House, Wolverhampton. Reproduced by permission of Wolverhampton City Council. *Page 172.*

Sedgley Park School. Drawing and aquatint engraving (*c.*1797) by R. Paddey in Staffordshire Views, viii. 152. *Page 176.*

John Philip Kemble as Hamlet. Engraving (1827) by H. Dawe (from a painting by Sir Thomas Lawrence) dedicated to Sarah Siddons, Kemble's sister, in S1905, v. 21. *Page 178.*

The Chapel at Sedgley Park School. F. C. Husenbeth, *The History of Sedgley Park School, Staffordshire* (1856), facing p. 56. *Page 180.*

Swynnerton Hall. Drawing by J. Buckler, 1841, in Staffordshire Views, x. 61. *Page 182.*

Chillington Hall: plan of the ground floor of the mid-Tudor house. Staffordshire Record Office, D590/571d. Reproduced by permission of the Record Office. *Page 186.*

Chillington Hall. plan of the ground floor of the house of the late 1780s. Drawing by John Soane, 1789, in Staffordshire Views, iii. 107a. *Page 187.*

Thomas Giffard the younger *c*.1784. Painting by P. Batoni at Chillington Hall, reproduced by permission of Mr J. Giffard. *Page 188.*

Chillington Hall. Drawing by J. Buckler, 1843, in Staffordshire Views, iii. 101*. *Page 191.*

The Chapel at Black Ladies. Drawing by T. P. Wood, 1837, in Staffordshire Views, ii. 140a. *Page 192.*

John Milner, Vicar Apostolic of the Midland District 1803–26. Engraving (1819) by W. Radclyffe (from a painting of 1816 by J. V. Barber at Oscott College) in S1905, vi. 7. *Page 208.*

John Kirk. Carved portrait at Oscott College. *Page 210.*

Francis Martyn. Drawing at Oscott College. *Page 214.*

St Mary's, Walsall. Photograph of *c*.1920, reproduced from the Collections of Walsall Local History Centre, Essex Street, Walsall. *Page 215.*

George Spencer (from 1846 the Passionist Fr Ignatius). *Page 216.*

Holy Trinity, Newcastle-under-Lyme. Drawing by J. Buckler, 1840, in Staffordshire Views, vii. 94. *Page 218.*

Detail from the Whitgreave memorial window in the church of SS. Joseph and Etheldreda, Rugeley. Photograph reproduced by permission of Fr Peter Stonier. *Page 222.*

The Benedictine Nuns at Caverswall Castle. Aquatint engraving (1817) by T. Sutherland in Staffordshire Views, iii. 43. *Page 226.*

St Mary's Convent, Handsworth. A. W. Pugin, *The Present State of Ecclesiastical Architecture in England* (1843; reprinted in facsimile by Gracewing, 2004), facing p. 102. *Page 230.*

The Chapel at Tixall. Drawing by J. Buckler, 1841, in Staffordshire Views, xi. 24. *Page 232.*

St Mary's College, Old Oscott (later Maryvale). Engraving (1819) by R. Roffe (from a drawing by F. C. Husenbeth) in Staffordshire Views, vii. 19b. *Page 240.*

Lord Shrewsbury, John Hardman junior, and A. W. N. Pugin. A window of 1987 by David Cowan of John Hardman Studios in the Oratory Chapel at St Mary's Convent, Handsworth, one of four telling the story of the coming of the Sisters of Mercy to Handsworth. Photograph reproduced by permission of the Convent. *Page 242.*

St Mary's, Uttoxeter. Drawing by J. Buckler, 1839, in Staffordshire Views, xi. 112. *Page 244.*

St John's Hospital, Alton. A. W. Pugin, *The Present State of Ecclesiastical Architecture in England* (1843; reprinted in facsimile by Gracewing, 2004), between pp. 86 and 87. *Page 245.*

St Giles's, Cheadle. Drawing by J. Buckler, 1847, in Staffordshire Views, iii. 64. *Page 250.*

St Giles's, Cheadle, the north aisle. *Illustrated London News*, 9 January 1847. *Page 251.*

The casket containing the relics of St Chad in St Chad's Cathedral, Birmingham. Photograph by Fr Peter Dennison, reproduced by permission of the Dean of the Cathedral. *Page 254.*

PREFACE

In the last half-century there has been a revolution in the study of English Catholic history since the Reformation in this country. In 1952 the subject could still be described as 'the Cinderella among historical studies' – despite the considerable amount of writing over the previous century, including the work of the Catholic Record Society. By 1965 a reviewer could see the subject as 'almost a major historical industry nowadays'. (See Alan Davidson in *The Local Historian*, ix, no. 6). Forty years on the 'almost' can be dropped; it is no longer so much a question of what it felt like to be martyred by hanging, drawing and quartering as what it was to be an ordinary Catholic under Elizabeth I or Charles II or George III. The revolution, in part an aspect of the revolution in local history over a similar period, has produced books, articles, journals, theses and conferences, with an abundance of source material becoming steadily more available.

Staffordshire has been well to the fore. The trigger here was Archbishop Grimshaw's opening of the archives at Archbishop's House, Birmingham, with listing begun in 1956 and a diocesan archivist appointed in 1957; there is now a repository in Cathedral House which is a model of a modern record office. As a result fresh archive material for Staffordshire has become readily available. The Staffordshire Catholic History Society was formed in 1961 and produced twenty-four issues of a journal, *Staffordshire Catholic History*. The journal was merged with that of the Worcestershire Catholic History Society in 1991 to produce *Midland Catholic History*, and the two societies were merged in 1996 to form the Midland Catholic History Society. Both journals include editions of archive material as well as articles. In 1984 the Archdiocese of Birmingham Historical Commission was established by Archbishop Maurice Couve de Murville mainly to produce booklets on the history of the area covered by the archdiocese, an area of which Staffordshire is the most northerly county; to date eighteen such booklets have been published. The Staffordshire Victoria County History includes accounts of Catholic missions in all its topographical volumes, and its general volume on ecclesiastical history has a section on the history of Catholicism in the county. The Staffordshire Record Society too has included Catholic material in its volumes. And only last September two dissertations on Catholicism in two different parts of the county were submitted for the Keele University MA in Local History

It therefore seems useful to attempt an overview of Staffordshire Catholicism since the Reformation. Some further original research has been necessary, but in the main the story has been told from printed sources, primary and secondary, local and national. Much detail has had to be omitted and remains to be written up in a different context, and many topics have still to be investigated. Too few missions have had their history written; subjects such as the inter-marriage of Catholic families and Irish immigration await their chronicler; and questions have still to be answered such as what was it to be a Catholic in, say, Wolverhampton or Brewood or the Potteries or even in Staffordshire generally as compared with, say, County Durham. The year 1850 has been taken as a convenient and indeed significant terminus; but the ever-lengthening story since then has still to be told.

The Staffordshire treated here is the historic county, before the changes of the nineteenth century and after. Harborne and Handsworth, transferred to Birmingham in 1891 and 1911, therefore appear in the story, Handsworth being particularly relevant with the mission centred on Old Oscott (now Maryvale), the Stamford and Hardman families, and the convent of the Sisters of Mercy. The borough of Dudley on the other hand remained an enclave of Worcestershire until 1966; Dudley Castle, however, was declared part of Staffordshire by papal decree in 1298 and has been included in chapter 3.

Very many people have helped in different ways in the preparation of this book, and I thank them all. Special thanks are due to Thea Randall, William Salt Librarian and Staffordshire County Archivist, and to her staff: in particular to Dominic Farr and Margaret Heath at the William Salt Library, to Joanna Terry and Matthew Blake at the County Record Office, and to Martin Sanders at Lichfield Record Office. Similar thanks are due to successive Birmingham archdiocesan archivists, and especially the present archivist, Dr John Sharp. I also want to thank fellow members of the Midland Catholic History Society and the Archdiocese of Birmingham Historical Commission, in particular Fr Brian Doolan and Michael Hodgetts. Further thanks are due to the owners of items used in the illustrations as noted in the list of illustrations and to those who have helped with photographing and supplying items – Margaret Heath again, Judith Champ and Christopher Howard of Oscott College, Sister Barbara Jeffery, archivist at St Mary's Convent, Handsworth, Julie Pate of the Regeneration and Environment Marketing Team, Wolverhampton City Council, Corinna Rayner, archivist at Walsall Local History Centre, Walsall Metropolitan Borough Council, Nigel Tringham, editor of the Staffordshire Victoria County History, and David Wakefield of Peter Rogers (Photographic) Ltd., Stafford. I owe a special debt to Ian Atherton and George Baugh, each of whom has read the whole book in manuscript, corrected many mistakes, and made a great number of valuable suggestions for improvements.

At Wimbledon College in the early 1940s the Jesuits made us preface our homework with the letters A.M.D.G. (Ad Maiorem Dei Gloriam – To the Greater Glory of God) and round it off with L.D.S. (Laus Deo Semper – Praise to God Always). It has to be admitted that much of the work presented between those sentiments was unworthy of them. I hope, however, that after placing them before this latest piece of homework I have been able to do some honour to those teachers who laid the foundations so many years ago.

Michael Greenslade
Pentecost 2005

PUBLISHER'S NOTE

It is very sad to record that, just under four weeks after writing the Preface to his book, Michael Greenslade died. During the book's course through the press the proofs were checked by Michael's friends and colleagues George Baugh and Michael Hodgetts, and the index was compiled by George Baugh.

1

THE END OF CATHOLIC STAFFORDSHIRE: 1500-1559

In 1232 a grant of property was made to Hulton abbey in north Staffordshire with the condition that the monks should celebrate a daily Mass for the souls of the benefactor and others 'all the days of the world'. In the event that world lasted three centuries, and the days came to an abrupt end on 18 September 1538 when the monks surrendered their abbey to Henry VIII.

Yet it was part of a Reformation which few in Staffordshire seem to have expected or wanted. In the early sixteenth century the pious practices of the Middle Ages were alive and well. Religious guilds flourished along with chantries and other commemorations. Lights before statues in churches continued to be endowed. Church building continued, and schools were founded. Clerical life, secular and religious, was ticking over, even though fervour was not much in evidence. As for heresy, Lollardy had never had much influence in Staffordshire.

∼

Religious guilds offered spiritual welfare now and hereafter. Even villages had their guilds, though records are sparse. In his will of 1534 Sir Lewis Bagot of Blithfield left land and a two-year-old heifer to Our Lady's guild in nearby Abbots Bromley.[1] Several such guilds existed at the time of the suppression under the Chantries Act of 1547. The Moorlands parish of Alstonefield had a guild of the Blessed Mary. At Eccleshall the inhabitants had established two guilds, St Catherine's and Our Lady's. The two priests, who were supported partly from rents and partly from 'gatherings' among the inhabitants, had the duty of celebrating Mass daily and teaching poor children free of charge. Penkridge had a Trinity guild with a priest paid a salary of 8 marks (£5 6s. 8d.) a year from endowments.[2] At Wednesbury Our Lady's guild may have been founded in the early sixteenth century: at least it was receiving endowments in 1528. Its purpose was the maintenance of a priest celebrating at Our Lady's altar in the parish church 'for ever'. He was being paid a salary of £4 3s. at the time of the guild's suppression in 1548, and he was then given a pension of £4.[3]

At Lichfield the guild of St Mary and St John the Baptist attached to St Mary's church was founded in 1387 as an amalgamation of two earlier guilds.[4] Annual admissions had peaked at 160 in the late fifteenth century and averaged ninety-three in the early sixteenth century. In the early 1540s the figure was fifty, and even in 1546–7, with dissolution imminent, the last enrolment totalled eleven. Membership, which included men and women, continued to be drawn not just from Lichfield but from a wide circle of ecclesiastical notables, including bishops of the diocese and heads of Midlands religious houses, and from Staffordshire gentry with a sprinkling of nobility; even Henry VII was enrolled in 1487 and his queen in 1494. The clergy were well represented. Posthumous admissions were made from the time of the guild's establishment, a reflection of its role as an intercessor for the dead as well the living, and such admissions became particularly numerous in the sixteenth century. The guild had always played an important part in the government of Lichfield. It also exercised influence in the affairs of St Mary's church in the centre of the city. The guild's four chaplains were active in the liturgy there, and it supported two children who sang daily in the church. It supported two parish clerks, and the churchwardens evidently presented their accounts to the guild. When the cathedral and the diocesan authorities were in dispute over the right of appointing the vicar of St Mary's in the early 1530s, the master of the guild intervened 'with the counsel of my brethren and of all and singular other inhabitants of the city and suburbs': the settlement of the dispute in 1532 was sealed by him in the guildhall.

The guild continued to rule from beyond its grave. In 1545 the master, Hector Beane, seeing which way the wind was blowing, proceeded to thwart the Crown's designs on the guild. Acting with the consent of the guild, he settled most of its land lying outside Lichfield on trustees for the maintenance of the town's water supply and for the general good of the inhabitants; that part of the guild's property was thus saved from falling into the hands of the Crown. The trust continued to supply water to the town until the twentieth century and has been extensively involved in other public works including education. The presence of coal under the land resulted in a sharp rise in the trust's income from the 1840s.[5] The guild's influence also continued in the town's government. When Lichfield received its incorporation by royal charter in 1548, the senior of the two bailiffs and twelve of the twenty-four brethren were former masters of the guild and another six of the brethren had been guild wardens. Council meetings were held in the former guildhall in Bore Street.[6]

Walsall had two guilds, which were amalgamated in 1520. That of St John the Baptist was founded by 1390 and attached to the chapel of St John in the parish church.[7] In the early sixteenth century it had over 300 members, both men and women, of whom well over half lived outside the parish and included persons of importance. Its guildhall in High Street was also the town hall of the borough. There was a guild of St Mary by 1471. The chantries in the parish church were subject to the supervision of one or other of the guilds: borough ordinances of the early sixteenth century laid down that when chantries fell vacant the officials of the relevant guild were to ensure that the patrons swiftly appointed priests 'able in conyng of pryksonge' and of good life, 'neither disars ne cardars'. The guilds were amalgamated in 1520 when St

The Guild of St Mary and St John the Baptist, Lichfield, guild book:

(a) Portrait of John Jennens (Gennings), master 1535.

The Guild of St Mary and St John the Baptist, Lichfield, guild book:

(b) Rebus of Richard Watwode, master 1538 ('wat' being a dialect word for a hare).

John's was refounded and attached to both St John's chapel and that of St Mary. It had seven chaplains, celebrating daily for the King, the Queen and the guild members.

At Burton a guild, with a chapel dedicated to St Luke, was apparently open to all parishioners. In the 1530s and 1540s several testators made gifts of 3s. 4d. in return for which their names were inscribed in the guild book and prayers were said for their souls. The four guild priests had £4 13s. 4d. a year each, raised by festivities to which parishioners brought 'a dish of meat . . . to make merry'; any deficit was met from the lands of the guild. As at Lichfield some of this land found its way into the lands owned by the inhabitants of Burton.[8]

Concern for the dead was also reflected in the continuing support and foundation of chantries and other forms of provision for prayers for the dead. At Kinver in 1514 Thomas Perot assigned the income from land there to the existing chantry of St Mary in the parish church, with the unusual condition that after ninety years the money was to be used 'in the maintenance of God's service' and other charitable works. More land was later given by other benefactors.[9] At nearby Wombourne John Woodhouse by will proved in 1523 left 3s. 4d. to the chantry of St Mary in the parish church and money to provide tapers at St Mary's altar. His son Stephen left the chantry a further 3s. 4d. in his will proved in 1528.[10] The founding of perpetual chantries was forbidden by statute in 1532, but temporary endowments persisted. In 1533 Edmund Wetton of Stockley Park in Tutbury left £5 to support a priest chosen by the vicar of Tutbury to pray for him and his wife for a year.[11] Sir Lewis Bagot provided not only for the Abbots Bromley guild in 1534 but also for his own soul, leaving 40s. a year and meat and drink for a priest 'to sing for me' in Blithfield church for two years.[12] At Leek Edmund Washington in his will proved in 1537 left £26 13s. 4d. to the new chapel of St Catherine in the parish church to provide a stock for the support of a priest to pray for the souls of Edmund's father and mother and their children; he directed that his son William 'shall sing for me if he will as long as the stock doth last'. Edmund further directed that he was to be buried 'in my own form before St Catherine'.[13] In 1538 Robert Swynnerton, rector of Blymhill, made numerous bequests to secure prayers for his soul, notably £5 to John Collins, probably his confessor and probably a curate at neighbouring Sheriffhales, 'to sing a year in Blymhill church to pray for my soul and my father's and mother's souls if my goods will perform it'.[14]

Endowments continued almost up to the Act of 1547 which completed the attack on chantries begun by an Act of 1545. In a will of 1544 Stephen Dolman of Seisdon in Trysull parish not only left 8d. to the Lady altar in the parish church, where there was already a chantry, but also directed his son and heir Thomas to find a priest to pray in the church for the souls of Thomas, his wife and his ancestors for a year. In 1545 Thomas Barnsley of Seisdon provided for a trental of Masses at the Lady altar for his soul, those of his father and mother, and all Christian souls.[15] At Leekfrith in 1544 William Gent left 2s. to the stock of St Anthony for the maintenance of God's service in the chapel at Meerbrook, a reference to either a chantry or a religious guild.[16] In 1546 Henry Slany, vicar of Bushbury, made bequests to local priests to secure Masses for his soul.[17] As late as January 1547 Robert Lees, an ironmonger of Stafford, having directed in his will that he should be buried in St Mary's collegiate church there, provided for four obits a year to be said by one of the priests; 5d. was to be paid to the priest and 1d. to the bellman.[18]

Another way of providing for the souls of the departed is to be found in a document of the early 1530s listing families in the archdeaconry of Stafford grouped by parish and town.[19] They were probably contributors to the fabric fund of Lichfield cathedral earning spiritual benefits thereby. There are nearly 55,000 names. A large number were deceased, marked with a cross and usually the parents, wives or children of the living listed; in the case of the Bagots of Blithfield grandparents were named, while eight generations were given for the Griffith family of Wychnor. The Colwyke family of Town

St Peter's, Wolverhampton.

Well Street, Wolverhampton, were also determined to be inclusive: besides Nicholas, his wife Joan and ten children there were Nicholas's deceased wife Margery and 'the sowlis of xiij departed'.[20] It is clear that the living were concerned to secure benefits not only for themselves but for their deceased relatives as well.

∽

Popular devotions flourished. St Chad's richly adorned shrine in Lichfield cathedral continued to attract pilgrims and their offerings.[21] At Burton the island in the Trent known as Andresey remained sacred to the memory of St Modwen, the Irish abbess who was supposed to have built a church there dedicated to St Andrew at some date between the fifth and ninth centuries and to have been buried there until her remains were translated to the nearby abbey endowed at the beginning of the eleventh century. Her shrine attracted pilgrims, and by the 1530s there was an image of the saint 'with her red cow and her staff which women labouring of child in those parts were very desirous to have with them to lean upon and to walk with it'. The annual income from offerings at the chapel on Andresey dedicated to the saint was given in 1535 as £2.[22] At Ingestre, east of Stafford, William Chetwynd built a chapel during the reign of Henry VII. He endowed it with lands for the support of a priest celebrating divine service there for the benefit of sick persons coming to the adjoining well of St Erasmus. This was highly esteemed for its medicinal properties, and offerings were valued in 1535 at £6 13s. 4d.[23]

The period saw some new ecclesiastical building. Much of St Peter's, Wolverhampton, was rebuilt in the later fifteenth century, including the fine tower dating from the late 1470s.[24] An elaborate high altar was erected in the earlier 1530s, with a picture of Our Lady, a gilded Resurrection and a canopy. In 1533–4 the carver was paid £45 and two gilders received £50. The money came from individual bequests and donations, including £55 from the Leveson family, who held the two Wolverhampton manors.[25] The main range of St John's hospital

St John's Hospital, Lichfield, in 1833.

St James's, Barton-under-Needwood, in 1839.

at Lichfield, dating from Bishop William Smith's refounding of
the hospital in 1495 and a little later, is a striking example of the
early use of brick in the county.[26] One building, however,
stands out: the church of St James at Barton-under-Needwood
built by Dr John Taylor on the site of the cottage where he was
born, the eldest of triplets. He was a churchman active in the
service of Henry VIII at home and abroad and served as
Master of the Rolls from 1527 to 1534. The church is an
outstanding architectural whole. The tower bears the date 1517
and Taylor's initials, and work on the church was still in
progress in the later 1520s and evidently in 1531 when Taylor
had permission from the Crown to cut thirty-three trees in the
nearby Highlands park. The date 1533 in the east window may
mark the completion of the church. A blank arch in the north
chancel wall may have been intended as the site of Taylor's
tomb. The nave arcade contains shields with inscriptions celebrating the founder.[27]

A number of schools were founded.[28] Bishop Smith's
refoundation of St John's hospital in Lichfield in 1495
included the endowment of a grammar school. Thomas
Countre, rector of Ingestre (d. *c.*1500), left property to
support a chantry priest in St Mary's church at Stafford who
was to act as a schoolmaster; the gift may have been an
endowment of an existing school. The school was recognised
as a grammar school by the chantry commissioners in 1548.
At Kinver a priest was engaged in 1511 to teach grammar, a
group of twenty-two men agreeing to pay him eight marks a
year until he was appointed to the chantry in Kinver church.
When the chantry was suppressed in 1548 its property
included a schoolhouse. In 1512 the Merchant Taylors'
Company received licence to acquire lands for the support of
a grammar school at Wolverhampton. This was at the instigation of one of their number, Sir Stephen Jenyns, who was a
native of Wolverhampton and lord mayor of London 1508–9;
in 1513 he received licence to increase the endowment. The
schoolhouse in John's Lane (later St John's Street) was apparently built by Jenyns on the site of his family home. William
Bene, abbot of Burton from 1502 until his death in 1530 or

1531, endowed a school at Burton, probably in 1517. A school seems to have been in existence by 1531, and in 1535 the then abbot of Burton appointed a master at a salary of £5. The formal establishment took place in 1538, when lands were settled in trust to maintain a school for all, rich and poor, who came to Burton to study grammar. At Tamworth under a royal licence of 1536 the executors of John Bayley of nearby Syerscote founded a chantry in St Edith's collegiate church, the incumbent of which, in accordance with Bayley's wishes, was to keep a free grammar school. The intention was probably to produce a flow of candidates for the fellowship which Bayley and his brother Robert had founded at St John's College, Cambridge, in 1526, stipulating that preference was to be given to Tamworth men.

꙰

In the early sixteenth century the clergy, secular and regular, probably accounted for one in every forty people. Staffordshire was part of the Diocese of Coventry and Lichfield, the third most extensive diocese of pre-Reformation England. The bishops of the period were typically royal servants, but they were not neglectful of the diocese, which was run through a sophisticated administrative machinery.[29] The diocese shared in the general boom in ordinations to the priesthood: between 1503 and 1531 an average of 167 a year were ordained in the diocese. Only a minority, however, secured a benefice. A tax list of 1533 for the diocese records over 930 stipendiary clergy as against fewer than 420 with parochial livings. The boom may in fact reflect the openings for the unbeneficed as a result of the general growth in guilds and chantries. The clergy of Coventry and Lichfield diocese seem to have been of the normally fair standard found elsewhere, although they were notably poor. According to the *Valor Ecclesiasticus* of 1535 nearly half of the Staffordshire incumbents had an income of between £10 and £30; a quarter had between £5 and £10, while ten per cent had less than £5.[30] Pluralism was lower than elsewhere. In 1533 some twelve per cent of the

Croxden Abbey: remains of the east range of the cloister and of the south transept of the church in 1839.

livings in the diocese (fifty livings) were held in plurality by just over five per cent of the parish incumbents (twenty-two clergy). Staffordshire, however, possessed the most extreme example: Richard Egerton, besides being prebendary of Whittington in Lichfield cathedral and master of the two hospitals at Lichfield and Stafford, held the livings of Enville, Ingestre, Stoke-upon-Trent and Stone, all in Staffordshire, and Frodsham in Cheshire. In 1535 he was living in Lichfield and the parishes were served by curates. He died in 1538, aged about eighty.[31]

It was a similar story with the religious of the county, monks, friars and nuns. There was little sign of spiritual fervour or intellectual distinction; but neither was it a period of marked decline. During Bishop Geoffrey Blythe's visitations of 1515–25 none of the Benedictine and Augustinian houses visited registered a decline in numbers, and all managed to attract novices except for the tiny priory of Calwich with its two monks.[32] Two of the three Cistercian houses, Croxden and Dieulacres, had the required number of thirteen monks at the Dissolution.[33] Cardinal Wolsey suppressed three Benedictine houses in Staffordshire as part of his general attack on small houses in the interests of other beneficiaries: Canwell and Sandwell, each with only two monks, in 1525 for the benefit of his new college at Oxford, and Farewell, with five nuns, in 1527 for the benefit of the choristers of Lichfield Cathedral; the monks and nuns were transferred to other houses.[34] About 1530 Burton Abbey had the distinction of a sub-prior who was on the waiting list for admission to a cell which was being founded by the Carthusians of Mount Grace in North Yorkshire. In 1533 the abbot of Burton, William Boston, was elected abbot of Westminster, the highest office known to have been attained by a Burton monk.[35]

⟢

The first impact of the Reformation to be felt locally was the attack on the monasteries. Wolsey had to some extent pointed the way. Then in 1532 Calwich priory, reduced to one monk by the death of the prior in 1530, was suppressed by the Crown working in agreement with the patron, who secured a lease of the priory's property.[36] The main attack came with the Act of 1536 suppressing religious houses worth less than £200 a year. Some Staffordshire houses were duly dissolved, others bought exemption. In August 1538 the county's four friaries were dissolved. All remaining religious houses were dissolved in 1538 and 1539, the last to go being the oldest, Burton Abbey. It was reconstituted as a college of secular priests in 1541, but that too was dissolved in 1545. The other more ancient colleges were dissolved under the Chantries Act of 1547.[37]

The monks and nuns were assigned pensions, and some continued to live locally. The last abbot of Croxden was buried in Checkley parish church in 1544. The last prior of Ranton was living at Seighford when he made his will in 1555, asking to be buried in the chancel of the parish church and leaving that church, 'to be prayed for', his best cope and his best vestment'.[38] The abbot of Dieulacres, who died in 1558, then had a house in Mill Street in Leek. The abbot of Rocester was buried at Rocester in 1576. Some monks secured parish preferment. Richard Whytell, prior of St Thomas at its dissolution in 1538, became vicar of the priory's church at Audlem in Cheshire in 1539 and held it until his death some eighteen years later. In 1546 John Stanley, a monk of Croxden, became vicar of Alton, a church which was part of the abbey's original endowment; he continued there until his death in 1569. Nuns were more dependent on their families. When she died in 1551 the last prioress of Black Ladies was living with her sister and nephew as a paying guest, probably at her native Beech in Stone parish.[39]

The Dissolution started a scramble for the lands of the religious houses seized by the Crown. An early example was the priory of Augustinian canons at Ranton west of Stafford. In April 1536 Sir Simon Harcourt, descendant of the founder, wrote to Thomas Cromwell offering him and the King money to secure the priory's exemption from dissolution and if that failed offering to buy the property: 'I desire to have it as it adjoins such small lands as I have in that country.' Later the same month Henry (later Lord) Stafford, put in his bid, begging Cromwell to

> use means with the King that I may have the farm of the Abbey of Ranton if it be dissolved; it is within four miles of my house and reaches my park pale, and I will give as much for it as any man. I heard that the Queen had moved the King to have me in remembrance for it, and he was content, saying it was alms to help me, having so many children on my hands. I heard that George Blount endeavours to obstruct my suit.

The next day Stafford wrote to the Earl of Westmorland urging his claim against Blount's; he asked Westmorland to intercede with Cromwell but added that he was willing to take the nunnery of White Ladies just over the Shropshire border instead. In May Cromwell's nephew wrote to him passing on Cromwell's promise to obtain Ranton for him 'when the surveying of the abbeys is at an end'. Henry Stafford later turned his attention to the Augustinian priory at Stone, but having heard that its prior was optimistic about its survival, he wrote to Cromwell in March 1537 from 'my poor house beside Stafford' urging his claims to Ranton against Harcourt's: 'I have twelve children and my living £40 a year less than it has been. I will give as much to the King as anyone and your lordship £40 to get it for me.' In the event Ranton was dissolved later in the year and a lease was granted to Harcourt; when the Crown sold the property in 1538, Harcourt secured it from the new owners in exchange for a manor in Kent.[40]

It is ironical that some of the monastic sites later became Catholic centres. In 1536 and 1538 Rowland Lee, the Bishop of Coventry and Lichfield, put in a bid for the Augustinian priory of St Thomas near Stafford for 'the poor boys my nephews'. On Lee's death in 1543 the site and the bulk of the property passed to his nephew Brian Fowler; most of the remainder went to three other nephews.[41] Under the Fowlers

Trentham c.1680, showing the church of the former Augustinian priory, retained as the parish church, and the house built on the priory site in the 1630s by the Leveson family, who had bought the site in 1540.

St Thomas flourished as a Catholic centre for well over a century and a half. The Benedictine nunnery in Brewood known as Black Ladies was the subject of rival bids by Thomas Giffard of Stretton in Penkridge and Edward Littleton of Pillaton, also in Penkridge. In 1539 it was sold to Giffard, who succeeded his father as lord of nearby Chillington in 1556.[42] Black Ladies thus became part of the Catholic enclave which centred on Chillington for three centuries under the wing of the Giffards. At Burton-upon-Trent the former monastic site was granted in 1546 to Sir William Paget (created Baron Paget in 1549). The remaining claustral buildings were used as a house by his son, the third baron, in the 1570s and early 1580s, and this was then a recusant centre. The memory of St Modwen persisted, and Burton girls were still being christened Modwen in the 1580s.[43]

It was not only the nobility and gentry who were involved in the scramble for the property of the religious. In August 1538 the royal agent for the dissolution of the friaries, Richard Ingworth, Bishop of Dover, received the surrender of the Franciscan friary at Lichfield in the presence of the town's two constables and Richard Watwode, the master of the town guild; the house and its goods were left in the keeping of the three men. Bishop Rowland Lee and his cousin Dr Thomas Legh, who was employed in the suppression of religious houses, tried to persuade Cromwell to grant the house to Watwode, who had 'formerly shown great favour' to both of them. In the event it was put up for sale.[44] The Bishop of Dover moved on from Lichfield to Stafford, where he received the surrender of the two friaries, and then went on to Newcastle-under-Lyme to dissolve the Dominican friary. There he found himself courted by John Booth, 'a great builder in these parts', who wanted to buy the slate and shingle from the friary. 'Master Booth', Ingworth informed Cromwell, 'for your sake showed me many pleasures and gave me venison; wherefore I may no less do but write to your lordship, beseeching you to be good lord to him.'[45]

At the same time various popular devotions were suppressed. In 1538 Thomas Cromwell ordered the removal of

Canon Arthur Dudley removing some of St Chad's bones from Lichfield
Cathedral in 1538.

images 'abused with pilgrimages or offerings . . . for avoiding of that most detestable offence of idolatry'. At Lichfield Bishop Lee persuaded Henry VIII to give St Chad's shrine to the cathedral for its 'necessary uses', but the jewels and ornaments were presumably seized for the Crown. Some of St Chad's bones were removed by Canon Arthur Dudley and entrusted by him to two female relatives at Russells Hall in Dudley.[46] St Modwen's statue at Burton and her red cow and staff were removed by Sir William Bassett, of Meynell Langley in Derbyshire; he sent them to Cromwell along with a statue of St Anne which he had taken from Buxton. In an accompanying letter he stated that in order to ensure 'that there should no more idolatry and superstition be there used, I did not only deface the tabernacles and places where they did stand but also did take away crutches, shirts and sheets, with wax offered, being things that did allure and entice the ignorant people to the said offering'. He warned the keepers of the shrines to see that no more offerings were made, pending further instructions.[47] At Wolverhampton the same year the churchwardens spent 2s. on 'setting out' (evidently painting over) St George and St Peter and 4d. on 'setting up' Our Lady and King Harry. The next year, in obedience to royal injunctions, they removed the candlesticks from the high altar, the holy water pot, and seven iron bars for tapers and five candlesticks from Our Lady's and St Catherine's chapels. In 1542 they sold the shoes and black velvet coat of Our Lady, her broken crown, her nine pairs of beads, and the red satin coat of Jesus.[48] The chapel of St Erasmus at Ingestre survived until the Chantries Act of 1547. Having then been seized by the Crown, it was sold in 1549 to two speculators, who in turn sold it to Thomas Chetwynd, the son and successor of its founder.[49]

The government's religious policy became more firmly Protestant after the accession of Edward VI in 1547. Parishioners would have noticed a steady change in the liturgy accompanied by a change in the appearance of their churches; in 1553 at the end of the reign commissioners were appointed to confiscate church goods, leaving only what they judged necessary for the new services. At Wolverhampton in 1548–9 out went images and the rood, including the image of St George. Next year the castle of St George was removed from his chapel and the wall whitened; in 1552–3 the chapel was dismantled. The elaborate high altar was removed, but the communion table which replaced it was a makeshift board in 1550–1 and was not completed until 1552–3. Old service books were sold in 1548–9, and two communion books and two psalters were bought in 1549–50 and two Books of Common Prayer in 1552–3. A new desk for the Bible was set up in 1549–50.[50]

There was widespread selling of church goods, many of which were also lost or stolen. In some cases the aim was the support of the new liturgy and the repair of churches. At Lichfield the new corporation of 1548 sold goods from the three city churches and used the proceeds not only for repairs but to take down altars, remove 'idols and images' and provide required books, including the Bible in English.[51] At Penkridge one of the five bells belonging to the former collegiate church was sold and part of the proceeds were used partly to pull down the altars and 'deface' the church, to buy and paint thirty-seven yards of cloth to go over the rood loft, to paint the table at the high altar with scriptures, and to glaze the church. The rest of the money was spent on hiring a young man to teach in a writing school and to provide a gift for 'three lame creatures' who were housebound.[52] At Clifton Campville there was a similar mixture: church goods were sold for £6, of which £5 was spent on church repairs and £1 was given to the poor; at the chapel of ease at Harlaston one of two bells was mortgaged for 20s. to buy shingle for the chapel.[53] Public works were sometimes the object. At Rushton Spencer, a chapelry in Leek parish, one of the two bells was sold for 26s. 8d. in about 1549 to repair Hug bridge carrying the Leek–Macclesfield road over the river Dane.[54] At West Bromwich three candlesticks were sold for the repair of a local bridge.[55]

There was little resistance to the changes from either clergy or laity. No parochial incumbent in Staffordshire was deprived under Henry VIII or Edward VI; six resigned during Henry's last three years, but their reasons are not known. Only three resigned under Edward VI, one because of promotion to a better living and two pluralists who gave up one of many livings.[56] It is arguable that clergy who conformed to whatever programme was being imposed from above were not necessarily vicars of Bray but rather pastors serving their flock through thick and thin and in some cases preserving a devotion to the ways of their youth. Thomas Wilson was vicar of Abbots Bromley from 1527 until his death in 1561 and thus lived through the whole cycle of change from Henry VIII to Elizabeth I. In his will of 1561 he not only bequeathed his soul to Almighty God and placed his special trust in Christ but retained the Catholic custom of 'beseeching the Blessed Virgin Mary and all the holy company of Heaven to pray for me'. He left 4d. to every child who could say the *De profundis* and attended his funeral, and he asked to be buried in the chapel of St Nicholas in the parish church where the statue of the Trinity once stood. Similarly Thomas Tunstall, curate at Wolstanton from 1531 until his death in 1565, commended his soul in 1565 to 'Almighty God, there to be kept with the holy company of Heaven' and left his body to be buried 'within Our Lady's chancel, before there as the altar was before time'.[57]

The monks and nuns went quietly. They were however the object of some sympathy and even optimism. As already seen, Sir Simon Harcourt tried to buy the exemption of Ranton priory in 1536. Bishop Rowland Lee did the same for St Thomas's priory near Stafford, writing to Cromwell: 'if it shall stand the King's highness shall have not only a certain sum but you also for your goodness.' Like Harcourt he went on to put in a bid for the house if the dissolution went ahead.[58] Although Stone priory came within the terms of the Act of 1536 for dissolving the lesser monasteries and the royal commissioners were due in Staffordshire in mid-March 1537, Henry Stafford reported a few days before that the prior of Stone 'thinks his house shall

stand, whereof the country is glad'. Stone was in the event
dissolved that year, and Henry Stafford with persisting optimism removed his ancestors' alabaster tombs from the priory
church to the Austin friars' house in Forebridge, the southern
suburb of Stafford, where the friars hung up a pedigree of the
Stafford family. That house too was dissolved the following
year.[59] In 1538 the Bishop of Dover, reporting his suppression
of friaries in Staffordshire, Shrewsbury, Chester and North
Wales, stated that the friars in the area had many active supporters; people hoped to see them restored 'and some have gone up
to sue for them'.[60]

Two towns showed some opposition to the Crown's depre-
dations. The ruse of 1545 by which much of the Lichfield
guild's property was saved from the clutches of the Crown has
been described above. At Tamworth the suppression of the
college in 1548 caused resentment. The collegiate church was
the parish church, and when the chantry commissioners
dismissed the clergy and seized the church goods, the towns-
people petitioned the Duke of Somerset, the Lord Protector.
He wrote to the commissioners, rebuking them for having 'no
further consideration than to leave a number of people to so
loose a disorder' and ordering them to restore to the church
ornaments and utensils necessary for services. Some vestments and plate were promptly returned. In addition he
ordered the commissioners to make similar restitution
throughout Staffordshire.[61]

On the other hand the evidence of active support for the
changes is ambiguous. The scramble for monastic property
was hardly a sign of Protestant zeal. The disposal of church
goods was sometimes recorded as having been with the
consent of the parish, but it is not possible to check the reality
of such consent. The sales were often simply a chance to
secure the means to repair the church or to perform charitable
or secular works. Even where the money was spent on the
new liturgy, it is not possible to say how much enthusiasm
there was. The new Lichfield corporation showed some zeal
in promoting the new liturgy. It also adopted for its seal a
depiction of the legendary massacre of early Christians at

Lichfield in what may have been an attempt to advertise its break with the cult of St Chad. The corporation's attitude could be variously interpreted as Protestant zeal or politically correct prudence; it could also have been an expression of newly found independence from the bishop and the cathedral authorities.[62] At any rate, when the Catholic Mary Tudor faced rebellion on her accession in 1553, Lichfield was one of eleven towns which supported her and were duly rewarded with charters, Lichfield receiving a grant of county status.[63]

❦

With the advent of Mary it was soon all change once more. The kingdom was formally reconciled with Rome in 1554 by the new Archbishop of Canterbury, Reginald Pole – a native of Staffordshire, born in 1500 at Stourton Castle in Kinver, originally a royal hunting lodge.[64] There was some opposition in Staffordshire. At least forty-two married clergy in the diocese were immediately deprived; they included the Dean of Lichfield, two canons and two vicars choral of the cathedral, and eleven parish incumbents in Staffordshire. A further six incumbents resigned in 1557 and 1558.[65] Of the seven people in the diocese burnt for heresy under Mary three suffered at Lichfield. One of them, Joyce Lewes of Mancetter (Warwickshire), received comfort from the sheriff of Lichfield and a group of women including the wife of the junior bailiff and the wife of a former junior bailiff. Nearly all the Staffordshire MPs went along with the new regime as they had done in the previous two reigns. The exception was one of the two members for Newcastle-under-Lyme, Sir Ralph Bagnall of Dieulacres, the site of a Cistercian monastery near Leek which he had secured from the Crown in 1552. When the rest of the MPs knelt for the papal blessing during the 1554 session, he refused to do so: 'who said he was sworn the contrary to King Harry the Eighth, which was a worthy prince and laboured twenty-five years before he could abolish him [the Pope]; and to say that I will now agree to it, I will not.' By 1556 he was living in France.[66]

Stourton Castle in the late eighteenth century.

Otherwise there was once again a general acquiescence in the religious changes. At Wolverhampton three altars were quickly set up, but it was not until 1556–7 that the high altar was put back, two men spending five and a half days in setting it up. Mr Horton received 2s. for the boards which he had had from the altar when it was taken down, and Mrs Thackerde was paid 4d. for dusting the gilding. At the same time the rood loft, the rood and the images were set up, mended and painted. Plate and service books were recovered, and two chalices which had been in pledge were redeemed. A bucket for holy water and a chrismatory were bought. Vestments were recovered, including, it would appear, a cope of crimson velvet embroidered with gold which was bought from Robert Cutt for 27s., the exact sum which he paid the churchwardens for a cope in 1551–2. Orphreys were sewn back on the vestments, and an altar cloth and the banner of St George were repaired.[67]

Mary also restored the college of Wolverhampton, dissolved in 1548. Its deanery had been united with the deanery of St George's chapel in Windsor Castle in 1480, and in 1553 Mary declared the dissolution of Wolverhampton college invalid since exemption had been granted to St George's. It survived until 1846, when it succumbed to another wave of church reform. Its lands had been granted to the Duke of Northumberland at the end of Edward VI's reign, but with his fall at the beginning of Mary's reign they were given back to the college.[68] A general restoration of lands belonging to religious houses was, however, impossible: too many people had a vested interest in that side of the Reformation. There was nonetheless some nostalgic optimism about a restoration of the religious. In her will of 1556 Margaret Sutton of Stafford stated: 'I will that my fine kercher be made a corporas and given to the friars if it go up again.'[69] The last abbot of Dieulacres, Thomas Whitney, left a silver-gilt chalice to his nephew in his will of 1558 'on condition that if the monastery of Delencres be hereafter re-edified, the said chalice to be restored to the said monastery'; he also wished to be buried in the revived Westminster Abbey.[70] There was also optimism about the revival of chantries. Robert Jackson of Stanshope in Alstonefield left two sheep in his will of 1556 'towards the beginning of Our Lady's service again at Alstonefield', adding that he wished to be buried as near as possible to 'Our Lady's choir door' in the church.[71] At least the Crown was able to use some 300 acres of former chantry land in Walsall, Tipton and Norton Canes to endow Queen Mary's Grammar School in Walsall in 1554; the foundation was made in answer to a petition by local inhabitants, echoing a recommendation by the chantry commissioners in 1548.[72]

The will of Sir Philip Draycott of Paynsley in Draycott-in-the-Moors, made in September 1558, showed a confidence in the revival.[73] He was to be buried in the chancel of Draycott parish church 'where a stone of marble may be laid upon me with images of me and my wife, my vi sons and vi daughters and with letters graven in the same stone in English as my brother doctor shall think good without any plate of metal in the stone sculpture'. He left 20s. to the high altar in the church and directed 'dirge and mass to be solemnly made and kept in the cathedral church of Lichfield for my soul and all Christian souls'. His legacies to his grandson and heir, John Draycott, included linen to 'make three altar cloths for my chapel', a chalice and paten of silver, a silver pyx and 'my vestments, mass book, and other things to my chapel belonging'. Sir Philip died in February 1559 and was duly buried in the chancel.[74] The Catholic church at Cresswell, successor of the Paynsley mission, has a number of chasubles on which are mounted orphreys dating from the early sixteenth century and depicting Christ, Our Lady and several saints. The vestments were discovered in the nineteenth century in or behind a chimney at the nearby Rookery Farm and were possibly rescued from a religious house at the Dissolution. It is tempting to identify them with the vestments mentioned in Sir Philip's will, but evidence is lacking.[75]

Mary and Cardinal Pole both died on 17 November 1558. Mary was succeeded by her sister Elizabeth, and in the following year came a new settlement of religion, one which this time was going to last.

Orphreys on the Vestments at St Mary's, Cresswell.

(a) The Virgin and Child.

Orphreys on the Vestments at St Mary's, Cresswell.

(b) St Peter.

Orphreys on the Vestments at St Mary's, Cresswell.

(c) A Seraph.

Notes

1 S.R.O., D4038/I/2.
2 *S.H.C.* 1915, pp. 10, 88–9, 205–6.
3 Ibid., p. 306; J. F. Ede, *History of Wednesbury* (Wednesbury, 1962), pp. 68–9, 190.
4 *V.C.H. Staffs.* xiv, pp. 75, 87, 131–2, 138; A. G. Rosser, 'The Town and Guild of Lichfield in the late Middle Ages', *Transactions of the South Staffordshire Archaeological and Historical Society*, xvii (1987), pp. 39–47.
5 *V.C.H. Staffs.* xiv, pp. 96–8.
6 Ibid., pp. 78, 82.
7 Ibid., xvii, pp. 214, 228–9.
8 *V.C.H. Staffs.* ix, pp. 91, 110–11. For other religious guilds at Lichfield and Wolverhampton see ibid. xiv, p. 131; Shaw, *Staffs.* ii, p. 160.
9 *V.C.H. Staffs.* xx, p. 154.
10 Ibid., p. 219.
11 L.R.O., B/C/11/Edm. Wetton (1534).
12 S.R.O., D4038/I/2.
13 *V.C.H. Staffs.* vii, p. 134.
14 G. T. O. Bridgeman, 'An Account of the Family of Swynnerton', *S.H.C.* vii (2), pp. 83–4 note; *S.H.C.* 1915, p. 31.
15 *V.C.H. Staffs.* xx, p. 194.
16 Ibid., vii, pp. 198–9.
17 T. Cooper, *The Last Generation of English Catholic Clergy* (Woodbridge, 1999), p. 145.
18 G. P. M[ander], 'A Register of Stafford and other local wills', *S.H.C.* 1926, p. 7.
19 Edited by A. J. Kettle, *S.H.C.* 4th ser. viii (1976).
20 Ibid., pp. vii–x, xiv, 106–7, 157.
21 M. W. Greenslade, *Saint Chad of Lichfield and Birmingham* (Archdiocese of Birmingham Historical Commission, publication number 10, 1996), pp. 13–14.
22 *V.C.H. Staffs.* iii, pp. 199, 212; ix, p. 108–9.
23 [F. P. Parker, ed.], 'Collections for a History of Pirehill Hundred. By Walter Chetwynd of Ingestre, Esq. A.D. 1679', *S.H.C.* new ser. xii (1909), pp. 150–1.
24 N. Pevsner, *The Buildings of England: Staffordshire*

(Harmondsworth, 1974), p. 314; S.R.O., D593/B/26/6/26/11.

25 P. Heath, 'Staffordshire Towns and the Reformation', *North Staffordshire Journal of Field Studies*, xix (1979), pp. 9–10.

26 *V.C.H. Staffs.* ii, p. 255; iii, pp. 280–1, 286 and plate facing.

27 Ibid., x (forthcoming); R. Plot, *The Natural History of Staffordshire* (Oxford, 1686), pp. 277, 296; *Oxford D.N.B.* liii, p. 928.

28 See the relevant sections in *V.C.H. Staffs.* vi; for Kinver see ibid., xx, p. 157.

29 Ibid., iii, pp. 27–8, 44.

30 Ibid. 42–3; Cooper, *English Catholic Clergy*, pp. 37, 92–5; C. Haigh, *English Reformations* (Oxford, 1993), pp. 37–8; C. Harrison, 'The *Valor Ecclesiasticus*: a Re-appraisal based on the Staffordshire Returns', *Staffordshire Studies*, xi (1999), p. 48.

31 Cooper, *English Catholic Clergy*, pp. 65, 67; *S.H.C.* 1915, pp. 99–100, 132, 249, 259.

32 P. Heath (ed.), *Bishop Geoffrey Blythe's Visitations c. 1515–1525* (*S.H.C.* 4th ser. vii, 1973).

33 *V.C.H. Staffs.* iii, pp. 228, 233.

34 Ibid., pp. 215, 218, 224.

35 Ibid., pp. 208, 210.

36 Ibid., p. 239.

37 See the relevant sections of *V.C.H. Staffs.* iii.

38 'A Register of Stafford and Other Local Wills', *S.H.C.* 1926, p. 11.

39 *V.C.H. Staffs.* iii, p. 137, n. 34.

40 Ibid., pp. 246, 254.

41 Ibid., pp. 265–6.

42 Ibid., p. 222; ibid. v, pp. 36–7.

43 Ibid., ix, pp. 9–10, 50, 109; below, pp. 77–8, 189–90, 223.

44 *V.C.H. Staffs.* iii, pp. 269–70; above, p. 5.

45 T. Wright (ed.), *Three Chapters of Letters relating to the Suppression of Monasteries* (Camden Society, 1843), p. 206.

46 Greenslade, *Saint Chad*, 14.

47 Wright (ed.), *Suppression of Monasteries*, p. 143; *Letters and Papers of Henry VIII*, xiii (2), p. 101.

48 *N. Staffs. Jnl. of Field Studies*, xix, p. 10.

49 *Calendar of Patent Rolls 1549–1551*, pp. 126, 128; *S.H.C.* new ser. xii, p. 151.
50 *N. Staffs. Jnl. of Field* Studies, xix, p. 11.
51 *V.C.H. Staffs.* xiv, pp. 140–1, 146, 149–50.
52 *S.H.C.* 1915, p. 203.
53 Ibid., pp. 67–9.
54 Ibid., pp. 147; *V.C.H. Staffs.* vii, p. 224.
55 *S.H.C.* 1915, p. 309.
56 Ibid., pp. xl–xli.
57 Cooper, *English Catholic Clergy*, pp. 8, 148, 185–9; *S.H.C.* 1915, p. 1.
58 *V.C.H. Staffs.* iii, p. 265; above, pp. 16–17.
59 *V.C.H. Staffs.* iii, p. 246, 274; L. Toulmin Smith (ed.), *The Itinerary of John Leland*, v (1910), p. 21.
60 *Letters and Papers of Henry VIII*, xiii (2), p. 67.
61 *V.C.H. Staffs.* iii, p. 45.
62 Ibid., xiv, pp. 38, 85–6; D. Johnson, '"Lichfield" and "St Amphibalus": the Story of a Legend', *Transactions of South Staffordshire Archaeological and Historical Society*, xxviii (1988), p. 8.
63 *V.C.H. Staffs.* iii, p. 76.
64 Ibid., xx, pp. 131–2; *Oxford D.N.B.* xliv, p. 715.
65 *V.C.H. Staffs.* iii, pp. 45–6, 169; *S.H.C.* 1915, p. xli.
66 J. C. Wedgwood, *Staffordshire Parliamentary History*, i (*S.H.C.* 1917–18), p. 325–7; *V.C.H. Staffs.* vii, p. 100.
67 *N. Staffs. Jnl. of Field Studies*, xix, p. 11.
68 *V.C.H. Staffs.* iii, p. 325–6, 329.
69 Ibid., p. 137.
70 Ibid., p. 234.
71 Ibid., vii, p. 22.
72 Ibid., vi, p. 174.
73 W. F. Carter, 'Notes on Staffordshire Families', *S.H.C.* 1925, pp. 129–30.
74 National Archives (Public Record Office), C 142/119/185 (his inquisition post mortem August 1559); S.R.O., D3455/1/1, f. 6. His wife Elizabeth (d. 1568) left instructions for her burial in the chancel of Draycott church as near her husband's body as possible 'and on that side of the tomb that my picture is made': *S.H.C.* 1925, p. 131.
75 P. Bailey, *Painsley: A History of Cresswell's Roman Catholic*

Community 1570–2000 (Market Rasen, 2005), pp. 52–3. The date of the discovery is given as 1846 by Mr Paul Adams and as during the time when Thomas Scott was the priest at Cresswell (1882–1921) by *Roman Catholic Registers* (Staffordshire Parish Registers Society, 1958–9), p. 140.

2

A NEW CATHOLIC STAFFORDSHIRE: 1559–1603

The religious settlement of 1559, reinforced by an Act of 1563, restored the royal supremacy and a slightly revised version of the second prayer book of Edward VI and imposed a 12d. fine for every failure to attend the parish church on Sundays and holy days. Office holders and future MPs had to take the oath of supremacy, and anyone who persisted in upholding the authority of a foreign potentate was guilty of treason. The government's policy was initially pragmatic in the hope that Catholicism in the kingdom would gradually wither away. On the other side Rome was slow to issue an official condemnation of the widespread practice of minimal conformity, whereby people attended church as required but avoided any active participation. The settlement was widely seen to be just one more change with no better chance of survival than its predecessors.[1]

It was, however, sufficiently clear cut for many of the higher clergy to make a stand at last. In the Diocese of Coventry and Lichfield the bishop, Ralph Baynes, was examined by the Privy Council in April 1559, fined heavily in May and deprived in June; he died in November at Islington.[2] The Dean of Lichfield, John Ramridge, was sent to the Tower; although appointed divinity lecturer at the cathedral by Archbishop Cranmer at the beginning of Edward VI's reign, he had become dean early in Mary's reign. He was released on bail and escaped with his nephew and amanuensis to Flanders,

where he settled in Louvain. In 1568 he set out to take alms
to fellow exiles and was murdered in an attempted robbery by
tramps at Hever near Mechlin. The cathedral precentor,
Henry Comberford, was also deprived. In a letter to the Privy
Council at the end of February the bailiffs of Lichfield
accused him of 'lewd preaching and misdemeanour'. He was
summoned before the Privy Council in March and kept in
prison until April. A schedule of recusants (those refusing to
accept the 1559 settlement)[3] drawn up by the recusancy
commissioners in the early 1560s pronounced him 'learned but
wilful and meet to be considered'. He had by then been
ordered to live in Suffolk but was allowed to travel twice a
year to Staffordshire for six weeks at a time. He was before
the Yorkshire ecclesiastical commissioners in 1570 for defending the Mass, and in 1579, at the age of eighty, he was in
prison at Hull for his religious beliefs. The chancellor of the
cathedral, Dr Alban Langdale, was appointed in February
1559, being already Archdeacon of Chichester. He never
came to Lichfield and was deprived the same year. Described
by the commissioners in the early 1560s as 'learned and very
earnest in papistry', he was then in the custody of the Catholic
Viscount Montagu, of Battle Abbey and Cowdray Park in
Sussex, and served as chaplain to the family until his death
in the late 1580s. The treasurer, George Lee, who had
been in office since 1541, took the oath of supremacy but
resigned in 1560. Four of the canons of the cathedral were
deprived in 1559 and a fifth about 1561. Ten more vacated
their prebends between 1559 and 1564; their reasons are not
known, but one became a Jesuit.

Of the parish clergy in Staffordshire it has been argued that
over a third were deprived of their livings or abandoned them
on conscientious grounds in the early years of Elizabeth's
reign.[4] The county as a whole proved resistant to change. A
metropolitical visitation of the Diocese of Coventry and Lichfield, held early in 1560 before the consecration of a new
bishop, found that many churchwardens had failed to replace
their altars with communion tables, with the Staffordshire
parishes of Biddulph, Church Eaton, Sandon and Stone among

the offenders.[5] In the schedule of the early 1560s the ecclesiastical commissioners complained that 'a great part of the shires of Stafford and Derby are generally evil inclined towards religion and forbear coming to church and participating of the sacraments, using also very broad speeches in alehouses and elsewhere'. In 1564 the new bishop, Thomas Bentham, reported the county as 'too much hinderly in all good things pertaining to religion'.[6]

There was clearly much time-serving and a feeling of 'wait and see'. After a rebuke from the Queen and the Privy Council Bentham issued a set of injunctions to the clergy of the diocese in 1565. Altars were to be 'clean taken away' and replaced by 'a decent and simple table', and rood lofts were to be taken down. The Commandments were to be set up where the Sacrament used to hang, and 'all monuments of idolatry and superstition' were to be removed, such as 'holy water stocks, sepulchres which were used on Good Friday, hand bells and all manner of idols which be laid up in secret places in your church where Latin service was used'. Bases on which statues had stood were to be smashed and niches in church walls filled in. The church interior was then to be whitewashed. The clergy were to throw away Latin service books and adhere rigidly to the Prayer Book communion service. There were to be no candles at funerals, and parishioners were to be forbidden to set corpses down at wayside crosses and to pray for the dead. They were to be urged to throw away their rosaries and reminded to work on those holy days abolished by Parliament.[7] Staffordshire's 'hinderliness' presumably included such clinging to old ways. It was one of the 'barbarous counties' to which John Aylmer, Bishop of London, suggested in 1577 that leading puritans should be sent to preach against the papists.[8] In 1584 Bentham's successor William Overton suspected the survival in the diocese of 'vain popish trish-trash' such as images and relics.[9] As late as 1588 the Earl of Shrewsbury, the Lord Lieutenant of Staffordshire, was informed that crosses had been erected in the county; describing them as 'the very badges of old idolatry and superstition', he was indignant that 'such folly remaineth as yet unrooted out from amongst the people' and ordered the deputy lieutenants to look into the matter.[10]

The main trouble was what Bentham described as 'mastership' – the influence of Catholic gentry and nobility, who encouraged Catholic tenants and servants and provided refuges and centres in their houses for Catholic priests. In their schedule of the early 1560s the Bishop of London and fellow commissioners attributed recusancy in Staffordshire and Derbyshire to the example of Sir Thomas Fitzherbert of Norbury in Derbyshire and Mavesyn Ridware in Staffordshire, John Draycott of Paynsley in Draycott-in-the-Moors in Staffordshire and John Sacheverell of Derbyshire, 'being by us committed to prison and so remaining, and through the bearing and supporting of their wives, friends, kinsfolk, allies and servants'. All were imprisoned in London, Fitzherbert in the Fleet, Draycott in the Counter, Poultry, and Sacheverell in the Counter, Wood Street; Draycott's great-uncle Dr Anthony Draycott, who had been deprived of the rectory of Checkley and several other benefices for refusing the oath of supremacy, was also in the Fleet.[11] In 1564 the Privy Council asked the bishops to report on the reliability of justices of the peace, the men who had an important share in the task of enforcing the new settlement. In Staffordshire Bishop Bentham considered ten out of seventeen justices to be hostile to the changes. They included Brian Fowler, whose home was on the site of St Thomas's priory near Baswich, south-east of Stafford. He was sheltering David Pole, the deprived Bishop of Peterborough, and as a result, commented Bentham, 'many people think worse of the regiment and religion than they would do, because that divers lewd priests have resort thither, but what conference they have I cannot learn'.[12] One such priest was John Felton; he had conformed to the Elizabethan settlement but came to Fowler's house where, as he later reported, Dr Pole 'reconciled him to the Catholic Church . . . shriving him, absolving him and enjoining him penance of fasting etc.'[13]

It was however not only the gentry who were a problem. Bentham complained that many people fled into places of peculiar jurisdiction, areas which were exempt from the bishop's authority, 'and so avoid ordinary correction, not without great offence and slander both of the gospel and ministers thereof'. He also claimed that 'the greatest disorder within my whole diocese hath been in the great towns corporate; for there when I have required the assistance of the bailiffs or other officers I have found open resistance in matters of charge, whereof it is needful to place good men in office there.'[14] In 1582 Bentham's successor William Overton repeated the complaint about peculiar jurisdictions, singling out those in Staffordshire and the Lichfield jurisdiction of the dean and chapter in particular: the existence of such peculiars helped to make the diocese 'the den of fugitives, the very receptacle of all the refuse that is thrown out of other dioceses round about me'.[15]

꿴

After the Northern Rising of 1569 there was a general stiffening of policy on both sides. In 1570 Pope St Pius V abandoned Rome's policy of 'wait and see' and excommunicated Elizabeth in a belated attempt to help the rebels, releasing her subjects from obedience to her. The government replied by making it treason to deny that Elizabeth was lawful Queen. In January 1573 the Earl of Shrewsbury informed Lord Treasurer Burghley that he had arrested Thomas Comberford, of Comberford near Tamworth, 'where Masses were frequented', along with two very active Mass priests. It was his wish 'that bishops and others in authority . . . would have more regard unto their charges and not suffer such dangerous vagabonds to rest unpunished in their jurisdiction'.[16] From 1574 exiles ordained abroad (later styled seminary priests by the government) returned to bring new fervour to the congregations served by Marian priests (those ordained under Mary and earlier and had not conformed and who were styled massing priests) and to dash the government's hope that Catholicism in the kingdom would gradually wither away. Their mission was the reclamation of the lapsed and not the conversion of heretics; they were also forbidden by their superiors to meddle in politics, however much those superiors were so meddling abroad.

The Privy Council was informed in 1579 that in Staffordshire 'do lurk certain Mass priests disguised in serving men's apparel or like other lay persons and are secretly received and entertained in sundry men's houses'; three justices were ordered to search for them, including Sir Walter Aston of Tixall and Richard Bagot of Blithfield, notable hammers of Staffordshire recusants and their priests.[17] It is likely that the Jesuit St Edmund Campion spent a night at Throwley Hall, Lady Fuljames's house in north-east Staffordshire, in January 1581 during his missionary journey to the north of England.[18] The same year the council ordered the examination of a group of men including 'one Worsley' of Staffordshire – perhaps Erasmus Wolseley of Wolseley – in connection with the harbouring of Campion. Dr Henshawe, a secular priest, stated in 1582 that he and the Jesuits William Holt and Jasper Heywood had spent three months in Staffordshire and converted 228 persons.[19] Dr Thomas Worthington, who had been trained at Douai, escaped from Maer Hall, the home of the Macclesfields (otherwise Maxfields), when it was raided in 1584.[20] The first recorded arrest of a seminary priest in the county was in 1587 when Richard Bagot apprehended Nicholas Marwood alias Chichester, described by Lord Shrewsbury as 'that Jesuit'; Bagot thereby earned the special approval of the Queen, the Lord Chancellor and the Privy Council. Marwood was a prisoner in London in 1588, but in 1593 he was released from Stafford gaol on a recognizance of £100 to appear before the recusancy commissioners on twenty days' notice, to be given him at the house of Isabel Warner of Whittington.[21] It was evidently in Staffordshire that the Jesuit John Gerard won a convert in 1591. He was on a visit to a relative, possibly one of the Gerards of Gerrards Bromley, and made the first contact with his convert by joining a hunting party.[22] A few years later a Jesuit, Robert Jones, was reported at Paynsley in Draycott-in-the-Moors, the home of John Draycott.[23]

Marian 'Massing' priests continued to be recorded in the

Hamstall Ridware: the church and manor house in the late eighteenth century.

county into the 1590s.[24] The John Buckland who was buried at Castle Church in 1578 may have been the priest named Brucklande who was chaplain at Stafford Castle in the later 1540s and the 1550s.[25] Thomas Cheddleton, a canon of the collegiate church of St Mary, Stafford, became the first vicar there after the dissolution of the college in 1548; he continued to hold office along with other preferment under Mary but refused to conform under Elizabeth and was deprived. He was living in Castle Church parish in 1577 along with his nephews Thomas and Henry Tulley, probably in the Forebridge suburb of Stafford. He appears regularly as a recusant in the quarter sessions records of the 1580s, and the St Mary's register records his burial in June 1589, describing him as 'an old priest'.[26] John Bradbury was chaplain to Dorothy Heveningham at Aston in Stone in 1577 and was still there in the late 1580s.[27] The Fitzherberts sheltered Marian priests at Hamstall Ridware. Thomas Collier, deprived as vicar of Uppingham in Rutland and as a canon of St Paul's Cathedral in 1560, came to Staffordshire and secured a farm at Hamstall Ridware. He was still there when convicted of recusancy in 1588 but was 'a supposed fugitive' in 1589.[28] Walter Barlow, a Marian priest living at Hamstall Ridware in 1582, was probably chaplain to the Fitzherberts; he was in the Marshalsea for four months that year and in Stafford gaol in 1586. He was perhaps the old priest called Barlow who was received by Alice Tulley at Forebridge in the early 1590s.[29]

Robert Parton was another 'old priest' received by Alice Tulley. A priest of that name was born about 1516 and ordained during Mary's reign. He conformed under Elizabeth but returned to Catholicism when he was deprived of his benefice about 1568. He was imprisoned in Newgate about 1583 and later stated that, having been released and rearrested, he spent five years in Stafford gaol from about 1587. At the end of 1592 he was taken from Lichfield to Hampton Court, and after being examined by the Privy Council he was committed to the Marshalsea. He was again examined in April 1593, and although refusing to attend church, he agreed to have conference with the Dean of Westminster. As a result he decided to conform again, and he signed the oath of allegiance apparently in Staffordshire in the presence of Richard Bagot.[30]

෴

In 1575 Elizabeth went on progress through Staffordshire and was evidently disturbed by what she saw there.[31] On 12 August, a few days after she had left the county, the Privy Council summoned a number of Staffordshire gentry to appear before it for failing to attend church: Brian Fowler of St Thomas, John Giffard of Chillington in Brewood (who had entertained the Queen at his house for the last night of her stay in Staffordshire), John Draycott of Paynsley in Draycott-in-the-Moors, Francis Gatacre of Swynnerton and Gatacre in Shropshire,[32] Erasmus Wolseley of Wolseley, Thomas Peshall of Horsley in Eccleshall, Hugh Erdeswick of Sandon and his son Sampson, and William Macclesfield of Maer. Fowler and Giffard were justices of the peace; Giffard had also been sheriff in 1573–4. All except Peshall appeared on 17 August and admitted their defaulting, 'alleging their consciences and examples of their forefathers who taught them so'. They were referred to four bishops and other learned men for 'conference'.

After two days the bishops reported that they had made no progress. The recusants were then called back before the Council and told that they would not be allowed home unless they obeyed the Queen's laws, 'the breach whereof in men of their calling for example sake could not be tolerated'. Several, however, were released for brief periods. Brian Fowler was allowed home to settle a debt but had to report back to the Bishop of Worcester. Sampson Erdeswick was allowed back to Sandon to fetch his books and notes and was also ordered to return to the Bishop of Worcester; his father had meanwhile to remain with the same bishop. William Macclesfield was permitted to return to Staffordshire to sit on a commission provided that he surrendered at Michaelmas to the custody of the Bishop of Coventry and Lichfield. John Giffard had permission to go back to Chillington, which was, 'as he alleged, by reason of Her Majesty's late being there, out of order and unfurnished', but he had to return to the custody of the Bishop of Rochester. Francis Gatacre was committed to the Bishop of Coventry and Lichfield, Erasmus Wolseley to the Bishop of Rochester, and John Draycott to the Bishop of Rochester and a Dr Pieres.

They all remained obstinate, and in November the Privy Council lost patience and started to imprison them. Gatacre and Draycott were put in the Fleet in the city of London, the latter in solitary confinement. Wolseley was sent to the Gatehouse in Westminster, and Macclesfield to the Marshalsea in Southwark. Fowler and the two Erdeswicks were allowed to have 'further conference', but in December they too were imprisoned. Fowler was sent to the Fleet and allowed one servant; for six weeks he was to have 'the liberty of the Fleet and the repair of his friends', but if he then failed to conform, he was to lose those privileges. Sampson Erdeswick was sent to the Marshalsea with one servant, and his father was put in the Fleet. John Giffard was more pliant. He was allowed home, having promised to attend his parish church at Brewood while pointing out that he could not do so every Sunday and holy day as his house at Chillington was a mile and a half from the church. The Council ordered that when he was not at church he and his family were to be present at Common Prayer in the chapel at his house; they also instructed the Dean of Lichfield, who held the rectory of Brewood, to notify them of Giffard's attendance at the church.

In January 1576 conditions began to improve for the group. Gatacre 'yielded from henceforth to better conformity' and was released. Fowler fell seriously ill as a result of his close confinement, while at the same time there was some hope that he would conform; he was duly released 'for some trial to be made of him'. Draycott had a law suit pending, and his counsel was allowed to visit him in the Fleet; in addition he too was ill because of close confinement and permission was given for him to walk in the garden. In April the Erdeswicks were released on bonds that they would return on the first day of Trinity term unless they conformed in the meantime. In

Chillington Hall: the (east) entrance front of the mid-Tudor house in the early eighteenth century. The cross on the left gable may indicate the site of an attic chapel.

Sandon Hall *c.*1680.

June Draycott was released, and, along with the Erdeswicks, Fowler and Wolseley were respited until the beginning of the Michaelmas term.

In 1577 the Privy Council required the bishops to make returns of recusants in their dioceses. Having made a return in November, Bishop Bentham followed it with a more detailed return for Staffordshire in February 1578.[33] Besides the centres dependent on the eight gentry listed above there was a wide distribution of recusants. The place with the highest number listed was Hamstall Ridware, home of Sir Thomas Fitzherbert, who had been a notable public figure in the county until 1560. He was in prison for recusancy in the early 1560s, as already seen, and in 1570 he was in the Fleet prison. In 1578, besides Sir Thomas and two members of his family and their five servants, thirty three recusants, all tenants or servants of the Fitzherberts, were listed in Hamstall Ridware.[34] The next largest collection of recusants mentioned was at Swynnerton with Francis Gatacre and his wife, three servants and nine others.

The only peer listed in 1578 was Thomas, third Lord Paget, who had succeeded in 1568 and was frequently at his house on the site of Burton Abbey. In the mid-1570s his household steward was a Catholic priest, William Botrell, and he maintained a choir which provided secular entertainments but probably had a liturgical function as well. He was patron of William Byrd, a Catholic who managed to retain his position as a gentleman of the Chapel Royal. Byrd was paid money by Paget from 1576, probably a £10 annuity, and he stayed at the Burton house for over a week in August 1580, his room over the gatehouse containing a pair of virginals. In 1580 the Privy Council found that Paget had 'perverted to Popery' by his example many who had earlier conformed and committed him to the custody of the Dean of Windsor for persuasion. After fourteen weeks he promised to conform, but in 1581 he was the first to speak in the Lords against the new anti-recusancy Bill. In 1582 Bishop Overton complained that Paget had chosen the time of the Easter Communion to send his officers into Colwich church to execute warrants of arrest issued some time before. At Burton, where he was obliged to provide Communion bread, his officers produced 'little singing cakes, after the old popish fashion, varying nothing at all in form from massing bread, save only somewhat in the print'.[35]

Suspected of complicity in the Throckmorton Plot, Paget fled to Paris in 1583, and his lands were seized, those in Staffordshire being committed to Richard Bagot's administration. Although Paget's heir, a minor, was brought up a Protestant, his influence persisted. Sir Amias Paulet, who secured the stewardship of the Staffordshire lands in 1585, wrote to Sir Francis Walsingham in 1586 that 'divers of the better calling of the late servants of the Lord Paget's are ill-affected in religion, come seldom to the church, and that for fashion's sake only, and come not to the Communion at all'. Paulet stated that he had desired the stewardship in order to keep the tenants 'in the better obedience to Her Majesty's laws and proceedings in matter of religion, wherein they had been greatly seduced by the Lord Paget and his ministers'; he added that he had had some success. He also had a search made of suspect houses, and the study of one of Paget's servants 'was found furnished with Popish books of all kinds'.[36]

✍

With the growing number of priests arriving from abroad and the increasing threat from Spain, the 1580s saw harsher measures against Catholic priests, those who helped them, and recusants generally. In 1581 it became treason to reconcile another to Rome or to be reconciled oneself. Saying and hearing Mass were punishable by a fine of 200 marks and 100 marks respectively, and the fine for refusal to attend the parish church was raised from the 12d. a time collected by the churchwardens to £20 a lunar month with the justices in quarter sessions hearing charges for non-attendance. In 1585 priests ordained abroad who remained in the realm and refused the oath of supremacy were declared guilty of treason, and those who sheltered them guilty of a capital offence. An

Act of 1587 tightened up the 1581 Act: defendants failing to attend after indictment at assizes were to be deemed convicted and liable to a series of monthly fines until they conformed; if they failed to pay, they were to have two-thirds of their lands and all their goods confiscated.

Already in 1580 there was a new crackdown in Staffordshire. On the Privy Council's instructions Richard Bagot summoned nine leading recusants to Stafford by 10 a.m. on 15 August to be bound over to appear before the Council. Three of them, John Giffard, Brian Fowler and Erasmus Wolseley, were examined by the Council on 29 August and bound over to appear before the Bishop of London in September.[37] Giffard was sent to the Marshalsea but was allowed out in November on health grounds provided that he lived in or near the city of London. He took a house in St Helen's parish in the city, where he remained under house arrest. He was later put in the Gatehouse but was released in July 1581, having been given permission to go to 'the new wells' at Newnham Regis in Warwickshire for fourteen days and his manor of Marston near Stafford for eight days. In November and December he appeared three times before the Privy Council.[38] Fowler was sent to the Fleet but was released in May 1581 provided that he stayed within three miles of his home and did not admit any recusants, including priests and servants.[39] In 1582 William Stapleton of Littywood in Bradley, west of Stafford, was sent to the Clink in Southwark and his half share of Littywood seized in 1585. The other half was held by his brother John, but, although he too was convicted in 1588, he escaped forfeiture.[40] Walter Blount, a prisoner at Southwark, had his lands at Kingstone and Uttoxeter seized in 1585.[41] Also in 1585 Erasmus Wolseley had his manor of Wolseley and lands in Little Haywood seized and leased out in satisfaction of his debt of £500. In 1586 Draycott's recusancy debts of £600 were assigned by the Queen to William Ashbye, 'our well beloved servant', for unspecified services to the Crown; in 1587 all Draycott's future fines at the rate of £260 a year (£20 a lunar month) were similarly assigned.[42] Sir Thomas Fitzherbert on the other hand cleared fines of £140 in October 1588 and a further £260 12 months later.[43]

The Erdeswicks were in special trouble in the early 1580s. Hugh 'very violently used' a pursuivant sent to attach certain Staffordshire recusants in 1581,[44] and in 1582 he was described by Bishop Overton as 'the sorest and dangerousest papist one of them in all England'. The bishop was making a report to the Privy Council on a fracas at Sandon in May. He and other justices were meeting in the churchyard to discuss the repair of Sandon bridge when Hugh became involved in an argument with John Chetwynd and struck him with his crabtree staff.

> Immediately began a number of swords and daggers to be drawn, and had we not with diligence applied ourselves forthwith to appease the outrage, or rather had not God blessed our business at that time and stayed the hands and hearts of the people from further mischief, I think there had been such a bloody day as hath not been seen this great while in Staffordshire.[45]

In 1582 Sampson married Elizabeth Dixwell, his first wife, 'at a mass'. In June that year the Council ordered the Erdeswicks' house at Sandon to be searched for suspect persons, including Doctor John, a massing priest, and 'one Price', and for 'popish trumpery'.[46]

Meanwhile there were problems in the enforcement of the law. In November 1581 the Privy Council ordered the sheriff of Staffordshire to arrest fifteen jurymen impanelled for the finding of recusants and to take bonds for their appearance before the Court of Star Chamber 'to answer their disordered proceedings'. In December the Council complained that at the last assizes the grand jury of Staffordshire, when faced with the bishop's certificate of recusants, had 'found the Bill of some of the number certified and put out other some at their pleasure, such as are known to be the most obstinate and dangerous recusants of that county'. The jurors were ordered to acknowledge their offence at the next assizes or else appear before Star Chamber.[47]

Large-scale prosecution under the 1581 Act began in 1582, and by 1586 several hundred recusants had been indicted at Stafford. The great majority, however, were not convicted since they failed to appear and therefore the new fines could not be collected; the ultimate penalty was outlawry with loss of property and perpetual imprisonment. Several hundred Staffordshire recusants were so outlawed, but many were of too humble status – husbandmen, labourers, craftsmen – for loss of property to be relevant. In addition women could not be outlawed and some half of the defendants were women; it was not until 1593 that an Act made a husband responsible for the penalties incurred by a recusant wife. Finally the gaols were totally inadequate to hold hundreds of people.[48] At one of the assizes in 1587 the Chief Baron of the Exchequer, Sir Roger Manwood, refused to 'be troubled with the indicting of so many of them, saying they were most of them beggars', and he ordered the clerk of the peace for Staffordshire 'to collect some twenty or thirty of them of the most hablest to satisfy the penalty of the statute'.[49] Some humbler people, however, did suffer. John Wynckle had his goods worth £23 seized by the sheriff on 18 March 1586 and was in prison by April; he was presumably the John Wynckle who was described as a yeoman, late of Hixon in Colwich parish, when indicted in 1582 and who at last appeared at the county court in April 1586.[50]

Even leading recusants slipped through the net for a time at least. Francis Gatacre, John Giffard and William Macclesfield were indicted in 1582 for non-attendance at church. It was only after the passing of the 1587 Act that their lands were seized – Macclesfield's in 1587, Giffard's in 1588, and Gatacre's in 1592.[51] Sampson Erdeswick and Brian Fowler, indicted in 1582, seem to have escaped forfeiture altogether.[52] On the other hand eight leading Staffordshire recusants had their armour confiscated in 1585 as part of a national campaign.[53]

Richard Topcliffe, a leading priest-hunter, suggested in 1589 that one reason why Staffordshire recusants had been 'winked at' was the connivance of the clerk of the peace of

Staffordshire, 'that lewd fellow Blackewell'.[54] Nicholas Blackwell, who held office from 1586 to 1587, lived in Hamstall Ridware and was examined by the Privy Council in 1588 on several counts of devising ruses that enabled his neighbours there to escape the full force of the law, all of which he denied. He admitted that he had not received communion for nineteen years but protested that he did 'not abstain for religion but by reason of suits of law and other controversies'; he also stressed that he had taken the oath of supremacy when admitted at Clement's Inn some twenty years before. His wife was clearly a recusant: he stated that she had not received communion at least since the time of their marriage. He also admitted to using his influence with the sheriff to secure the release of a number of his neighbours in Hamstall Ridware; there were indeed 'a great number of his neighbours and friends Papists, but he hath not been a favourer of them in their Papistree'. Blackwell shows all the signs of being a church papist.[55]

In 1586 the government hit on a way of producing an immediate and sure source of income from recusants. In February the Privy Council notified sheriffs and justices that the Queen, impressed by the willingness of recusants in 1585 to meet their assessments for providing light horsemen for the expedition to the Netherlands, was now ready to allow them to compound annually for relief from fines and sequestrations.[56] In April Sir Walter Aston and Richard Bagot reported that they had discussed the matter with certain recusants who had duly made offers in writing, offers which Aston and Bagot considered to be realistically as much as could be squeezed out of them. There were twenty-five offers, headed by £20 from Erasmus Wolseley and £10 from Dorothy Heveningham for herself and a maidservant. The imprisoned John Wynckle offered 10s. with a promise to 'daily pray for Her Majesty'. Another prisoner, George Walker, offered £1. Hamstall Ridware was the most extensive source. Richard Fitzherbert, though described as a gentleman, offered only 3s. 4d. since his annual income was only 13s. 4d., but eleven other people there offered £1 each, while 'a poor serving man' offered 6d.[57]

Tutbury Castle about the time of the imprisonment there of Mary, Queen of Scots.

༄༅

A complication in Staffordshire was the presence of Mary, Queen of Scots, who had fled to England in 1568. As a claimant to at least the succession to the English throne and as a focus for Catholic discontent she remained an embarrassment to Elizabeth until her execution in 1587. Mary spent part of that time as a prisoner in Staffordshire. She was brought to Tutbury Castle in February 1569, with the Earl of Shrewsbury as her keeper; his countess (Bess of Hardwick) had furnished apartments for her and acted as a companion in the embroidering which filled so much of Mary's time. In April Mary was removed to Derbyshire, but she returned to Tutbury in September. With the Northern Rising in November and fear of a rescue attempt she was taken to Coventry, but she was again at Tutbury from January to May 1570. She returned in January 1585 in the reluctant custody of Sir Ralph Sadler, the Chancellor of the Duchy of Lancaster, of which Tutbury formed part. A stricter gaoler, the Puritan Sir Amias Paulet, took over in April.[58]

Mary at Tutbury was considered a security risk. When she returned there in September 1569 Elizabeth, having 'doubt of some escape of the said Queen', ordered that Mary's household, 'much enlarged of late time', was to be reduced to the thirty persons originally allowed; in addition 'common resort' to her was to stop, and she was not to send or receive messages and letters without Elizabeth's knowledge. Indeed any suggestion for a 'meeter place to keep her' was to be passed on to Elizabeth.[59] In October Mary complained that severity was being shown to her servants and that she was not allowed to receive news from Scotland or France; 'they have forbidden me to go out and have rifled my trunks, entering my chamber with pistols.' On her return from Coventry in January the lock on the door of her outer chamber was removed.[60]

Soon after his arrival with Mary in 1585 Sir Ralph Sadler told Sir Francis Walsingham that the Tutbury area was 'a perilous country, for both men and women of all degrees are almost all papists'; two in particular, 'which both do lurk' on the Derbyshire side of the nearby county boundary, 'nourish certain massing priests which do haunt their houses'. Sadler had thirty soldiers in the castle but had a low opinion of its strength. All the same Mary was allowed to go out of the castle to take the air; as in other places where she had been imprisoned, she used such occasions to distribute alms, and thus, as Walsingham noted, she won the hearts of the local people. In one day she distributed nearly 20 marks (£13 6s. 8d.) in the town of Tutbury. She had also been able to continue her customary charity on Maundy Thursday, distributing cloth and money to forty-two young girls and eighteen little boys; on Good Friday she bestowed £6 on the elderly poor. Sadler also allowed Mary to accompany him when he went out hawking, incurring Elizabeth's displeasure when she found out; he protested that he always took a large number of servants and others, some armed with pistols, sufficient to prevent any rescue attempt.[61]

Sir Amias Paulet too considered the area insecure. Walsingham told him of a report that letters between Mary and her son, King James of Scotland, were being passed by a local gentlewoman. Paulet agreed that there were 'many recusants and other suspected papists within twelve miles of Tutbury whose wives are not unlikely to do bad offices'. He singled out Grace, the wife of Henry Cavendish, who was the son of Bess of Hardwick by her second marriage and who owned a house built by his father on the site of Tutbury priory: 'the Lady Grace ... is an old acquaintance with this Queen, and with all the retinue, as you know.'[62]

Paulet quickly stopped members of Mary's retinue from walking on the walls by the castle gate and so having 'a full view of all comers and goers'.[63] He was advised that coachmen, laundresses and other servants were Mary's principal means for the conveyance of letters and messages. He therefore had her coachman closely watched, prevented him 'from riding abroad without my privity', made him move his lodging inside the castle, and stopped him, along with Mary's other servants, from eating with Paulet's own servants.[64] Washing carried by the laundresses who served members of her household was searched at the castle gate. Mary's own three laundresses, however, lived without restriction in a house in the park adjoining the castle and had always been allowed access to her chamber; Paulet observed to Walsingham that to search the clothes which they carried, 'as it cannot be comely, so it will be as little profitable, unless the women be also stripped unto their smocks'. He suggested that the only solution was to replace the women by others specially chosen.[65] Paulet suspected, correctly, that Camille de Preau, the member of Mary's household described as her reader, was 'a massing priest'; he reported his suspicions to Walsingham but no action was then taken.[66] Mary was still allowed to go out of the castle in her coach or on horseback, on occasion for coursing and hunting, but in line with his instructions Paulet would not allow her to travel further than two miles.[67] He also restrained her almsgiving.[68]

Mary hated Tutbury. She found the two rooms now allocated to her cold and thus a danger to her already poor health; they were also dark, and the stench from the castle privies, especially one below her window, was offensive.[69] By June she was constantly asking to be moved elsewhere.[70] Various Staffordshire places were considered, including Sir Walter Aston's home at Tixall, John Giffard's at Chillington, and Chartley Hall, which belonged to the Earl of Essex. Despite the Earl's objections, it was to Chartley that Mary was removed on Christmas Eve 1585.[71] Paulet rejoiced in the greater security: 'the laundresses being lodged within the house as now they are, and the residue of this Queen's train watched and attended in such precise manner as they be, I cannot imagine how it may be possible for them to convey a piece of paper as big as my finger.'[72] It was also the place where Mary was trapped into involvement in the Babington Plot of 1586, a conspiracy which was partly inspired by Walsingham and which aimed to place Mary on the English throne with foreign aid after Elizabeth had been despatched. Letters to and from Mary were hidden in casks conveyed by William Nicholson,[73] a Burton brewer who supplied beer to Tutbury

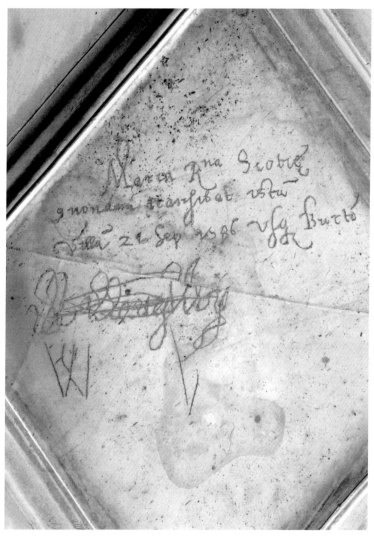

A pane from a window formerly at Hall Hill, Abbots Bromley, with the inscription: Maria R[egi]na Scoti[orum] quondam transibat ista[m] villa[m] 21 Sep[tembris] 1586 usq[ue] Burto[n] (Mary Queen of Scots once passed through this town 21 September 1586 on the way to Burton). It has been suggested that the word 'Willoughby' below the inscription may indicate that one of that family made the inscription, a William Willoughby having married into the Paget family who owned the house and whose arms are depicted elsewhere on the window: William Salt Library, Stafford, M 1118.

Castle and then to Chartley Hall. The link man at Burton was Walsingham's double agent Gilbert Giffard, a younger son of the staunchly recusant John Giffard. On 11 August, unaware of the collapse of the Babington Plot, Mary was taken out hunting by Paulet, arrested, and held at Tixall for a fortnight while her apartments at Chartley were ransacked. She was then brought back to Chartley; on being met outside Tixall gatehouse by a number of poor persons, she could only protest that she was a beggar like them.

Elizabeth, now thoroughly alarmed and convinced of 'the unsoundness' of Staffordshire, decided to remove her prisoner elsewhere.[74] On 21 September Mary left Chartley on her way to Fotheringhay in Northamptonshire and to trial and execution the following year. The first night of the journey was spent at Burton, but on the way Mary rested at Hall Hill in Abbots Bromley, where a room had been prepared for her. The visit was recorded a few years later on a window pane there, now preserved at the William Salt Library in Stafford.[75]

⁂

With the Armada crisis of 1588 the Privy Council ordered new measures against Catholics. In January Lord Shrewsbury as Lord Lieutenant of Staffordshire ordered the sheriff and deputy lieutenants to provide details of the most 'noted and obstinate' recusants and the 'not so obstinate'. A fortnight later he issued a stinging rebuke after receiving only a list 'of the most ignorant and base' and himself provided a list of leading recusants to be arrested. Of these John Draycott had by mid-February been committed by Archbishop Whitgift into the custody of a Shropshire vicar and Walter Fowler to Dr Adam Squire, master of Balliol College, Oxford, and Archdeacon of Middlesex; Fowler's wife, being 'somewhat sickly', was in the custody of Sir Walter Aston at Tixall pending further instructions. Of the remaining four, Draycott's son Philip, Sampson Erdeswick, and Walter Wolseley, had managed to be out of the county. The fourth, Richard, son of Francis Biddulph of Biddulph, was not at home and his whereabouts were allegedly unknown, but in the event he was committed to the custody of the chancellor of the diocese. In July, with the Armada advancing on England, Erdeswick was one of a number of recusants sent as prisoners to the bishop's palace at Ely.[76] The same month Lord Shrewsbury ordered that recusants already in prison should be held in close custody, while other suspect persons were to be arrested; special care was to be taken 'in those parts of the county towards Lancashire and the sea side'.[77] A week later John Giffard was committed to the custody of Thomas Phelippes, an agent of Walsingham who had played a leading part in trapping Mary, Queen of Scots, into the Babington Plot and who held the two-thirds of Giffard's sequestrated estate. Phelippes was instructed to allow no one access to Giffard but in the event treated him leniently as the father of Gilbert Giffard, who had worked closely with Phelippes in the plot against Mary. Phelippes claimed that it was the Queen's wish that John should be rewarded for his son's actions, although John was kept in ignorance of the reason for the leniency. Already in 1586 he had been released from prison and given permission to take the waters at Newnham Regis in Warwickshire or Bath and even to return to Chillington – although only for a month at a time so long as Mary, Queen of Scots, was in Staffordshire. In August 1588 he was allowed, 'upon some necessary occasions of his own', to return to Chillington for a time under the supervision of a servant of Phelippes. Richard Bagot was put fully in the picture by Phelippes and asked to counter any criticism of John's light treatment.[78]

It was at the time of the Armada that the first Staffordshire priest was executed. Blessed Robert Sutton was born in 1545 at Burton-upon-Trent, the son of a carpenter. He became rector of Lutterworth in Leicestershire in 1571 but resigned in 1577 and went abroad. He was ordained as a Catholic priest at Cambrai the same year and sent to England. Captured in 1585, he was banished but returned. He came to Stafford in 1587 and was arrested there apparently on 18 July 1588 (the day before the Armada arrived off the English coast) while saying Mass – according to one account in the house of

Erasmus Wolseley, according to another in the gaol. Wolseley and several others were taken with him, and all were condemned to death at the next assizes. Sir Walter Aston carried out the priest's examination and gave evidence against him at the trial. Such was the public outcry that the laymen were fined and released, but Sutton suffered the traitor's death on 27 July. The town annals of Stafford record the event:

> The priest was a very reverend learned man and at his arraignment disputed very stoutly and learnedly. He only was executed, that was hanged and quartered. And it was done in a most villainous butcherly manner by one Moseley who with his axe cut off his head (while he had yet sense and was ready to stand up) through his mouth.

Another account records how he blessed his fellow prisoners as he left the gaol on his way to execution with the words 'God comfort you all, for I am comforted' and continues:

> When he came to the place he desired he might speak, but they would not permit him. Then he took his handkerchief out of his pocket, lapped it together, made a fine discourse of the candle we receive in baptism and in the hour of death, and in remembrance of what he said, he held up the handkerchief in token he lived and died in the light of the Catholic faith. He was put off the ladder and cut down very lively, for he stood upon his feet, was taken by great violence, dismembered, spoke these words, 'O! thou bloody butcher! God forgive thee.' So calling upon Jesus and Mary, he gave up his spirit.

His quarters were fixed on the four gates of the town, but Wolseley's wife Cassandra secured the remaining bones for a bribe when they were taken down a year later. Three relics survive in England and a fourth in Brittany. One is a thumb, formerly at Stonyhurst College in Lancashire and in 1987 transferred to the church of Our Lady of Victories at Lutterworth. It was given by Sutton's brother to the Jesuit John

Gerard; a note in the reliquary believed to have been written by Gerard states that the thumb and first finger, which had been consecrated to hold the Body of Christ, were found to be intact when the remains were taken down. Robert Sutton was beatified in 1987 and is commemorated on 27 July.[79]

Another seminary priest, James Harrison, was captured in April at Comberford Hall near Tamworth, and the Comberford family's tenant there, Thomas Heath, was also arrested. They were imprisoned in London but eventually released; Harrison was rearrested in Yorkshire in 1602 and executed at York.[80]

Despite the anxiety of the gaolers of Mary, Queen of Scots, the optimism of her supporters about her popularity in Staffordshire, and the suspicions of Lord Shrewsbury,[81] there seems to have been little to fear from Staffordshire Catholics – or indeed from the general run of Catholics elsewhere in the kingdom. In 1585 the firmly Catholic Sir Thomas Fitzherbert, asking Walsingham for 'merciful consideration' because of his 'poor estate', protested that there was no one more willing to serve the Queen than he.[82] Even 'the sorest and dangerousest papist' Hugh Erdeswick, begging Lord Shrewsbury in 1587 to let him have 'such armour and furniture as he is charged to have in readiness for Her Majesty's service', protested that

> I shall not only show myself willing (according to my duty) to make or do any service which shall be acceptable to Her Majesty and your Honour to my most ability, but will continually pray for the good and prosperous estate of Her Majesty and your Honour's good government under the same long to continue to God's pleasure.[83]

In October 1588 the recusants imprisoned at Ely subscribed their allegiance, acknowledging that Elizabeth was their only sovereign, notwithstanding any excommunication, that she and no foreign power had jurisdiction over the realm and over persons spiritual and temporal, and that they would hazard their goods and persons in defending her against the Pope or anyone else; they were then released. In November John

Giffard agreed to do the same – 'so as his example shall be no stay to any of the rest in that country', as Phelippes informed Richard Bagot. Although Giffard persisted in his recusancy, Phelippes told Bagot in 1592 that he was otherwise completely law-abiding and 'ready by oath or otherwise to testify his duty to Her Majesty and his country'. Richard Biddulph too had subscribed his allegiance by January 1589 when the Privy Council ordered his release into his father's custody.[84] It was on a secret press in Staffordshire that the Jesuit Robert Southwell's *An Humble Supplication to Her Majestie*, written in the early 1590s, was later printed. In it he solemnly protested that 'the whole and only intent of our coming into this realm is no other but to labour for the salvation of souls, and in peaceable and quiet sort to confirm them in the ancient Catholic Faith in which their forefathers lived and died these 1400 years.' He assured the Queen 'that what army soever should come against you, we will rather yield our breasts to be broached by our country swords than use our swords to the effusion of our country's blood.'[85]

∽

After the defeat of the Armada measures against recusants were intensified. Topcliffe wrote to Richard Bagot in March 1589, commending his zeal, all the more so as 'much of the weight of that backward shire lieth upon your shoulders' and urging that if he would persevere and 'see that the fattest be not spared and the poorest sent into the Exchequer, it will breed a good alteration in your country'.[86] In September of that year Walter Whittall, gentleman, of Bloxwich and Edward Birch, husbandman, of Walsall had two-thirds of their lands seized. At Hamstall Ridware Richard Fitzherbert, Thomas Collier, the Marian priest, and Agnes Knowles, a widow, had goods and two-thirds of their lands seized, while two labourers and two husbandmen had their goods seized. At Blithbury in Mavesyn Ridware Isabel Blount, a widow, had half her house seized.[87] In 1592 Francis Gatacre suffered the loss of two-thirds of the manor and advowson of Swynnerton and of his lands in Shropshire.[88] Simon Rider of Dunkirk at Greets Green in West Bromwich, a member of a long established yeoman family, forfeited two-thirds of his house and estate there in 1594, including a water mill on the Tame.[89]

John Giffard continued to receive lenient treatment. He was still at Chillington in April 1589, and having apparently again taken the waters in Warwickshire in 1590 and returned home, he was still there in September 1592.[90] On the other hand Sir Thomas Fitzherbert and John Draycott were once more imprisoned, being released on bond in June 1589 provided they returned to prison by the beginning of the new law term. Fitzherbert was sent to the Tower in January 1591 and died there the same year, being buried in the chapel. Draycott had a somewhat easier time. He was released on bond from the custody of Archbishop Whitgift in November 1590 so that he could sell land in Lincolnshire and Shropshire in order to meet his recusancy fines. He returned from Lincolnshire to his home at Paynsley early in January intending to continue to Shropshire but was promptly seized 'with such a crick and pain in my back that I was not able never since either to ride or go'. Being due back in London under the terms of his bond, he wrote a fortnight later to Richard Bagot, begging him to come over and certify 'the extremity of my cause'. Bagot obliged, and the Privy Council gave Draycott leave of absence until he was fully recovered. He was back in London by September.[91] Similar leniency was shown to Hugh Erdeswick in 1590; he was then living on his estate at Leighton in Cheshire, and the Council accepted that he was too weak to appear before it.[92]

One long-established Staffordshire recusant had evidently succumbed by 1591. Thomas Peshall, 'an obstinate recusant' since the 1570s, found himself faced with confiscation and in January 1591 wrote to Richard Bagot protesting that he was 'no recusant'. He stated that he had not been in Staffordshire on any Sunday for a year but that while living elsewhere 'in a strange country where I have little acquaintance and few friends', he was nonetheless able to find twelve men to swear before the Lord Chief Justice 'that I came to church orderly according to the laws'. He escaped confiscation, and in 1608 he was appointed sheriff of Staffordshire, evidently dying while still in office.[93] He may well be another example of a church papist.

Late in 1591 the government, fearing a new threat from Spain, appointed recusancy commissioners for each county who were to inquire into the activities of seminary priests and Jesuits. In December Bishop Overton summoned his nine fellow commissioners for Staffordshire to meet at Eccleshall church for a discussion of their duties; they consisted of leading gentry and churchmen, including Richard Bagot. The following June the high commissioners for recusancy ordered the Staffordshire commissioners to arrest 'all Jesuits, seminary and popish priests' and lay people refusing to go to church; suspect houses were to be searched for popish writings and objects. The high commissioners had also been advised that Mass was being said in recusants' houses, 'whereunto is great resort of people', a report which was to be given special attention.[94]

It was in this spirit that Edward, Lord Stafford, a justice of the peace although not a recusancy commissioner, promptly carried out a search for a seminary priest in his manor of Forebridge to the south of Stafford. In Henry Tulley's house he broke open a closet and found unlawful books and some images. There were other locked places, but he notified three of the commissioners that he would await their arrival the next morning before taking further action. He committed Tulley's wife Alice to prison as an obstinate recusant but in September bound her over to appear at the next quarter sessions. He noted that her neighbours would 'depose that she is a continual recettor both of recusants and of one Perton and Barlow being old priests and of other such like disobedient persons against Her Majesty's laws'.[95]

The persecution of the early 1590s produced a saint for Staffordshire.[96] Edmund Gennings was born at Lichfield in 1567. He went to France in 1583 and was ordained at Soissons in 1590. Returning to Lichfield and finding his parents dead, he sought out his brother John in London. He was

St Edmund Gennings, with depictions of his arrest and his hanging, drawing and quartering.

arrested by Topcliffe while still in his vestments after saying Mass at the house of Swithun Wells in Grays Inn Fields in November 1591, and he and Wells were executed outside that house on 10 December.[97] Edmund's brother recorded the execution in the biography which he published in 1614:

Mr Topcliffe cried out with a loud voice, 'Gennings, Gennings, confess thy fault, thy Popish treason, and the Queen, by submission, no doubt will grant thee pardon.' To which he mildly answered, 'I know not, Mr Topcliffe, in what I have offended my dear anointed Princess, for if I have offended her, or any other, in anything, I would willingly ask her and all the world forgiveness. If she be offended with me without a cause, for professing my faith and religion, because I am a priest, or because I will not turn minister against my conscience, I shall be, I trust, excused and innocent before God' . . .

After he had been dismembered the violence of the pain caused him to utter these words in a loud voice, 'Oh, it smarts'. Which Mr Wells hearing, replied, 'Alas, sweet soul, thy pain is great indeed, but almost past. Pray for me now, most holy saint, that mine may come.' After he was ripped up, and his bowels cast into the fire, if credit may be given to hundreds of people standing by, and to the hangman himself, the blessed martyr, while his heart was in the hangman's hand, uttered these words, 'Holy Gregory, pray for me'. Upon which the hangman swore a most wicked oath, and cried out, 'Z . . . ds! See, see! His heart is in my hand, and yet Gregory is in his mouth! Oh, egregious Papist!'

Edmund Gennings and Swithun Wells were canonized among the Forty Martyrs of England and Wales in 1970, and Edmund is commemorated on 10 December.

In August 1592 the Privy Council ordered the committal of leading recusants to the charge of sound Protestants or else to gaol, in all cases at their own expense. Of those who appeared before the Staffordshire justices, John Giffard was still in the

The Tomb of Sampson Erdeswick in Sandon Church.

charge of Thomas Phelippes, Sampson Erdeswick was committed to Richard Bagot, Edward Stanford, son of Robert Stanford of Perry Hall in Handsworth, was sent to the Dean of Lichfield, and Humphrey Comberford was put in prison. John Draycott had gone to London on bond to appear before the high commissioners. Three others had 'reformed themselves'. Fifteen failed to appear, including Brian Fowler, three members of the Macclesfield family and three Draycotts; these were to be arrested and sent to the bishop's palace at Lichfield with 'some sufficient man to see unto their safe keeping'.[98]

∽

Sampson Erdeswick's committal to the custody of Richard Bagot is a reminder that matters were not black and white – that whatever those at the centre might decree, the local scene presented a different picture.[99] For all their division over religion, both men were keenly interested in antiquarian pursuits, and in 1590 Richard described Sampson as a gentleman 'of good knowledge and experience' in such studies. With Richard's son Walter, who succeeded his father in 1597, relations were friendly; Walter indeed was much less enthusiastic than Richard about applying the laws against recusants. Sampson corresponded with him 'as so dear a friend to me' and was on visiting terms at Blithfield, Walter's home. Walter had been party to an Erdeswick family settlement in 1593 and stood surety for a loan to Sampson which was still outstanding at the latter's death in 1603.

Sampson in fact, despite being in constant trouble as a recusant, was able to play a part in local life. Even before succeeding his father Hugh in 1596, he was prominent in running the Sandon estate. Both appear as hard-nosed landlords in an undated petition from a group of inhabitants and freeholders of Sandon to the assize justices; it accused the Erdeswicks of inclosing much of the land and converting arable to pasture, 'not having the fear of God before their eyes ... fraudulently, against all Christianity ... nothing more coveting than the extreme destruction of your poor orators and the having of the whole manor to themselves, whereby (as the prophet sayth) they may live alone upon the earth'.[100] In 1592 Sampson contributed, like fellow gentry (including other recusants such as John Giffard), towards the building of a new shire hall in Stafford. Although a Catholic, he was patron and impropriator of Sandon church, and he also left his heraldic mark on the building, decorating the walls and east window with his ancestral arms. In 1601 he erected his own tomb in the chancel, probably to the design of Joseph Hollemans of Burton. It has a more than life-size effigy of himself and figures of his two wives kneeling in niches above; it too was adorned with arms along with the Erdeswick pedigree from 1086. The tomb of his father Hugh (d. 1596) is also in the chancel.

Sampson was Staffordshire's first county historian, compiling 'A View of Staffordshire' in the last ten years or so of his life. He was involved with other antiquaries locally and nationally. He was a member of the Society of Antiquaries, which met in London from about 1582, introduced probably by William Camden. The two corresponded, and the entry for Sandon in the 1600 edition of Camden's *Britannia* describes Sampson as 'a most illustrious man' (*vir clarissimus*) and an outstanding student of antiquity. Sampson's 'View' is personal in style and yet contains little or nothing to suggest his recusancy. When he criticises the bishop, it is not for heresy but for failing to restore wall paintings in the palace. When he speaks of 'the iniquity of this age', he is referring to the removal of the copper from a tomb in Caverswall church. The dissolution of the monasteries gets a single dry comment in connection with Calwich Abbey:

Now a Lancashire gentleman is owner thereof; who, as I have heard, hath made a parlour of the chancel, a hall of the church, and a kitchen of the steeple, which may be true, for I have known a gentleman in Cheshire, who hath done the like.

The records of the 1590s reveal recusancy among all social degrees throughout the county, illegal but not underground, with its leaders extensively but not consistently persecuted. Even sequestration did not necessarily spell ruin. John Giffard, sequestrated in 1588, survived to be buried in 1613 in a fine alabaster tomb in the chancel of Brewood parish church – one of four such Giffard tombs dating from 1556 to 1632. At a somewhat humbler level Simon Rider of West Bromwich, sequestrated in 1594 and dying in 1640, continued as a Catholic farmer and miller with a keen interest in local affairs. Indeed when officers arrived to seize his goods in 1598, they were forcibly resisted by a crowd of at least thirty, including several women and two members of the Rider family.[101] In all, only twelve Staffordshire recusants had had their lands seized by 1595–6, though very many more stood convicted.[102]

It was Staffordshire that made the Diocese of Coventry and Lichfield the third most recusant diocese in England, after Chester and York, when James I succeeded Elizabeth in 1603.[103]

Notes

1 See A. Walsham, *Church Papists* (1993), chapters 1 and 2.

2 For this para. see H. E. Savage, *The Cathedral under the Elizabethan Settlement* (Lichfield, 1930), pp. 11–13; M. W. Greenslade, 'The Popish of Lichfield', in P. Morgan (ed.), *Staffordshire Studies: Essays presented to Denis Stuart* (Keele, 1987), pp. 129–30. For Ramridge see also H. de Vocht, 'John Ramridge, Exul pro Fide Catholica', *Sacris Erudiri*, vii (1955), pp. 367 sqq. For Langdale see also R. B. Manning, *Religion and Society in Elizabethan Sussex* (Leicester, 1969), pp. 44n, 54n, 160.

3 The first use of the term (from the Latin *recusare*, to refuse) in this context. According to Sir Edward Coke it was used from 1568 to describe persons who refused to attend the Prayer Book services prescribed by the Settlement; in 1583 a divine referred to 'our recusants, as we call them, that is, our refusing papists to come to church'. It remained unusual for

the term to be used for Protestant seceders from the Church of England. See *Cal. S.P. Dom. 1601–1603; with Addenda 1547–1565*, pp. 521–5; H. Bowler (ed.), *Recusant Roll No. 2 (1593–1594)* (*C.R.S.* lvii), pp. viii–ix, xxxvi–xxxvii. In contrast the term 'church papist' was by 1582 applied to one who conformed minimally by being present at church while remaining a Catholic at heart – and often having a recusant wife: Walsham, *Church Papists*, p. 1.

4　*S.H.C.* 1915, pp. xliii–xliv.

5　*V.C.H. Staffs.* iii, p. 47.

6　*S.H.C.* 1915, pp. 367–8.

7　Ibid., p. 369; *V.C.H. Staffs.* iii, pp. 47–8.

8　P. McGrath, *Papists and Puritans under Elizabeth I* (1967), p. 155.

9　Walsham, *Church Papists*, pp. 15–16.

10　*S.H.C.* 4th ser. ix, p. 37.

11　*S.H.C.* 1915, p. 367; *Cal. S.P. Dom. 1601–1603; with Addenda 1547–1565*, p. 524; *Oxford D.N.B.* xvi, pp. 892–3. Draycott died at Draycott-in-the-Moors in 1571 and was buried near his family's chapel in the parish church, where he had been rector until he resigned in 1547: *S.H.C.* 1915, p. 83.

12　M. Bateson (ed.), 'Collection of Original Letters from the Bishops to the Privy Council', *Camden Miscellany*, ix (1895), p. 41.

13　V. M. Webster, 'Two Marian Priests in Worcestershire: John Felton and Symon Southern', *Worcestershire Recusant*, i (1963), p. 21.

14　*Camden Miscellany*, ix, p. 41.

15　*V.C.H. Staffs.* iii, p. 53.

16　*S.H.C.* 1915, p. 371.

17　*Acts of the Privy Council 1578–80*, p. 57.

18　M. Hodgetts, 'Campion in Staffordshire and Derbyshire', *Mid. Cath. Hist.* vii (2000), pp. 52–3.

19　*Cal. S.P. Dom. 1581–1590*, p. 75.

20　T. Dunn, 'Pedigree & History of the Macclesfield Family ...' (1995; copy in W.S.L.), pp. 165, 167; Anstruther, *Seminary Priests*, i, pp. 387–8.

21　*S.H.C.* 4th ser. ix, pp. 22–3.

22　P. Caraman (ed.), *John Gerard: The Autobiography of an Elizabethan* (1956 edn), pp. 37–8.

23   Historical MSS Commission, *Salisbury*, xvii, pp. 500–1. The letter to the Earl of Salisbury is dated 1605 but refers to 'the haunts and residence which Jesuits were wont to have a good while since'. Cf. National Archives (Public Record Office), SP 14/7/50.

24   A Puritan survey of Staffordshire parishes in 1604 described the vicar of Baswich and the rector of Blymhill as Mass priests: *S.H.C.* 1915, pp. 25, 32.

25   *Castle Church Parish Register* (Staffordshire Parish Registers Society, 1903), p. 78; National Archives (Public Record Office), E 134/12 Jas. I Hil/11, m. 7.

26   *S.H.C.* 1915, pp. 245, 375; S. A. H. Burne (ed.), *The Staffordshire Quarter Sessions Rolls. Vol. I. 1581–1589* (*S.H.C.* 1929), pp. 37, 53, 131; *S. Mary's, Stafford, Parish Register* (Staffs. Par. Regs. Soc. 1935–6), p. 98.

27   *S.H.C.* 1915, p. 375; H. Bowler and T. J. McCann (eds), *Recusants in the Exchequer Pipe Rolls 1581–1592* (*C.R.S.* lxxi, 1986), 25.

28   *C.R.S.* lxxi, pp. 39–40.

29   Ibid., p. 15; below, p. 65.

30   *S.H.C.* 4th ser. ix, pp. 65–6.

31   For the next four paragraphs see *Acts of the Privy Council 1575–1577*, pp. 13, 15, 17–18, 20–1, 40–1, 44, 46, 57–8, 75, 80–1, 105, 145–7.

32   He married Elizabeth, widow of William Fitzherbert; she inherited Swynnerton from her father, Humphrey Swynnerton, in 1562 and conveyed it in 1608 to her strongly Catholic grandson, Edward Fitzherbert: T. B. Trappes-Lomax, *Swynnerton* (*Staffs. Cath. Hist.* ix, 1967–8), pp. 1–3, 27.

33   *S.H.C.* 1915, pp. 373–5.

34   For Sir Thomas see also J. C. Wedgwood, *Staffordshire Parliamentary History*, i (*S.H.C.* 1917–18), pp. 314–15; *Cal. S.P. Dom. 1547–1580*, p. 372.

35   *V.C.H. Staffs.* iii, pp. 99–100; ix, pp. 10, 130; C. Harrison, 'William Byrd and the Pagets of Beaudesert: a musical connection', *Staffordshire Studies*, iii (1990–1), pp. 51 sqq.

36   J. Morris (ed.), *The Letter-books of Sir Amias Poulet* (1874), pp. 32–3, 35, 174, 179–81.

37   *S.H.C.* 4th ser. ix, pp. 5–7.

38   *S.H.C.* new ser. v, pp. 132–5.

39   *Acts of the Privy Council 1581–1582*, p. 42.

40 *C.R.S.* lxxi, p. 161; *V.C.H. Staffs.* iv, p. 80. Joyce Stapleton, spinster, of Bradley was convicted in 1582.

41 *C.R.S.* lxxi, p. 23.

42 Ibid., pp. 53, 195.

43 Ibid., p. 62.

44 *Acts of the Privy Council 1581–1582*, p. 30.

45 Ibid., pp. 444–5; *V.C.H. Staffs.* iii, pp. 102–3.

46 *Acts of the Privy Council 1581–1582*, pp. 425, 437.

47 *V.C.H. Staffs.* iii, p. 101.

48 *S.H.C.* 1929, pp. xxxii–xxxvi.

49 *S.H.C.* 4th ser. ix, p. 35.

50 *S.H.C.* 1915, p. 381; *S.H.C.* 1929, pp. 36, 62, 125.

51 *C.R.S.* xxi, pp. 66–7, 116.

52 Leighton, the Erdeswicks' property in Cheshire, was due to be seized after Hugh's death: M. M. C. Calthrop (ed.), *Recusant Roll No. 1, 1592–3* (*C.R.S.* xviii, 1916), pp. 21–2.

53 *S.H.C.* 4th ser. ix, pp.15–18.

54 Ibid., p. 43. For what follows on Blackwell see ibid., pp. 32–6; Sir Edgar Stephens, *The Clerks of the Counties 1360–1960* (1961), p. 158.

55 For the term see above n. 3.

56 *Cal. S.P. Dom. 1581–1590*, p. 307.

57 *S.H.C.* 1915, pp. 380–1.

58 *V.C.H. Staffs.* x (forthcoming). For the embroidery see A. Fraser, *Mary Queen of Scots* (1970 edn), pp. 487–9.

59 P. Collinson, *The English Captivity of Mary Queen of Scots* (Sheffield, 1987), p. 40.

60 *V.C.H. Staffs.* i, pp. 250–1.

61 Ibid. x (forthcoming); Shaw, *Staffs.* i, appendix, pp. 16, 19–20; Morris (ed.), *Letter-books of Poulet*, pp. 6, 53–4, 161–2.

62 Morris (ed.), *Poulet*, pp. 64, 67, 125; *V.C.H. Staffs.* x (forthcoming).

63 Morris (ed.), *Poulet*, pp. 14, 43.

64 Ibid., pp. 11, 14, 41, 43, 50.

65 Ibid., pp. 49–52.

66 Ibid., pp. 24, 31, 57, 60–2, 109–10. For action taken after the Babington Plot see ibid., pp. 269, 328, 339.

67 Ibid., pp. 52–3, 60–1, 91.

68 Ibid., pp. 39–40, 53–4.

69 Ibid., pp. 63, 77, 87, 93, 106–8; R. Somerville, *Guide to Tutbury Castle, Staffordshire* (1968 edn), p. 11.

70 Morris (ed.), *Poulet*, p. 63.
71 For the rest of this paragraph, unless otherwise stated, see Fraser, *Mary Queen of Scots*, chapter 24.
72 Morris (ed.), *Poulet*, p. 126.
73 *S.H.C.* 4th ser. ix, pp. 38, 45–6; Morris (ed.), *Poulet*, p. 33.
74 Morris (ed.), *Poulet*, pp. 272, 275.
75 M. A. Rice, *Abbots Bromley* (Shrewsbury, 1939), chapter 3.
76 *S.H.C.* 4th ser. ix, pp. 17, 24–6, 31, 40–1.
77 Ibid., p. 37.
78 Ibid., pp. 38–9; *Acts of the Privy Council 1586–7*, p. 19.
79 Anstruther, *Seminary Priests*, i, p. 343; F. Grady and A. W. Neal, 'Blessed Robert Sutton', *Staffs. Cath. Hist.* xxiii (1988), pp. 1 sqq.
80 Anstruther, *Seminary Priests*, i, pp. 150–1.
81 *V.C.H. Staffs.* iii, p. 102; *S.H.C.* 4th ser. ix, p. 24.
82 *Cal. S.P. Dom. 1581–1590*, p. 286.
83 *S.H.C.* 4th ser. ix, pp. 23–4.
84 Ibid., pp. 38, 41–2.
85 McGrath, *Papists and Puritans*, pp. 268–9.
86 *S.H.C.* 4th ser. ix, p. 43.
87 *C.R.S.* xviii and lxxi.
88 Ibid., xviii, pp. 265, 299.
89 H. Bowler (ed.), *Recusant Roll No. 3 (1594–1595) and Recusant Roll No. 4 (1595–1596)* (*C.R.S.* lxi, 1970), pp. 86–7; *V.C.H. Staffs.* xvii, pp. 21, 31, 60.
90 *S.H.C.* 4th ser. ix, pp. 39–40, 59.
91 Ibid., pp. 45, 52–3, 59; *S.H.C.* 1917–18, p. 315.
92 *Acts of the Privy Council 1590*, p. 34.
93 *S.H.C.* 4th ser. ix, pp. 51–2.
94 Ibid., ix, pp. 53–5.
95 Ibid., pp. 55–6.
96 For this para. see Anstruther, *Seminary Priests*, i, p. 128; *The Life and Death of Blessed Edmund Gennings by his brother John Gennings* (published 1960 by the Office of the Vice-Postulation for the Canonisation of the Forty Martyrs of England Wales as an abridged version of John Gennings' *The Life and Death of Mr. Edmund Geninges, Priest . . .* (St Omer, 1614).
97 Anstruther, *Seminary Priests*, i, p. 128.
98 *S.H.C.* 4th ser. ix, pp. 58–9.
99 For the next three paras. see M. W. Greenslade, *The Stafford-*

shire Historians (S.H.C. 4th ser. xi, 1982), pp. 21, 24–6 and sources cited there. For the tomb see also S. A. Jeavons, 'The Monumental Effigies of Staffordshire, Part III', *Transactions of the Birmingham Archaeological Society*, lxxi (1955), pp. 2, 5–7, and plate 3a.

100 S.R.O., HM Chetwynd 67.

101 S. A. H. Burne (ed.), *The Staffordshire Quarter Sessions Rolls. Vol. IV. 1598–1602 (S.H.C.* 1935), p. 41; *S.H.C.* 4th ser. xi, p. 19; *V.C.H. Staffs.* xvii, pp. 31, 60.

102 *C.R.S.* lxi, pp. 215–23.

103 McGrath, *Papists and Puritans*, p. 399. The return made by the bishops recorded 2,482 recusants in the Chester diocese (which included Lancashire), 720 in York and 650 in Coventry and Lichfield; the next largest figure was 526 in Durham.

3

CONSOLIDATION AND WAR: 1603–1649

Catholics had high but exaggerated hopes of King James. The son of Mary, Queen of Scots, and married to a Catholic convert, Anne of Denmark, he made promises of some religious toleration before his accession to the English throne. Once in England in 1603 he showed friendliness to Catholics and even remitted a year's fines as part of his coronation celebrations. Catholic numbers promptly grew, or at least more Catholics came out into the open.

Catholic enthusiasm was evident in Staffordshire at the parliamentary election of March 1604. Sir Edward Littleton of Pillaton in Penkridge, a Protestant who took one of the county seats, reported that 'the common speech is that the assembly at Stafford on Thursday was rather to choose a pope than a knight for the Parliament because they were all of that tribe'. The other county seat went to Sir Robert Stanford of Perry Hall in Handsworth, perhaps a church papist. His wife Anne, daughter of John Leveson of Wolverhampton, was a recusant, and his eldest son Edward, having been committed as a recusant to the custody of the Dean of Lichfield in 1592, evidently persisted in his recusancy.[1]

A Puritan survey of most of Staffordshire's parishes in 1604 showed recusancy throughout the county.[2] A large number of parishes were described as having many or some recusants (or 'popish'). At Brewood there were 'very many recusants', a reflection of the influence of the Giffards of

Chillington. The only precise figures given were for Penkridge, where recusants numbered four men and fourteen women. At Cannock, an area of peculiar jurisdiction belonging to the Dean and Chapter of Lichfield, the population of 400 were 'almost all Papists, as is commonly seen in the jurisdiction of the Dean and Chapter of Lichfield' – an echo of the earlier complaints by Bishops Bentham and Overton.

A return of 1607 covering much of the county parish by parish and listing individual recusants and 'half recusants' (church papists) presents a similar over-all picture.[3] There is a classic example at Sedgley of a mixed recusant and church papist family. The wife of Edward Hall, gentleman, and two sons and a daughter were presented by the vicar as

> absolute recusants, refusing both to frequent divine service and to receive the holy communion. I present that Edward Hall aforesaid the elder, gent., doth not as yet conform himself to the receiving of the holy communion although he doth resort unto the church and there stay the whole time of divine service and sermons.

James seems to have been willing to grant *de facto* toleration provided Catholics remained docile and a minority. Their growth in number was not to his liking, and by 1604 he was making public statements condemning Catholicism. Even his protestation that he 'would be sorry to punish their bodies for the error of their minds' had its limits: in that same year a Staffordshire priest suffered the ultimate penalty. John Sugar was born at Wombourne near Wolverhampton in 1557 or 1558 and is said to have served as minister at Cannock. He went to Douai in 1599 and was ordained in 1601, being then sent to England. He worked in his native Staffordshire as well as in Worcestershire and Warwickshire, serving 'the meaner and poorer sort of Catholics'. He was arrested in Warwickshire with his servant Robert Grissold in 1603. They were committed to Warwick gaol in July and convicted at the summer assizes. Judgement was respited so that they could sue the King for a pardon, the judges urging them meanwhile to conform. No pardon had been forthcoming by the Lent assizes 1604, but the judges again deferred judgement until the summer assizes, when they offered to approach the King themselves provided the two would conform. Sugar and Grissold persisted in their refusal to conform and were executed at Warwick on 16 July. They were beatified in 1987 and are commemorated on 17 July.[4]

꙼

Catholic disappointment with James was keen, but only a few turned to violence and gunpowder treason. It was in Staffordshire that the Gunpowder Plot of 1605 was finally broken in a shoot-out at Holbeach just south of Himley in the south-west of the county. It was the home of a branch of the Littleton family, one of whom, George, had been in trouble for recusancy in the 1590s; the house contained two priest holes.[5]

With the capture of Guy Fawkes on 5 November Robert Catesby, the ringleader, and the other plotters dispersed to the Midlands, hoping to gather support.[6] They were joined in Warwickshire by the dashing Sir Everard Digby of Gayhurst in Buckinghamshire, stepson to Sampson Erdeswick and knighted by James at the beginning of the reign, and also by Stephen Littleton of Holbeach. The group's hopes dwindled as they proceeded, and at 10 o'clock on the night of 7 November they arrived at Holbeach, hoping to fortify it against the pursuing force of the sheriff of Worcestershire, Sir Richard Walsh.

The gunpowder which the conspirators had with them was damp and they put it in front of a fire to dry. A spark flew out of the fire on to the powder, and in the blaze which followed one of them was blinded and three, including Catesby, were badly burnt; the house too was damaged. Meanwhile some slipped away, including Digby who intended to give himself up honourably in Warwick. There were eight of the plotters still in the house as well as a number of their servants when Walsh and his troop arrived about noon on 8 November. Four were wounded trying to escape across the

A marginal drawing on a Horton court roll, October 1644. The profile resembles that of Charles I, and the man's Spanish headgear and clawed hand suggest a link with Catholicism and Anti-Christ; see *Staffordshire Studies*, xiii (2001), p. 77.

courtyard. Catesby and another were shot down at the door of the house and the besiegers rushed in. Three of the plotters were stripped as they lay dying. Catesby crawled back into the house and died clutching a picture of the Virgin. This and the gold crucifix round his neck were seized by the sheriff's assistant and sent up to London as 'superstitious and popish idols'.

Digby was captured before he could reach Warwick.[7] Stephen Littleton and Robert Winter, one of the original plotters, found various hide-outs together in Rowley Regis before crossing into Worcestershire where they were sheltered in a barn at Hagley before being taken into the Hall by Stephen's first cousin, Humphrey Littleton. Humphrey was living at the Hall in the absence of Meriel Littleton, widow of Humphrey's brother Sir John.[8] The cook betrayed the fugitives, who were caught while trying to escape. Humphrey fled to Prestwood in Kinver not far from Holbeach, where he too was captured.[9] The executions followed in 1606.

It gives a twist to the story to find that Staffordshire commemorates the Gunpowder Plot in a special way. Several streets on a housing estate south-west of Holbeach House are named after people connected with the Plot. They include Catesby Drive and Digby Road.

༄

Despite the Plot James continued his pragmatic approach to recusancy, but Parliament insisted on new anti-Catholic measures. They included an oath of allegiance of 1606 denying the temporal supremacy of the Pope and various Catholic doctrines. It was a similar story under Charles I, who succeeded in 1625. There was, however, no Parliament between 1629 and 1640, and the French Catholic Queen Henrietta Maria had more influence than Anne of Denmark. In general Catholics had an easier time under the first two Stuart kings than under Elizabeth I. In 1623 William Bishop arrived as Vicar Apostolic for England and Scotland with the title of Bishop of Chalcedon. He promptly established archdeaconries and deaneries and set up a chapter of twenty-four canons under a dean. With the withdrawal of his successor Richard Smith from the country in 1631 the chapter exercised powers of government until the next appointment of a vicar apostolic in 1685, a situation tolerated but never officially recognised by the Pope.

There were ten secular priests working in Staffordshire in 1610. Staffordshire and Cheshire together formed one of the new archdeaconries of 1623, containing thirty-one seculars in 1631.[10] Four Benedictines died in the county in the earlier seventeenth century, and two can be identified to a definite place. Nicholas Becket was born at Moseley in 1583 and died in 1618 at Cannock, where he was apparently chaplain to the Coleman family. Francis Forster, alias Henry Clark, was born in 1572 and died in 1631 at Stafford Castle, the home of his sister Isabel, dowager Lady Stafford.[11] There was a Dominican at St Thomas for many years: William Fowler, son of the Walter Fowler who died in 1621. William went abroad to study for the secular priesthood in 1609 at the age of eighteen but soon joined the Dominicans. He returned to St Thomas, possibly in the 1620s and in succession to a secular priest named Fisher, and was based there until his death in 1662.[12]

The Jesuits were the only religious order to have an organised presence in the county before the nineteenth century. A few Jesuits had been at work in Staffordshire in the 1580s and 1590s,[13] and the order became settled in the county about 1614, possibly at Biddulph under the wing of the Biddulphs. A hostile account, reflecting the clash between secular priests and the Jesuits, was given in 1634 by Richard Button, Archdeacon of Staffordshire and Cheshire, who had been at loggerheads with the order since his time as a student in Rome:

> About thirty years ago, when I first came to these parts, no member of a religious order lived in or visited Cheshire or Staffordshire. At that time the secular clergy administered religion in great charity and peace. Concord reigned, not only among the priests but also the laity. And so, for about ten years, matters continued and the cause of God smoothly

prospered until a certain lady, who was devoted to the
Society of Jesus, arrived from London, and with guile won
over her brother's wife to a like opinion as her own.

As a result a secular chaplain was replaced by a Jesuit. At
Biddulph in 1632 there was a Jesuit chaplain who had taken
the place of a secular.[14] In 1622–3 there were ten priests on
the Jesuits' *missio Staffordiensis*, with John Worthington as
superior; the *missio*, however, seems to have included
Cheshire and possibly Shropshire and was part of the newly
created college of Blessed Aloysius which also included
Lancashire and Westmorland.[15] A few years earlier the Jesuits
had established a school at Ashmore in Wednesfield, a moated
house belonging to a Catholic branch of the Leveson family.
The priest running it was arrested in 1635 along with eight
pupils, including John Stanford of Perry Hall; the boys were
released, but the priest was imprisoned.[16] The Jesuit William
Southerne, who came to England in 1629 and died in 1658,
may have worked at St Thomas and been a member of the
Catholic Southerne family of nearby Acton Trussell.[17]

Details of the disguises worn by priests are given in *The
Boy of Bilson* (1622),[18] a tract claiming to be 'a true discovery of the late notorious impostures of certaine Romish priests
in their pretended exorcisme or expulsion of the Divell out of
a young boy, named William Perry, sonne of Thomas Perry
of Bilson, in the county of Stafford, yeoman'. In 1620 the boy
(who finally admitted to be feigning possession in order to get
off school) was visited by three Catholic priests who
performed various rites over him. According to the author of
the tract, they styled themselves 'Catholike gentlemen . . .
albeit by their outward garb one would rather suspect them for
serving men and attendants on such persons'. The first, who
arrived after the boy's father was persuaded by some papists
to seek such help, was described by the boy as 'of an indif-
ferent tall stature, with long black hair, in a greenish suit, his
doublet opened under the armpits with ribbons'. He later
brought along another priest, 'a short big fat man, with black-
ish long curled hair, in a kind of russet coloured suite, with a

THE BOY
OF BILSON:

O R,

A TRVE DISCOVERY OF
THE LATE NOTORIOVS IM-
POSTVRES OF CERTAINE ROMISH
Priests in their pretended *Exorcisme*, or expulsion of
the Diuell out of a young Boy, named WILLIAM
PERRY, *sonne of* THOMAS PERRY *of*
Bilson, *in the County of* Staf-
ford, *Yeoman.*

Vpon which occasion, hereunto
is premitted

*A briefe Theologicall Discourse, by way of
Caution,* for the more easie discerning of such
Romish spirits ; and iudging of their false
pretences, both in this and the
like Practices.

2. Thes. 2. 10, 11.
*Because they receiued not the loue of the truth, that they might be saued.
For this cause God shall send them strong delusion, that they should be-
leeue a lye.*

AT LONDON,
Imprinted by *F. K.* for *William Barret.* 1622.

Title-page of *The Boy of Bilson.*

sword by his side'. About a week later the fat priest returned accompanied by a 'third priest, being a reasonable tall old man, in a horseman's coat, with long head hair'.

✍

By the early seventeenth century a contraflow to the priests returning to their native country had begun as daughters from Catholic families entered convents abroad.[19] Several from Staffordshire were professed at the convent of the Augustinian Canonesses of the Lateran in Louvain. They included: the daughter of Walter Coleman of Cannock, in 1618; Bridget and Anne, daughters of Walter Giffard of Chillington, in 1621; and their niece Mary, daughter of Peter Giffard, in 1625. Mary had entered the convent young and lived there until her profession. Four years later she helped found a house in Bruges. Helen, daughter of Alban Draycott of Paynsley, was professed as a lay sister in 1625, 'who, being a gentlewoman by birth, yet having but small means and a strong body, was well content to be a work-sister'. Ursula, daughter of Viscount Stafford, was at school in the convent with her two elder sisters until 1653, when they were sent back to England on their mother's orders. Ursula returned as a postulant and was clothed in 1663 in the presence of her father, mother, elder brother and one of her sisters 'with a train of ten servants'. The chronicle of the house goes on to state that 'she had rich cloth-of-silver gown and petticoat. The church was hung round and all things accordingly in great state befitting her quality.' The chronicle also records her profession in 1664:

> At her profession were used vestments of cloth-of-silver made from her clothing gown etc., of which also were the antependiums of all three altars. Before her profession she gave a jewel of diamonds worth £50 and two pendants for adorning the monstrance worth £2. Her portion was £400 ready money.

Several members of Staffordshire gentry families joined the

Carmelites at Antwerp. Margaret, daughter of Francis Trentham of Rocester,[20] was professed in 1624 at the age of seventeen as Sister Mary of St Albert, and Margaret, daughter of Peter Giffard,[21] in 1627 at the age of twenty-seven as Sister Angela of the Holy Ghost. There were two daughters of Thomas Leveson of Willenhall.[22] Anne was professed in 1627 at the age of twenty as Sister Anne of St Teresa. As Mother Anne she was involved in foundations in what is now Germany – at Düsseldorf in 1649 and Münsterfeld in 1659, where she was prioress until 1652; she then became prioress of Düsseldorf until her death in 1678. Her sister Elizabeth received the habit in 1634 at the age of sixteen as Sister Eugenia of Jesus but had to leave because of poor health. She returned in 1640, and her second clothing took place the following year. She was one of the twelve chosen for a new foundation at Lierre in 1649 and died in 1652, noted for humility, courage, obedience and devotion to the Holy Souls. Anne, daughter of Francis Harcourt of Ranton,[23] was professed as Sister Anne of St Mary in 1641 aged seventeen and was prioress from 1659 to 1665. She went to Hoogstraeten, founded in 1678, as first prioress but died the same year; she was accompanied there by her sister Mary (Sister Mary of the Angels). Mary, daughter of Walter Giffard of Chillington (d. 1688), joined the Antwerp community in 1681 at the age of forty-two, taking the name of Sister Mary of the Martyrs. In 1698 her nephew Thomas Giffard granted her an annuity of £10.

A foundation was made from Antwerp at Lierre in 1649. Elizabeth Leveson was among the twelve for the new foundation; early recruits included her first cousin Magdalen, daughter of Sir Walter Leveson of Wolverhampton.[24] She was professed in 1657 at the age of thirty-eight. Her niece Catherine, daughter of Andrew Giffard of Wolverhampton and Magdalen's sister Catherine, was clothed in 1656 and professed the following year.

The Poor Clares at Gravelines attracted several from Staffordshire families, with a great granddaughter of John Giffard of Chillington joining in 1596. Four daughters of

Peter Giffard entered: Dorothy, professed in 1626 aged twenty-two; Ursula in 1630 aged twenty-three; Elizabeth in 1632; and Winifred in 1633 aged sixteen. Winifred went on to the Poor Clares at Rouen where she was abbess for thirty-five years, until her resignation in 1701; she died in 1706. Dorothy, daughter of Alban Draycott, entered in 1637 aged eighteen. Dorothy, daughter of William Stanford of Perry Hall, born in 1629, entered in 1649.

Marian, daughter of John Draycott, joined the Benedictine nuns in Brussels as a child in 1624. She was professed at the age of nineteen in 1637.

આ

A list of Staffordshire recusants indicted at the Epiphany and Easter quarter sessions of 1641 contains 1,069 names.[25] It again shows a spread throughout the county, and persisting areas of gentry influence are notable. Brewood, under the influence of Peter Giffard of Chillington (who does not appear in the list), continued to have by far the heaviest concentration (eighty-six names); the Giffards of nearby Water Eaton in Penkridge also appear. Other concentrations in this area centring on gentry families included Lapley (the Brooke family, thirty-four names), Ranton (the Harcourts, twenty-one names) and Swynnerton (the Fitzherberts, thirteen names). Stone had eighteen names; Walter Heveningham of Aston was listed under Farewell near Lichfield with ten others, presumably because he was living at his other home, Pipe Hall.[26] Baswich had twenty-three names, but no mention was made of the Fowlers of nearby St Thomas: the list is headed by three members of the gentry family of Butler.[27] Colwich had thirty names and Hamstall Ridware nineteen, although Nicholas Fitzherbert was noted with 'denies the charge'. Recusants were still numerous at Cannock (thirty-five names), with the Colemans as the leading Catholic family.

Further south there were concentrations at Bushbury (the Whitgreaves of Moseley, eighteen names), Sedgley (the Halls, twenty-four names), Handsworth (the Stanfords of

Perry Hall, forty-eight names, with eight more at nearby Barr and Aldridge) and Patshull (the Astleys, twenty-one names). Bilston's thirty-three recusants included several named Perry, presumably relatives of William Perry, the Boy of 1620; one of them may have been the Boy himself, there being a husbandman, a weaver and a yeoman all called William Perry.

In the north and east of the county there were Maer (the Macclesfields, eleven of the twenty-seven names being members of the family), Biddulph (the Biddulphs, thirty-three names), and Ellastone (the Fleetwoods of Calwich, thirty names); Draycott had twenty-five (although the Draycotts were not included) and nearby Checkley eighteen and Leigh twenty-four. The nine Catholics in Horton west of Leek, mainly husbandmen, may have been tenants of the Biddulphs, who owned Dairy House there, a building with the date 1635 on the service wing and Catholic symbols on the front; John Biddulph and his wife Mary were among thirteen Catholics recorded there in 1635.[28] At Rocester five members of the Chetwynd family were listed but only four other people.

Of the towns Tamworth had twenty-one names. Stafford had thirty-seven in St Mary's parish[29] and four in the small town-centre parish of St Chad. Wolverhampton with fifty-six names was second to Brewood as a recusant centre. Wolverhampton parish, an area of peculiar jurisdiction covering an extensive district outside the town as well as the town itself, included Bilston (thirty-three names), Pelsall (one), Wednesfield (fourteen) and Willenhall (five). Some years earlier Catholic influence in the town had been strong enough to secure the removal of the master of the grammar school, Richard Barnes. After taking up his appointment in 1605 he insisted that all pupils, including those with recusant parents, should attend Anglican services. The Catholics claimed that this was a reversal of established practice, and, although Barnes had the support of the trustees of the school and a number of townsmen, Catholic pressure was so strong that the trustees dismissed him in 1610.[30] In 1624 Richard Lee, the recently appointed Puritan prebendary of Willenhall in St

Peter's, Wolverhampton, declared that 'I never knew any part of this kingdom where Rome's snakie brood roosted and rested themselves more warmer and safer, and with greater countenance, then [*sic*] in this country'.[31]

Although not included in the 1641 list, a noble family had recently been added to the ranks of Staffordshire Catholics. Walter Aston of Tixall (1584–1639), the grandson of the Sir Walter Aston who had hammered Elizabethan recusants in the county, became a Catholic at the end of his life. Knighted at James I's coronation, he was made a baronet in 1611 on the institution of the order and was created Lord Aston of Forfar in 1627 as a reward for his services as ambassador to Spain (1620–5) during the unsuccessful negotiations for a marriage between Prince Charles and the Infanta. He was ambassador there again from 1635 to 1638.[32]

It was during his second embassy that he became a Catholic, losing his post and salary as a result. He wrote to a friend that he had with some reluctance abandoned the religion in which he had been brought up. He had however been persuaded by arguments from scripture and history that Protestantism was a new-grown thing while the marks of the true Church of Christ were to be found only in 'the Catholique Roman religion', which alone showed continuity through the ages. He hoped that his friend would not break with him as a result: 'howsoever, I am, I thank God, so resolved that I had rather loose the best worldly friends that ever I had than change againe from what I am.'[33] His wife was already a Catholic; she was confirmed in 1627 by Bishop Smith, and in 1629 Francis Foster, a Jesuit, was said to resort to Lady Aston's house in Staffordshire.[34] It was ironical that the grandson of the fiercely anti-Catholic Sir Walter should make Tixall a recusant centre which lasted some 200 years.

In 1640 the Stafford barony passed from the Staffords to the Howard family. Henry, 5th Baron Stafford, died in 1637 with his sister Mary as his heir. The barony passed to a cousin, but the King secured its surrender in 1639. Mary had married the Catholic William Howard, a younger son of the Earl of Arundel, in 1637, and in 1640 they were created Baron and

Sir Walter Aston, first Baron Aston of Forfar.

TAB. XXVIII.

Albuquerque sculp.

C. Stony Delin.

Tixall Hall and Gatehouse *c*.1680.

Tixall Hall in 1842.

Baroness Stafford; two months later William was created Viscount Stafford.[35]

❧

Charles I, desperately short of money, soon saw a way of securing a steady income from recusants by allowing them to compound for their fines.[36] Composition had been tried earlier, but from 1628 it became a regular system. Recusants agreed to pay an annual rent based on the assessed value of their sequestrated lands or goods; technically, though not always in practice, they were then not liable for further fines.

In Staffordshire by 1640 there were 109 compositions for lands and 39 for goods. There were also three husbands paying a £1 composition each for their wives' recusancy (under the terms of an Act of 1610). By far the highest sum was paid by Peter Giffard of Chillington, who in 1635 compounded at a rate of £140 a year; in 1640 the Barons of the Exchequer expressed surprise that Peter Giffard was being prosecuted for recusancy, 'seeing that he pays to the King the greatest rents of any recusant saving two or three'. Meantime in 1639 he was accused of having 'for many years past aided and relieved and received into his house Roman papistical priests, where living 120 miles from town he had been a partaker of Mass, etc.'[37] The next highest Staffordshire compositions were £66 13s. 4d. paid from 1636 by John Wells and his son Thomas, both of of Hoar Cross in Yoxall,[38] and £53 6s. 8d. paid by John Biddulph of Biddulph from 1635. The Stanfords of Perry Hall paid twice: Edward Stanford's widow Elizabeth (his second wife) compounded for £20 in 1635, and his son William, who succeeded him in 1631, compounded for £25 in 1636.[39] The assessments were lenient, and the wealthier Catholics were therefore better off under the system. The large number of people paying sums of £5 and under, however, suggests that the net was cast more widely than before and caught poorer Catholics who had earlier escaped fines. The system also showed how undervalued sequestrated property could be: the two-thirds of the real estate of Walter Coleman of Cannock sequestrated in 1611

Blessed William Howard, Viscount Stafford.

were valued at 13s. 4d., but in 1629 he compounded at £10 a
year.

⁂

The Irish rebellion of 1641 and the stories of atrocities
committed by Catholics against Protestants there roused fears
about the intentions of English Catholics. With refugees from
Ireland travelling along the two main routes through Staffordshire south from Chester, the chief port for Ireland, the county
shared those fears.[40]

When a party of troops passed through Stafford in December 1641, probably those on their way to reinforce the garrison at Dublin, a Stafford thatcher named Walter Hill greeted
them with 'God speed you, you are going to fight against our
enemies the papists'. He proceeded to tell them that there
were several rich local papists, including Peter Giffard, who
'had whole wain-loads of money', Lord Aston and Dorothy
Fowler. Nearer at Stafford Castle there was the dowager Lady
Stafford, 'a rank papist' and 'an alone woman'; he urged that
if they went to the castle 'they might have great store of
money and that she had no armour and but little company'.
Lady Stafford complained to the mayor, who promptly took
three witness statements and sent them to the justices. Hill
admitted some of the remarks and was gaoled.[41]

There were a number of scares. A new Gunpowder Plot was
thought to have been discovered at Burton in January 1642 when
William Pargiter, a local attorney, was told that two carriers had
brought fourteen hundredweight of gunpowder from London to
Philip Draycott at Paynsley. A local innkeeper and a pewterer
confirmed the story, saying that they had seen some of the
powder. Pargiter informed the House of Lords, and William,
Lord Paget, lord of Burton manor, was ordered to investigate.
He questioned a number of people, including Draycott who was
arrested and brought before Lords. After two weeks it turned
out that seven barrels of powder had been sent to a Cheshire
gentleman, and when Paynsley was searched only eight pounds
of powder were found along with a few fowling guns and the
arms with which Draycott was charged for the militia.[42]

Probably about the same time there was a report in Lichfield of a similar plot. The bailiff of Walter Heveningham of nearby Pipe Hall and the postmaster were said to have confessed to planning a massacre on the next fast day, having stockpiled thirty-eight hatchets; another version said that at least 200 had been ordered from Lichfield blacksmiths. When the story reached London it was claimed that the Protestants of Staffordshire dared not go to church unarmed.[43] In March Thomas Boughey of Brockton near Eccleshall complained to the Lords of his neighbour Sir John Peshall, a suspected papist, who was harassing him with lawsuits and whose servants had assaulted him and his family. Boughey added that the local papists were meeting tumultuously and that Sir John and his servants were suspiciously buying up large quantities of food in local markets.[44] In May 1642 a petition from Staffordshire to the House of Commons urged that

> the papists (who are a great number in this small county) may be thoroughly and speedily disarmed, and so disposed of; that they be not formidable to your petitioners, by being able either to keep us in jealousies by their practices at home or to foment that fire kindled by their party in Ireland.[45]

In June a pamphlet was published in London entitled *Strange Newes from Staffordshire*.[46] It related how a poor man was looking for his lost sheep on Mow Cop, a hill in north-west Staffordshire on the Cheshire boundary. Hearing a bell tinkling, he investigated and came across a gathering of people at an open-air Mass. Aghast, he ran to inform the local people, and eleven of the congregation were arrested, along with two Jesuits, John Kilsole and Arthur Roeley. Although the topographical setting is accurately described and most of the surnames of those arrested are associated with the neighbouring part of Cheshire, none of the persons named can be traced, and the Jesuits' names are an obvious invention. The pamphlet is clearly another piece of anti-Catholic fabrication – and incidentally anticipates in its choice of location the birth of Primitive Methodism on Mow Cop over a century and half later.

With the outbreak of the Civil War later in 1642 the Catholic gentry rallied to the King with more enthusiasm than many others of their class. This was notably true in Staffordshire where a large majority of Protestant landowners fought against the King and a number were neutral. The reverse was true of the Catholic landowners.[47] Indeed at the beginning of the war the Catholics of Staffordshire and Shropshire lent the King between £4,000 and £5,000.[48]

In 1643 the Catholic Thomas Leveson of Wolverhampton was appointed royalist commander in south-east and central Staffordshire. It had been a different story the year before. In April 1642, following an order by Parliament for the seizure of Catholics' arms, Sir Walter Wrottesley and a fellow deputy lieutenant had ordered a Wolverhampton armourer not to restore Leveson's arms. Wrottesley reported how Leveson went to the armourer to demand his arms, and on being told that the deputy lieutenants' permission was needed, he flew into a passion, called Wrottesley a knave and a fool and assaulted the armourer with his cane. Describing him as an active and dangerous recusant, Wrottesley further reported to the Earl of Essex that 'Leveson is going to France to breed up his son in Popery' and suggested the issue of a writ *ne exeat regno*.[49]

In May 1643, far from being disarmed, Leveson was given the rank of colonel by the King and authorised to raise a regiment of 1,500 foot. Soon afterwards he was appointed governor of Dudley Castle and in July was authorised to levy the inhabitants of Seisdon and Cuttlestone hundreds for the support of the Dudley garrison. He duly levied not only money but provisions, beds with sheets, blankets and bolsters, teams to carry materials, and men with tools for work on the castle's fortifications. He was also subsequently appointed royalist sheriff of Staffordshire and ordered in January 1644 to recruit as necessary in areas of the county 'whither your power for the present can extend'.[50] In August 1644, however, his wife was allowed by the parliamentary committee for Staffordshire to live at their

Dudley Castle c.1680. One of the last royalist strongholds in Staffordshire to surrender, in 1646, it was subsequently slighted.

house in Wolverhampton for a year with protection and to enjoy lands and rents in Ashmore and elsewhere for a payment of £40.[51] Despite stormy relations with superiors and unpopularity because of his levies Leveson remained governor of Dudley Castle until its surrender in May 1646. The garrison was allowed to march out, and Leveson died in Bordeaux in 1652.[52]

Several Catholics garrisoned their houses for the King. John Biddulph, who following the outbreak of war was made a captain in the Earl of Northampton's regiment, garrisoned Biddulph Hall. He was killed at the battle of Hopton Heath near Stafford in March 1643. His son Francis continued the garrison, and in August a passing parliamentary troop decided that the Hall was too strong for an attack. A siege was mounted after the siege of Nantwich was raised in late January 1644 and lasted about a month, becoming more effective after the cannon known as Roaring Meg was brought from Stafford. Some 150 prisoners were taken, and Francis Biddulph was one of the prisoners at Stafford ordered in March to be transferred to Eccleshall Castle. Much of the Hall was promptly demolished, but a month after the surrender the parliamentary committee ordered the remainder to be preserved so that Francis could use the materials to repair a little house belonging to him two miles away.[53]

The dowager Lady Stafford garrisoned Stafford Castle. Having captured Stafford town unopposed in May 1643, the parliamentary commander Sir William Brereton went up to the castle where Lady Stafford was holding out 'with divers considerable persons'. She ignored Brereton's blandishments and threats, an attitude which he attributed to 'the pernicious counsels of some priests, Jesuits or other incendiaries about her, who delight in nothing but fire and sword'. Before returning to the town Brereton set fire to some outhouses in the hope of weakening the garrison's resolve but instead they shot some of his men and horses. That so enraged his troops that they proceeded to burn down most of the dwelling houses and outhouses by the castle.[54] Late in July a royalist force arrived to relieve the garrison. They beat back a disorderly force from

The remains of the Elizabethan Biddulph Hall in 1844.

the town and brought supplies into the castle. A force under Brereton was then seen approaching and the whole garrison hastily evacuated the castle. When Brereton entered it he found it deserted but well stocked with 'good food, excellent beer, arms and ammunition'. In their haste the Royalists had also left behind 'their crucifixes, beads and many popish books in English'.[55] On 22 December the parliamentary committee for the county ordered 'that Stafford Castle be forthwith demolished'.[56]

Sir Richard Fleetwood had garrisoned Wootton Lodge near Alton by the summer of 1643. He was joined by a younger son William, one of Colonel Henry Hastings's captains, although his eldest son Thomas remained quietly in the family's other house nearby at Calwich. According to Sir John Gell, the parliamentary commander in Derbyshire, Sir Richard boasted 'that he feared not all the forces of Derbyshire and Staffordshire if they came against him'. Another parliamentary account, perhaps over impressed by the way in which the garrison were plundering traffic between Lancashire, Cheshire and Derby and between Manchester and London, called Wootton one of the strongest places in Staffordshire, 'exceeding well provided of all necessaries and manned with such a company of obstinate papists and resolute thieves as the like were hardly to be found in the whole kingdom'. Gell too described how the parliamentary troops at Derby referred to Sir Richard as 'one of Colonel Hastings's fraternity of robbers'. A small force was besieging the house in June and July in an attempt to prevent the plundering. A force of 300 men then came out from Derby and after a siege of two nights and a day captured the house, taking Sir Richard, two of his sons, a Master Vincent Eyre and seventy others to Derby as prisoners, 'tied together with ropes'. A few months later, however, Sir Richard was taking part in the royalist siege of Nantwich.[57]

Peter Giffard, then in his early sixties, garrisoned Chillington for the King, and in August 1643 Sir William Brereton marched from Stafford to besiege it with three pieces of ordnance and a set of drakes. He battered down much of the

Stafford c.1680, with the ruins of the castle in the background.

defences, and in the afternoon of the following day the house was surrendered. Peter, two of his sons and about eighty others including an old priest were taken prisoner along with arms for 200 men and a store of ammunition.[58] Within six weeks Thomas Leveson had recaptured Chillington, and the King then ordered it to be regarrisoned, it 'being a place of much importance for our service in those parts'.[59] Peter was imprisoned at Stafford, and in March 1644 the parliamentary committee ordered his removal with others to Eccleshall Castle, though allowing his servant to attend him. By June Chillington was again in parliamentary hands, and the committee ordered its demolition. A final order was made on 22 July, when the committee arranged for all available horse and foot to go to Chillington at 4 o'clock the next day and demolish it. In February 1645, however, Peter's daughter-in-law Anne, wife of his son Walter, was given permission to live in the house along with her children, Peter's wife and two servant maids. In April the committee ordered Peter's release with permission to live at Chillington provided that he gave security not to take up arms; for this he was to pay £165 down and a further £65 quarterly up to Christmas.[60] Andrew Giffard of Wolverhampton, a brother of Peter, was killed in a skirmish near Wolverhampton, and Francis Giffard of Water Eaton in Penkridge, a royalist captain, was killed in another skirmish near Dudley.[61]

Walter Astley garrisoned Patshull House in 1643 and still held it at the beginning of 1645. His son Richard was a captain in the Dudley Castle garrison from 1643 to 1645 and at his father's request was allowed to march to the Patshull garrison in 1643 and 1644. Sir William Brereton, describing Patshull as 'strongly fortified and moated about', reported how a small party marched against it in February under the command of the governor of Eccleshall Castle:

Taking the opportunity of the drawbridge being let down, he suddenly surprised the sentinels and fell in amongst the whole garrison, fought with them for some time in the house, killed many of them, and took the governor, with divers gentlemen of quality, two Jesuits and about sixty soldiers, which they have all prisoners.

Walter Astley's property was sequestrated, and he died in 1653.[62]

Philip Draycott garrisoned Paynsley, but it had fallen to the parliamentarians by February 1644. In March the county committee ordered it to 'be made unserviceable to be a garrison', but although the order was repeated in April, by May it was occupied by a parliamentary garrison.[63]

William Fitzherbert, who rose to the rank of colonel in the royalist army, may have garrisoned his house at Swynnerton: in February 1644 the committee ordered its demolition forthwith. His property was sequestrated, but in 1649 he succeeded his cousin Sir John Fitzherbert of Norbury in Derbyshire. He appears to have lived there until the Resoration.[64]

Among other Staffordshire recusants who fought for the King the young Walter Fowler was often seen 'with his sword by his side and his pole-axe in his hand'. In February 1643 he joined Sir Francis Wortley, one of the royalist commanders at Stafford, in repulsing an attack on the town by a force from the Staffordshire Moorlands. An eyewitness stated that 'he saw Mr Fowler ride forth of Stafford, having a buff coat and armour upon it, with a head-piece, sword and pistol. And further this deponent saw Mr Fowler, together with Sir Francis Wortley and others, charge the said Moorlanders.'[65]

The second Lord Aston (who had succeeeded his father in 1639) was commissioned at the beginning of the war to raise a regiment, but he met resistance because suspected of Catholic sympathies and abandoned the project. He fought for the King, however, and from Bridgnorth joined the garrison in Lichfield Close. He was one of the negotiators of the articles for the surrender of the Close in July 1646 after a three-month siege.[66]

Whereas Walter Heveningham of Aston and Pipe was noted at the Restoration as being loyal but also as having 'lived at home in time of war',[67] his brother Christopher took up arms for the King at the beginning of the Civil War. He was a captain in the Chillington garrison after its recapture by Thomas Leveson in September 1643 – and perhaps its commander. In December he seized thirty loads of wheat on their way to Sir William Brereton from nearby Weston-under-Lizard, home of Lady Brereton. Leveson promptly sent him to attack Lapley House, which he captured, sending over eighty prisoners to Chillington.[68] By August 1645 he was a prisoner at Eccleshall Castle, and arrangements were then made for his exchange for two parliamentary prisoners. He was in Dudley Castle at its surrender in 1646 and then went abroad. He returned to Pipe Hall at the end of 1647.[69]

Edward Stanford of Perry Hall had had a distinguished career in the royalist army by the time he was captured at Kidderminster in June 1644. He was a prisoner at Stafford in October when the committee ordered his removal to Eccleshall Castle. After being freed on exchange in June 1645 he continued in arms until the end of the war.[70]

Viscount Stafford stated at his trial in 1680 that

> thinking my presence might prejudice rather than serve the King, my wife and I settled at Antwerp when the war began, where we might have lived obscurely but safely. My conscience was not satisfied to see my King in such disorder, and I not endeavour to serve him what I could to free him from his troubles. And I did come into England and served His Majesty faithfully and loyally as long as he lived.

He was, however, in Amsterdam in 1643, and in 1644 he and his wife and mother-in-law visited the nuns at St Monica's, Louvain. He was at the battle of Naseby in 1645 and was still in England in 1647 when he received a pass to go to Flanders to collect his wife and children. He and his wife were in Rome in 1649 and Padua in 1650, and though she returned to England he remained abroad until the death of his mother in Holland in June 1654. He was in England in November that year when he received a pass to go to the Low Countries on business; further passes were issued in 1655 and early 1660.

Bellamour c.1800, showing the house of c.1638 on the right and that of c.1796 on the left.

On her return to England Viscountess Stafford leased back the sequestrated Tart Hall (later renamed Stafford House) by St James's Park in London, built by Lord Stafford's mother on land acquired in 1633 and left to him in her will.[71]

Some sixty Staffordshire Catholics had suffered sequestration of their property by 1648, ranging from Lord Aston and his mother through numerous gentry to the widow of Simon Rider of West Bromwich and William Perry of Bilston.[72] Victims, however, were to some extent able to buy relief. The arrangements made with Peter Giffard and his family over Chillington in 1645 have been described above. By 1650 he was a prisoner, and at the Restoration he claimed that his estate was sold to three men for £5,600 and that he had to pay upwards of £12,000 to redeem it.[73] On Christmas Day 1644 the county committee gave permission for troops to be quartered in the gatehouse of Tixall Hall provided that they 'molest not nor affright the Lord Aston's children which now live in Tixall Hall nor be in any way burthensome or chargeable unto them'. In March 1648 Lord Aston secured a discharge of sequestration, having evidently compounded.[74] Meanwhile in 1644 the dowager Lady Aston, then living at Colton, was given the chance to compound for her estate for £200, but she chose to hold only half with the undertaking to pay annuities of £140 out of the estate to three of her children. Her home may have been the house called Bellamour, built in Colton by her younger son Herbert about the time of his marriage in 1638.[75] In July 1644 John Coleman of Cannock was granted his estate until the following Lady Day for £40 with permission to live at his home provided he behaved peaceably.[76] In January 1645 Thomas Underhill of Northycote in Bushbury was granted his estate until Lady Day 1646 for £30.[77]

In 1645 the county committee granted the wives of three sequestrated Catholics their husbands' property over and above the fifth part which they already held under a parliamentary ordinance of 1643. In February Francis Biddulph's wife Margaret was granted all the Biddulph demesnes including a mill, coal pits and a bloomsmithy for a year for two payments of £40. The county committee went further when she expressed a suspicion that the tenants of the Biddulph pits might 'do her wrong': it made an order 'that the said tenants shall take the level before them and work it workmanlike and so leave the same at the expiration of their term'. She could then have an inspection by three or four men, and if the tenants were found at fault, they would be punished. At the same time a further order was made that no soldier was to take any cattle belonging to Mrs Biddulph or her tenants without a special order from the committee. A few weeks later it ordered that an occupant of a house belonging to her at Biddulph was to vacate it within a month unless he could come to an agreement with her.[78] In March Joyce, the wife of Richard Palin of Dearnsdale west of Stafford, was granted the remaining four parts of Richard's lands for a year for £15 spread over four quarterly payments; he was then with the garrison of Dudley Castle.[79] Later the same month Ann, the wife of William Fitzherbert, was granted all her husband's lands and rents for a year for £140, likewise spread over four payments.[80]

With the execution of Charles I in 1649 the crown passed to his nineteen-year-old son Charles. Staffordshire Catholics were soon to play a key role in the preservation of the new King.

Notes

1 *S.H.C.* v (2), p. 280; *S.H.C.* 4th ser. ix, pp. 67–8, 77. Robert, a younger son of Edward, had a distinguished career as a Jesuit, mostly abroad, although he died in London in 1659: T. M. McCoog, *English and Welsh Jesuits 1555–1650, Part II* (*C.R.S.* lxxv, 1995), pp. 301–2.

2 A. Peel (ed.), 'A Puritan Survey of the Church in Staffordshire', *English Historical Review*, xxvi (1911), pp. 338–52.

3 M. W. Greenslade, 'The 1607 Return of Staffordshire Catholics', *Staffs. Cath. Hist.* iv (1963–4), pp. 6–32 (pp. 27–8 for Sedgley).

4 Anstruther, *Seminary Priests*, i, pp. 341–2; F. Grady and A.

W. Neal, 'Blessed Robert Sutton', *Staffs. Cath. Hist.* xxiii (1988), p. 5; R. Challoner, *Memoirs of Missionary Priests*, ed. J. H. Pollen (1924), p. 275; *Proposed Supplement to the Roman Missal for the Archdiocese of Birmingham* (Liturgical Commission, Archdiocese of Birmingham [1999]), p. 23. He was presumably the John Suker of Staffordshire, clerk, who matriculated at St Mary's, Hall, Oxford, in October 1584 aged 26: J. Foster, *Alumni Oxonienses: the Members of the University of Oxford 1500–1714* (1891), iv, p. 1442. Another martyr of James's reign with a Staffordshire connection is Thomas Maxfield (Macclesfield), a younger son of William Macclesfield of Maer ordained at Arras in 1614, hanged, drawn and quartered at Tyburn in 1615, and beatified in 1929: Anstruther, ii, pp. 214–16.

5 *S.H.C.* 4th ser. ix, pp. 70, 74; M. Hodgetts, *Secret Hiding-Places* (Dublin, 1989), p. 167.

6 For this and the following paragraph see A. Fraser, *The Gunpowder Plot* (1997 edn), pp. 140–1, 165–6, 169–72, 180–7.

7 Ibid., pp. 195–6.

8 For Humphrey see also Foley, *English Province S.J.* iv, p. 219; Harvington Hall, Worcestershire, MS Pedigrees of Pakington etc. (reference supplied by Mr Michael Hodgetts).

9 Fraser, *Gunpowder Plot*, pp. 212–13; G. P. Mander and N. W. Tildesley, *A History of Wolverhampton to the early Nineteenth Century* (Wolverhampton, 1960), pp. 63–5; Shaw, *Staffs.* ii, pp. 227–8.

10 *V.C.H. Staffs.* iii, p. 104.

11 F. Roberts, 'Staffordshire Benedictine Monks', *Staffs. Cath. Hist.* i (1961), p. 14; *V.C.H. Staffs.* v, pp. 56–7, 68; *Complete Peerage*, xii (1), p. 186.

12 J. Gillow, *St Thomas's Priory* (no date but mid to later 1890s), pp. 36–8.

13 Above, p. 41.

14 *Staffs. Cath. Hist.* iii, p. 1.

15 Ibid., pp. 2, 4, 17.

16 *V.C.H. Staffs.* iii, p. 104; G. P. Mander, *Wolverhampton Antiquary* (privately printed, 1933), p. 209.

17 A. M. C. Forster, 'Venerable William Southerne', *Staffs. Cath. Hist.* xii (1972), pp. 1 sqq.; M. Greenslade, 'List of Staffordshire Recusants, 1657', *S.H.C.* 4th ser. ii (1958),

p. 79. Venerable William Southerne was long thought to have worked under the wing of the Fowlers and to have been executed at Newcastle-under-Lyme; in fact he came from a County Durham family, worked in Northumberland and was executed at Newcastle-upon-Tyne in 1618.

18 Printed in facsimile in *Staffs. Cath. Hist.* xi (1970); see especially pp. 4, 63–8.

19 For this section, see Sister Mary Catherine, '17th Century Nuns of Louvain, Antwerp and Lierre from Staffordshire Families', *Staffs. Cath. Hist.* i (1961), pp. 17–19; Sister Mary Catherine, 'Sister Ursula Giffard', ibid., iii, p. 25; P. J. Doyle, 'The Giffards of Chillington, a Catholic landed family, 1642–1861' (Durham University MA thesis, 1968; copy in W.S.L.), pp. 173–5, 179, 402–6; M. J. Galgano, 'Restoration Recusancy in the Northwest of England: a Social History, 1650–1675 (Vanderbilt University, Tennessee, Ph.D. thesis, 1971; copy in W.S.L.), pp. 209–11.

20 *S.H.C.* v (2), p. 289.

21 *S.H.C.* new ser. v, p. 197.

22 *S.H.C.* v (2), pp. 202–3.

23 Ibid., p. 169.

24 Ibid., p. 202.

25 A. J. Kettle, 'A List of Staffordshire Recusants, 1641', *Staffs. Cath. Hist.* v (1964), pp. 1 sqq. For the returns of recusants made at Archbishop Laud's visitation of the Diocese of Coventry and Lichfield in 1635 see J. Hampartumian, 'Staffordshire Recusants in 1635', *Staffs. Cath. Hist.* xxii (1984), pp. 5 sqq.; the visitation did not include peculiars, so that Catholic centres such as Brewood and Wolverhampton were omitted.

26 Pipe Hall was in fact in St Michael's parish, Lichfield: *V.C.H. Staffs.* xiv, p. 206; W. F. Carter, 'Notes on Staffordshire Families', *S.H.C.* 1925, p. 39.

27 St Thomas was in the parish of St Mary's, Stafford, although the Fowlers were buried in Baswich church.

28 *V.C.H. Staffs.* vii, pp. 71, 76.

29 One name has been omitted from the printed list.

30 *V.C.H. Staffs.* iii, p. 104.

31 R. Lee, *The Spirituall Spring. A Sermon preached at Paul's* (1625), epistle dedicatory dated 1624 (copy in W.S.L.); Mander, *Wolverhampton Antiquary*, pp. 305–11.

32 *Complete Peerage*, i, pp. 285–6.

33 A. Clifford, *Tixall Letters* (1815), i, pp. 63–70.
34 *Complete Peerage*, i, p. 286; Foley, *English Province S.J.* i, p. 510; ii, p. 233.
35 *Complete Peerage*, xii (1), pp. 187–90.
36 For this section see T. S. Smith, 'Sequestrations for Recusancy in Staffordshire in 1640', *Staffs. Cath. Hist.* xviii (1978), pp. 1 sqq.; T. S. Smith, 'The Persecution of Staffordshire Roman Catholic Recusants', *Journal of Ecclesiastical History*, xxx (3) (1979), pp. 327 sqq. For an Elizabethan example of compounding see above, p. 53.
37 *S.H.C.* new series v, p. 175; p. *Cal. S.P. Dom. 1639–1640*, p. 554. Giffard himself stated in 1640 that had compounded for his lands and goods six years before at the yearly rent of £180: ibid., *1640*, p. 91.
38 *S.H.C.* v (2), p. 302.
39 Ibid., pp. 280–1.
40 M. Cooksley and I. Atherton, 'Staffordshire and the Irish Revolt', *Staffordshire Studies*, xiii (2001), pp. 55–78.
41 Ibid., pp. 74–5; D. A. Johnson and D. G. Vaisey (eds), *Staffordshire and the Great Rebellion* (Staffordshire County Council, 1964 edn), pp. 21–2.
42 J. Sutton, 'Loyalty and a "Good Conscience": the Defection of William, Fifth Baron Paget, June 1642', *S.H.C.* 4th ser. xix (1999), pp. 147–8; *Staffs. Studies*, xiii, pp. 69–70.
43 *Staffs. Studies*, xiii, pp. 70–1.
44 Ibid., p. 72.
45 Ibid., p. 68.
46 Ibid., pp. 72–3 and sources cited there.
47 G. Wrottesley, *A History of the Family of Wrottesley of Wrottesley, Co. Stafford* (*S.H.C.* new ser. vi (2), 1903), pp. 331–2; *V.C.H. Staffs.* i, pp. 257–8.
48 *V.C.H. Staffs.* i, p. 259.
49 *S.H.C.* new ser. vi, p. 315.
50 Shaw, *Staffs.* i, general history, pp. 60–2; ii, pp. 144–5; 'Some Letters of the Civil War', *S.H.C.* 1941, pp. 142–3.
51 D. H. Pennington and I. A. Roots (eds), *The Committee at Stafford 1643–1645* (S.H.C. 4th ser. i, 1957), p. 157.
52 Shaw, *Staffs.* ii, 145–6; *S.H.C.* 1941, pp. 146–7; R. E. Sherwood, *Civil Strife in the Midlands 1642–1651* (Chichester, 1974), p. 212; Johnson and Vaisey, (eds), *Staffordshire and the Great Rebellion*, p. 68.

53   [F. P. Parker, ed.], 'Collections for a History of Pirehill Hundred. By Walter Chetwynd of Ingestre, Esq. A.D. 1679', *S.H.C.* new ser. xii (1909), p. 9; J. Hancock, 'The Civil War', in J. Kennedy (ed.), *Biddulph* (Keele University, 1980), pp. 39–42; Sherwood, *Civil Strife in the Midlands*, pp. 123–4; *S.H.C.* 4th ser. i, pp. 68, 80.

54   Shaw, *Staffs.* i, general history, p. 55; Sherwood, *Civil Strife in the Midlands*, p. 67.

55   W.S.L., S.MS 370/vii (1), p. 317 (reference supplied by Mr Roy Lewis).

56   *S.H.C.* 4th ser. i, p. 21.

57   M. T. Fortescue, *The History of Calwich Abbey* [1914?], pp. 64–8; Shaw, *Staffs.* i, general history, p. 57.

58   *S.H.C.* 1941, pp. 138–9.

59   Shaw, *Staffs.* ii, p. 145.

60   *S.H.C.* 4th ser. i, pp. 68, 79, 128, 148, 150, 265, 282, 296–7.

61   *S.H.C.* v (2), pp. 166, 173; J. A. Williams, '"Our Patriarch": Bishop Bonaventure Giffard, 1642–1734', *Recusant History*, xxvi (3) (2003), p. 426.

62   *S.H.C.* 4th ser. i, p. lxxi; Shaw, *Staffs.* i, p. 70; *Calendar of the Proceedings of the Committee for the Advance of Money, 1642–1656*, iii, p. 1415; *V.C.H. Staffs.* xx, pp. 164–5, 171.

63   *S.H.C.* 4th ser. i, pp. 57, 62, 68, 87, 125; R. Speake (ed.), *A History of Alton and Farley* (Keele University, 1996), p. 129.

64   T. B. Trappes-Lomax, *Swynnerton* (*Staffs. Cath. Hist.* ix, 1967–8), p. 4; *S.H.C.* 4th ser, i, p. 58.

65   J. Gillow, *St. Thomas's Priory* (no date, but mid- to later 1890s), p. 153; R. Hutton, *The Royalist War Effort 1642–1646* (1982), pp. 39–40.

66   T. and A. Clifford, *A Topographical and Historical Description of the Parish of Tixall, in the County of Stafford* (Paris, 1817), p. 260; H. Clayton, *Loyal and Ancient City: Lichfield in the Civil Wars* (Lichfield, n.d. but 1987), pp. 68, 107, 122; Clifford, *Tixall Letters*, ii, pp. 123–8.

67   R. M. Kidson, 'The Gentry of Stafford, 1662–3', *S.H.C.* 4th ser. ii (1958), p. 18.

68   W.S.L., S.MS. 370, vii (1), pp. 359–61 (transcript of *Mercurius Aulicus*, 26 December 1643); Sherwood, *Civil Strife in the Midlands*, pp. 94–5; E. R. O. and C. G. O. Bridgeman, *History of the Manor and Parish of Weston-under-Lizard, in the County of Stafford* (*S.H.C.* new ser. ii, 1899), p. 140.

69 *S.H.C.* 1925, p. 38; *S.H.C.* 1941, pp. 145–6.
70 R. N. Dore (ed.), *The Letter Books of Sir William Brereton*, i (Record Society of Lancashire and Cheshire, cxxiii, 1984), p. 122; *S.H.C.* 4th ser. i, p. 190.
71 S. N. D. [Rose Meeres], *Sir William Howard, Viscount Stafford* (1929), pp. 29–31, 49–50 55; J. M. Robinson, *The Staffords* (Chichester, 2002), pp. 61–8; *Cal. S.P. Dom. 1654*, p. 442; *1655*, p. 581; *1659–1660*, p. 572.
72 *S.II.C.* 1915, pp. 389–92.
73 *S.H.C.* new ser. v, pp. 178–9.
74 Ibid., pp. 219–20; *Calendar of the Proceedings of the Committee for Compounding, &c., 1643–1660*, iii, p. 1876.
75 *S.H.C.* 4th ser. i, pp. 73 (where she is wrongly identified as the wife of Lord Aston instead of his mother), 163, 180, 210–11, 306. For Bellamour see [F. P. Parker], *Some Account of Colton and of the De Wasteney's Family* (Birmingham, 1897), pp. 141–3.
76 *S.H.C.* 4th ser. i, p. 145.
77 Ibid., p. 244.
78 Ibid., pp. 247, 254, 280.
79 Ibid., p. 265.
80 Ibid., pp. 276–7, 293, 309; *Staffs. Cath. Hist.* ix, pp. 3, 27.

4

HOPES AND DISAPPOINTMENTS: 1649–1688

Having succeeded his father in 1649 the young Charles II arrived in Scotland from France in 1650 in a bid to secure his crown.[1] He advanced into England, but his hopes were finally dashed when he was defeated by Cromwell at the battle of Worcester on 3 September 1651.

His escape from the city of Worcester was covered by a force under Captain Thomas Giffard, son of the Francis Giffard of Water Eaton who had been killed near Dudley during the Civil War. Charles planned to go to London but headed first for Boscobel on the Shropshire side of the Staffordshire—Shropshire border near Chillington. This was on the advice of Lord Derby, who had been sheltered in a priest's hiding-hole there on his way south to Worcester. It was, he told the King, the home of a recusant, adding 'that those people (being accustomed to persecution and searches) were most like to have the readiest means and safest contrivances to preserve him'.

Having crossed from Worcestershire into Staffordshire the royal party became lost on Kinver heath, whereupon Charles Giffard, the youngest son of Peter Giffard of Chillington, offered his servant Francis Yates as a guide. At 3 a.m. on Thursday 4 September the party arrived at White Ladies near Boscobel, another Shropshire Catholic house. It was the home of Dorothy Giffard, widow of John Giffard of White Ladies and Boscobel, who had left her a life interest in both. Also living there was George Giffard, a younger brother of Peter and a royalist veteran.[2] The door was opened by a servant, George Penderel. He was the youngest of six brothers, all born at the nearby Hubbal Grange. Three had fought for Charles I and one had been killed; the remaining five all lived locally: William, the eldest, lived at Boscobel; John, like George, was a servant at White Ladies; Richard rented part of Hubbal Grange; Humphrey was the miller at White Ladies. William and Richard were sent for, and after being introduced to the King, they urged that the royal party should disperse, there being an enemy troop quartered at Codsall on the Staffordshire side of the boundary.

Charles himself was anxious to proceed alone, and all but he and Lord Wilmot departed. Within half an hour some of the Codsall troop arrived, but Richard Penderel had meanwhile hidden Charles in a nearby wood. It was near the home of Richard's sister-in-law and her husband, Francis Yates; they provided Charles with a blanket, and she brought him food during a day spent in the rain. Charles then changed his plan and that night, accompanied by Richard, attempted to escape west into Wales. They reached the Severn at Madeley, but the crossings were all guarded, and they returned east, arriving at Boscobel about 3 a.m. on Saturday 6 September. There they found William Careless of Broom Hall in Brewood, a royalist army officer and a Catholic.[3] He had been in charge of the garrison at Lapley House after its fall to the Royalists in December 1643. In April 1644 he was appointed governor of Tong Castle in Shropshire, but he was captured in a skirmish near Wolverhampton in December and confined in the High House at Stafford before being released nearly a year later. After two spells abroad he spent nine months in the Brewood area before joining the royal army on its way south in August 1651. He fought with the rearguard at Worcester, and after returning north and hiding in the woods at Boscobel he went to the house shortly before Charles's arrival to seek help from William Penderel, an old acquaintance. He and

Richard Penderel.

The Royal Oak Tree at Boscobel, with William Penderel.

Moseley Old Hall.

Charles spent the rest of Saturday hiding in what became the most famous of oak trees while soldiers searched the wood. The night was passed by Charles in the priest-hole.

Meanwhile on the previous Thursday John Penderel had guided Lord Wilmot from Boscobel into Staffordshire and through Brewood. After twice narrowly escaping capture John left Wilmot at the home of John Huntbach at nearby Brinsford, while he himself went into Wolverhampton to find suitable accommodation. The town was full of soldiers, and he turned back. At Northycote in Bushbury, the home of the Catholic Underhill family, he saw Frances, the wife of Thomas Underhill, and 'told her his errand over the pales of her garden, which having heard, she dismissed him forthwith, not daring to give him any encouragement at all in the absence of her husband and the disturbance of the country'.[4] At that moment John Huddleston, chaplain to the Catholic Whitgreaves at nearby Moseley and tutor to three boys there, passed by. John Penderel promptly confided in him and accompanied him back to Moseley, where Thomas Whitgreave was brought into the secret. He went over to Brinsford and arranged for Wilmot to come to Moseley that night along with his manservant.

The next day, Friday, Wilmot's horses were taken to Bentley Hall, six miles to the south-east, the home of Colonel John Lane, a royalist veteran and an Anglican. John Penderel was sent by Wilmot to White Ladies to find out how the King was, only to discover that Charles had left for Wales. He duly returned to Moseley with the news. In the meantime Colonel Lane had come there and recognised Wilmot as an old comrade in arms. He told Wilmot that his sister Jane had been granted a pass for herself and a manservant to go Abbots Leigh near Bristol where her cousin was expecting a baby, and he suggested that Wilmot should take advantage of this. Thinking the King in Wales, Wilmot duly went to Bentley on the Saturday night and sent John Penderel back home to White Ladies. There John found that the King had returned, and early on Sunday morning he was back at Moseley. After attending Mass said by Huddleston for the King's preservation, Thomas Whitgreave went over to Bentley accompanied by the priest and John Penderel. It was agreed that Charles should be brought to Moseley that night and that Wilmot should return there, with Jane Lane's journey postponed until the King's wishes were known.

Still footsore from his earlier journey, Charles left Boscobel accompanied by the five Penderel brothers and Francis Yates. Careless stayed behind at Boscobel, being too well known in the area for safety. Charles was mounted on Humphrey Penderel's carthorse and declared that 'it was the heaviest jade he ever rode on'; Humphrey replied: 'My Liege! Can you blame the horse to go heavily when he has the weight of three kingdoms on his back?'[5] At Pendeford mill Charles was persuaded to dismount and proceed on foot, since the footway was more private and shorter than the road. The party divided, William, Humphrey and George going back with the horse. The rest had gone on a little way when Charles turned and called to the three brothers: '"My troubles make me forget myself, I thank you all", and gave them his hand to kiss.' About 3 a.m. on Monday 8 September the party of four arrived at an appointed place where John Huddleston was waiting. He conducted them to Moseley, and Thomas Whitgreave later recalled that he had difficulty in recognising the King: 'When he came to the door, with the Pendrells guarding him, he was so habited, like one of them, that I could not tell which was he, only I knew all the rest.'[6] While Charles went upstairs for a reunion with Wilmot, Whitgreave took the rest of the party into the buttery for food and drink and sent two of them on their way, keeping John Penderel at Moseley.

A hiding hole under the closet adjoining John Huddleston's chamber had been prepared, and Charles asked to see it. It measured 5 feet by 4 feet 9 inches and was 3 feet 6 inches high, and Charles was described in the posters for his arrest as 'over 2 yards high'.[7] He nevertheless expressed his satisfaction and returned to Wilmot's chamber. Admitting that he had not changed his shirt since leaving Scotland, he accepted a brand new one from Huddleston, who also changed his stockings and dried his sore feet. Whitgreave brought some sack and biscuits. It was now daybreak, and a pallet having been placed in the hiding-hole Charles retired for some cramped rest.

After getting up he was introduced to Whitgreave's mother. When she brought dinner he insisted that she sat down with him, and her son and Huddleston waited on them. Charles now decided to go to Bristol with Jane Lane. John Penderel was sent to Bentley to collect Wilmot's horses, and that night Wilmot went to Bentley to make preparations for the King's departure. Charles passed the night on Huddleston's bed, with the priest and Whitgreave keeping watch. The next morning, Tuesday 9 September, he watched from the window of Whitgreave's study as soldiers from his own army, hungry and half-naked, passed along the road or called at the house for food and bandages.

That afternoon Charles was dozing on Huddleston's bed when a party of soldiers was seen approaching the house. Whitgreave shut the King in the hiding hole and went out to meet the soldiers. They accused him of having been at Worcester and would have arrested him if neighbours had not convinced them otherwise. The same afternoon word was received from Wilmot that Colonel Lane would come for the King about midnight. Whitgreave recalled that during the evening

> his Majesty wished Mr Huddleston to show him our oratory, saying he knew he was a priest, and he needed not to fear to own it to him, for if it pleased God to restore him to his kingdom, we should never need more privacies.[8]

When Lane arrived, he was taken to wait in the orchard. At Charles's request Whitgreave brought his mother to say goodbye. She gave the King some raisins, almonds and other sweetmeats and knelt with her son and Huddleston to pray for God's blessing on him. The two men took him to the orchard, and he rode off with Lane, out of the Catholic underground. It was fair comment that despite temptations and threats the King's identity 'was concealed by persons, for the most part, of that religion which has long suffer'd under an imputation

Charles II and Jane Lane, preceded by her cousin Henry Lascelles, *en route* from Bentley to Trent, in Dorset. The print may depict a near encounter with a Parliamentarian troop near Stratford-upon-Avon, when Jane's brother-in-law left the party.

(laid on them by some mistaken zelots) of disloyalty to their soveraign'.[9]

Later that day, 10 September, Charles set off from Bentley, dressed as a serving man and with Jane Lane riding pillion. Also in the party were Jane's cousin Henry Lascelles, who had served under Colonel Lane, and Jane's sister and the sister's husband. Charles was later rejoined by Wilmot, and after many more narrow escapes and after again passing through Catholic hands, the two sailed from Shoreham in Sussex on 15 October and reached France the next day.

Thomas Whitgreave died in 1702 and was buried in Bushbury parish church. The Latin inscription on his monument celebrates his 'unshakeable loyalty' in verse:[10]

> Stay, traveller, and admire the loyal dust
> Of one whose service earned his prince's trust;
> Service when skies are fair is nothing great:
> He served when storms had overwhelmed the state.
> For when the *KING*, defeated, coarsely dressed,
> A stranger to himself, was *Whitgreave's* guest;
> And when the regicides, a bloody crew,
> Belched thunderbolts and thirsted to pursue,
> While proclamations threatened dire alarms,
> And tainted silver hawked its specious charms,
> His swelling honour proved without a stain,
> Intractable alike to loss or gain.
> Thus marble teaches those who understand
> To love, like him, their King and native land.

❧

During the Interregnum Catholics were not only treated in the same way as the political delinquents with their property sequestrated. They were also subject to the oath imposed by Parliament in 1643 which abjured the temporal claims of the Pope and numerous Catholic doctrines – as the oath of 1606 had done. Refusal to take it was now the touchstone of recusancy rather than refusal to attend the Anglican church; under the Instrument of Government of 1653 Anglicans as well as Catholics were denied freedom to exercise their religion. Late in 1656, however, the French ambassador reported the great freedom allowed to Catholics and to their clergy who went openly about London.

In Staffordshire there are examples of the modification of sequestration. Peter Giffard was a prisoner by the beginning of 1650. His forfeited estate was valued at £2,000 in 1652 and was sold to three men who claimed to have paid some £5,600. Peter was allowed to redeem it for upwards of £12,000.[11] Despite the fact that he had been in arms for the King during the Civil War, Walter Astley's son Richard regained his father's property in 1654 on the ground that there was no proof that he was a papist.[12] Lady Aston had a lease of two-thirds of her estate at Colton by 1651 instead of the half for which she had settled in 1644. By 1655, however, she had given up the lease, saying that she had had a bad bargain, and the Committee for Compounding ordered that the estate should be let to the highest bidder.[13]

Catholic influence continued. In April 1654 the two Protestant ministers at St Peter's, Wolverhampton, found much for complaint:[14]

> ... the state of this miserable town is so much the more sad in regard it swarms with papists (and thence is by many styled little Rome), there being besides many of inferior rank above twenty families of recusants of the rank of the gentry by whom many are drawn to popery; and some of them were so turbulent the last summer and guilty of such high riots that could not be suppressed by the justices at their monthly meeting or a smaller party of soldiers without further assistance from a whole troop of horse.

In August the Council of State, having been informed about meetings of papists, Jesuits and ill-affected persons at Wolverhampton, set up an inquiry with a view to the prevention of such meetings, the arrest of dangerous persons and the taking of proceedings against priests and Jesuits.[15]

At Lapley, where the Catholic Thomas Petre had recently succeeded the Catholic Walter Brooke as lord of the manor, the Puritan vicar was horrified by the junketing at the wake in August 1655. In October he wrote to the county justices, urging them to suppress all wakes and the popery that encouraged them: 'Though the public ministry prevail with many against such courses, yet many others remain refractory, especially the papists and other careless livers.' Meanwhile articles of misdemeanour at Lapley were presented at Stafford assizes two days after the wake. Of the two companies of morris dancers involved, the one from Lapley contained several recusants. The women included two servants of Thomas Petre. Among the men were the five sons of the recusant widow Sibley Floyd, who was further accused, along with Thomas Floyd, another recusant, of 'selling ale without licence and harbouring tipplers in their houses by day and by night'.[16]

During the 1650s the Jesuits gained possession of the relics of St Chad which had been smuggled from Lichfield Cathedral by Canon Dudley in 1538. He had given them to two female relatives living at Russells Hall in Dudley, who became nervous about possessing such objects and gave them to their friends Henry and William Hodgetts of High Arcal Farm at Woodsetton in Sedgley. William died in 1649, and his widow gave his share of the relics to Henry. On his deathbed in 1651 Henry was attended by Peter Turner, a Jesuit whom he had known for nearly twenty years. He revealed to Fr Turner that the relics were on the tester above the bed wrapped in a piece of buckram. Turner placed them in a box, which Henry's widow subsequently gave him. After Turner's death in 1655 the relics passed into the custody of John Leveson of Willenhall. In 1658 a party of soldiers and others discovered the box at his house, broke it open, and after smashing one of the bones in two removed some of the contents. The Jesuits regarded the relics as their property, and in 1665 Fr William Atkins of Wolverhampton placed them in a silk-lined box covered in velvet with three embroidered monograms, IHS above the letters MRA. The relics remained

Fr Peter Turner with Henry Hodgetts and the relics of St Chad.

with the Jesuits until passing to the Fitzherberts of Swynnerton probably in or soon after 1740.[17]

In 1656 war broke out with Spain and the government proclaimed its fear of its 'Spaniolized' subjects; it also needed money for the war. An Act of 1657 ordered justices and judges to have presented the names of all suspect papists aged sixteen and over and to summon them to take the oath; those who failed to take it were to be adjudged convicted popish recusants and were liable to forfeiture of two-thirds of their estates.

The returns for Staffordshire under the 1657 Act list 1,019 papists, but Lichfield, Stafford and Newcastle-under-Lyme, which had their own sessions separately from the county, were not included.[18] The pattern of gentry centres persisted, but occupations are given for the first time and artisan centres can be distinguished, with locksmiths and nailers in Bilston, Sedgley, West Bromwich and elsewhere in south Staffordshire and potters in Hanley and Burslem. The Burslem potters were mainly at Rushton Grange and nearby Cobridge Gate – Bagnalls, Bucknalls and Rowleys making up most of the thirteen Catholics there. This was presumably through the influence of the Catholic Biddulphs. Rushton had belonged to the Cistercians of Hulton Abbey and soon after the Dissolution had passed to the Biddulphs, with the Bagnalls as their tenants by the mid-seventeenth century. It may already have been a Mass centre, as it was in the eighteenth century: there is a tradition that the Biddulphs' chaplain ministered to plague victims at Burslem in 1647.[19] Brewood and Wolverhampton still had by far the largest concentration of Catholics: Brewood had at least ninety-seven, led by Peter Giffard, and Wolverhampton 116, including several Giffards.

There were eight recusants at Harborne on the Warwickshire border: a joiner, a husbandman and his wife, two nailers with the wife of one, a tailor and a widow. Harborne was served by the Franciscan travelling mission established mainly for Warwickshire in 1657. It continued until its replacement by Franciscan missions at Birmingham and Warwick in 1687.[20] Meanwhile in 1654 Sir William Powell left money to

Rushton Grange in 1800.

support a Franciscan on his Rolleston Park estate at Tutbury in the east of the county.[21]

Catholics played a part in the royalist rising of 1659, the main force of which was defeated in Cheshire. Among those subsequently imprisoned at Stafford were three prominent Staffordshire Catholics – Lord Aston, Richard Biddulph and Walter Fowler.[22]

෴

In May 1660 Charles II was restored to the throne. His reign did not bring the relief for which Catholics hoped. The Act of Uniformity of 1662 revived the previous anti-Catholic legislation, the requirements of the Corporation Act of 1661 and the Test Act of 1673 prevented Catholics from holding public office, and an Act of 1678 excluded them from the House of Lords.

Some rewards for loyalty were forthcoming. Richard Astley was evidently knighted at the Restoration, and in 1662 he was made a baronet. His Catholicism is problematic. He regained his father's lands in 1654 on the grounds that there was no proof that he was a recusant. In 1678 his arms were seized because of recusancy, but the following year orders were given for their return after he had taken the oaths of allegiance and supremacy. In 1680, however, he was included in an official list of considerable Staffordshire papists. His first wife Elizabeth was a Catholic, but his second, Henrietta, was not, and in the later 1680s their children were baptised as Anglicans. He died in 1688 with an infant son John as his heir. In 1704 Henrietta described John as the first Protestant in that line of the Astley family.[23]

In 1661 Peter Giffard petitioned the King for the payment to him of all money remaining in the hands of the three purchasers of his estate; he stressed that he 'for his faithful and eminent services to your late father of blessed memory hath been several times imprisoned, his goods and houses ransacked, and he by the cruel edicts of the late bloody tyrant proceeded against as a traitor to the government and his whole

The coat of arms granted to William Carlos (formerly Careless).

estate seized and sold'. In 1662 he was granted all money arising from the sale.[24]

The members of the Catholic underground who had helped in the King's escape through Shropshire and Staffordshire were particularly remembered. Charles Giffard had guided the dispersed royal party north from White Ladies to Newport, but they had been captured soon afterwards. He managed to escape and went to Holland. He was back in England by 1657 as a prisoner in Shrewsbury Castle and was ordered to stand trial. He survived, and from 1660 until at least 1672 he was petitioning the King for grants in kind and in cash. His involvement in various commercial ventures landed him in debt and in prison. The King gave him financial help, including a life pension of £150 in 1668. Despite his problems he supported his stepson Daniel Coulster at the Jesuit college at St Omer for at least seven years from 1672. In 1691 he was in receipt of a government pension of £375.[25]

William Careless had secured a pass to go to London under an assumed name with the help of his friend the Catholic Henry Ironmonger of Wolverhampton and escaped to the Low Countries. In 1658 the King changed William's surname to Carlos and granted him a coat of arms depicting an oak tree and three crowns with an oak garland on the crest. In 1661 he was given a share in the proceeds of the tax on straw and hay brought to Westminster and also the office of inspector of livery horse keepers. In addition he received a grant to sell ballast to ships on the Thames, but after disputes with Trinity House he surrendered it in return for compensation of 1,000 marks. In January 1688, he received £300 from the secret service fund. After spending his last year in Worcestershire he died in London in 1689 but was buried in Brewood churchyard on Oak Apple day (29 May), the anniversary of Charles's restoration. A memorial plaque was unveiled in the chancel of the church in 1960.[26]

John Huddleston and Thomas Whitgreave, on Charles's advice, both left the Moseley area after his departure, returning only when they knew that he was safely in France and that nothing had been discovered about his stay at Moseley.[27] At the Restoration Huddleston, who had become a Benedictine monk about 1653, was invited by Charles to live at Somerset House under the protection of the dowager Queen Henrietta Maria. After her death he was appointed chaplain to Queen Catherine of Braganza with a salary of £100 and a pension of £100. When Charles was dying in 1685 his brother the Catholic Duke of York, about to succeed as James II, brought Fr Huddleston to him and Charles was duly received into the Catholic Church. When Catherine returned to Portugal in 1692, she asked Lord Feversham, her lord chamberlain and a recent convert, to look after Fr Huddleston, who was by then senile. He died at Somerset House aged ninety in 1698.[28]

It was not until 1666 that Thomas Whitgreave petitioned the King for an annuity as a reward for his part in the royal escape. He claimed that he had been encouraged to seek some signal mark of favour but had failed and been put to much expense by a long stay in town. He was granted a life pension of £200, quickly raised to £300.[29] As late as 1683 John Underhill of Northycote, despite his mother's recalcitrance in 1651, was granted on petition the restitution of a £60 fine for recusancy 'in consideration of his particular merit in being instrumental in the King's escape from Worcester'; it was not recorded what the service was.[30]

It was the Penderels who received the most generous treatment.[31] In June 1660 the brothers went to Whitehall where 'his Majesty was pleased to own their faithful service and dismissed them with a princely reward'.[32] In 1661 they received £400, and between then and 1675 William received some £600 and the others about £400 each. In 1673, however, Humphrey petitioned the King, complaining that he had only fifty marks a year whereas two of his brothers had £100, although the King had said that they should all have pensions alike. Humphrey stated that he had 'a very great charge of children' and that marrying two of his daughters had forced him to borrow £200, which his creditors were now demanding. He asked for a grant of £200 to meet the debt, a request which the King promptly met.[33]

Although such gifts continued irregularly until 1714, in

1675 the King settled a number of rents on three trustees to provide annuities.[34] One of £100 was granted to Richard's widow Mary for life and then to the heirs of Richard's body, and another of £100 to William and his heirs. Three of 100 marks (£66 13s. 4d.) each were granted to John, Humphrey and George and their heirs. An annuity of £50 was granted to Elizabeth Yates and her heirs. A kinsman of the Penderels, she was the widow of the Francis Yates who had guided the royal party to White Ladies and been hanged for doing so. In 1672, having already petitioned the King for relief, she petitioned again for confirmation that she was to be granted a pension when the brothers received theirs. Her son Richard received a separate gift of £50 in 1675.[35] Payments are still made under the 1675 grant, but over the years annuities have been sold and divided; by the late twentieth century the maximum payment was about £37, most being much smaller. The original trustees included John Giffard of Chillington, and since 1692 the Giffards of Chillington have been sole trustees.[36]

The Cavaliers' quip that the Act of Indemnity and Oblivion of 1660 provided oblivion for loyalty and indemnity for treason was therefore not wholly justified. Viscount Stafford accompanied Charles II on his entry into London on 29 May 1660 and his sequestrated lands were restored to him in June. In 1664 he tried to secure the restoration to his wife of the earldom of Stafford, forfeited in 1521, but his petition was turned down. This turned him against the King, whom he considered to have failed to reward him sufficiently.[37]

Lord Aston was similarly disgruntled. In April 1675, however, Lord Aston wrote to Sir Joseph Williamson, Secretary of State, indignantly repudiating the charge made by Protestant extremists that he was in any way a papist.[38] He stated that he approved earlier measures against Catholics as necessary at the time to curb papal threats to the Crown; but now it was the opposite extremists who were the threat. In protesting his own loyalty to the King against their accusations he slipped in a further observation:

My father and I have spent in his service and in his father's and grandfather's above £5,000 a year in land, and there is yet due to me of what his late Majesty intended my father £7,000. I have often ventured my life and all that was dear to me in expressing my loyalty. I have under his late Majesty's hand these words, 'Lord Aston, the greatest of my misfortunes is that I cannot reward so gallant and loyal a subject as you are as I would and ought.'

In a second letter to Williamson a few days later Lord Aston expressed the fear that if there were an election 'the Presbyterian interest and the Fanatics will carry it in most countries'.[39] There was, he said, a contrary view:

Some, who believe that the papists in this country [Staffordshire] have a great interest in many of the electors are endeavouring to persuade that it is not the Protestant party but the Episcopal Prelatical party which have now great influence in the present House of Commons, which at this time is the cause of putting the penal statues rigorously in execution against them, but on a new election persons would be certainly chosen of a disposition, if not for full toleration, yet at least so qualified that they would have no just cause to complain. Others have lately conceived that in regard this country, where his Majesty was preserved (and that Whitgrave and the Pendrells who were so eminent loyal in his preservation are now prosecuted for being papists) is more severely prosecuted than any other in this circuit, [they] should [unite] in a petition to the House of Commons not only of themselves, but joined with all the papists of England. Where I meet this discourse I cry it down all I can, for I would have no grace or mercy expected from any but his Majesty.

If this was meant as an oblique reminder to the King, it worked. Two months later Charles ordered the suspension of all proceedings for recusancy against Thomas Whitgreave, his nephew Francis Reynolds (who had been one of John Huddleston's pupils at Moseley in 1651), Richard Penderel's widow Mary, the four other Penderel brothers and Elizabeth Yates, 'persons very instrumental in his Majesty's preservation after the Worcester fight'.[40]

✍

The Jesuits consolidated their position in the county soon after the Restoration. In 1661 the Staffordshire mission became a separate 'residence' dedicated to St Chad with eleven priests; William Atkins, a former rector of the College of St Aloysius, was superior until 1665, evidently stationed at Wolverhampton. The number of priests was down to nine in 1663 and 1664 and seven in 1667. The residence became the College of St Chad in 1669 or 1670: it was described in 1670 as recently established. Its income was stated to be enough to support eight priests in 1672; there were six in 1674 and seven in 1678.[41]

Five of the six Jesuits present at a gathering at Boscobel in August 1678 are known to have been working in Staffordshire.[42] The occasion was the taking of final vows by John Gavan, who was based at Wolverhampton by 1672. The others present were Francis Evers,[43] Lord Aston's chaplain at Tixall by 1672; Edward Leveson, a younger son of John Leveson of Willenhall, working in Staffordshire by 1672; Robert Petre,[44] who was said to have come to Staffordshire in 1655 and to have been harboured by Richard Gerard at Hilderstone; and Richard Vavasour,[45] procurator in Staffordshire, who can be located only from 1679 when he came to Alton Lodge, the home of Richard Kerby, 'for his conveniency and the security of his person'. They were joined at Boscobel by over twenty recusant gentry, including Gerard, Walter Heveningham of Aston, his two sons-in-law Walter Fowler of St Thomas and Sir James Simeon of Britwell in Oxfordshire, and Robert Howard of Hoar Cross. After the prayers, several of the company went to view the oak tree in which Charles had hidden in 1651. A venison dinner followed, where the King's health was drunk.

Blessed John Gavan.

The Jesuits fell victim to the outbreak of mass hysteria follow-ing Titus Oates's lying revelations in 1678 about a plot, spear-headed by the Jesuits, to assassinate the King and overthrow the Protestant Establishment. Charles played a cautious game; he signed warrants for judicial murders, but the Queen recalled later that whenever he came to her boudoir he turned to the portraits of those who had suffered, kissed their hands and begged their forgiveness.[46] At least in January 1679 the King in Council, following a resolution by the House of Lords, granted exemption from the measures against Catholics to a number of recusants who had helped him after the battle of Worcester 'and have thereby merited as a reward of their loyalty to be distinguished from others of their religion'.[47]

At the Stafford assizes of August 1679 Chief Justice Scroggs described Staffordshire as 'swarming with priests; like scurvy elsewhere, papism was there spread about by a mere touch'. He ordered the sheriff to empanel 'a good jury'. One juryman had scruples about condemning a man to death simply for being a priest, and Scroggs remanded him in custody until he could produce sureties for good behaviour. Three others were removed for being 'popishly affected'. Nine men were then in prison at Stafford accused of being priests, and Scroggs condemned two of them to death for being seminary priests: 'it is to these sorts of men we owe all the troubles we are in, the fear of the King's life, the subver-sion of our government and the loss of our religion.'[48]

One of the condemned was the Jesuit William Atkins, then in his late seventies, paralysed, deaf and almost speechless. A witness stated that he had said Mass in a Mrs Stamford's house in Cock Street (now Victoria Street), Wolverhampton, and another that he had performed Romish rites at Wellhead in the town. The other priest was the secular Andrew Bromwich, newly returned from the English College in Lisbon to his family at Oscott House in Handsworth and described as 'a young, lusty, brisk fellow'. Neither sentence was carried out, the King having ordered that priests were to be kept in

Blessed William Ireland.

gaol during the royal pleasure. Atkins died in Stafford gaol in 1681. Bromwich petitioned the Privy Council for his release in 1683, stating that he had taken the oaths of allegiance and supremacy, but it was not until 1688 that he was pardoned and freed.[49]

Of seven other Jesuits living in Staffordshire during the Popish Plot frenzy only two avoided arrest, Francis Evers and Edward Leveson, despite a proclamation of 1679 putting a price of £100 on Evers and £50 on Leveson; Evers escaped to St Omer for a time.[50] Francis Cotton, chaplain to the Heveninghams, had been in Staffordshire at least since 1661 and possibly since 1658, and he was superior of the 'residence' from 1665 to 1667. He was arrested in 1679, but being in his mid-eighties and infirm, he was kept in the custody of the constable. Within a few days he died after being thrown downstairs by his captors.[51] John Gavan left Wolverhampton disguised as a servant, planning to escape via London to Flanders. He hid for several days with the family of the Imperial ambassador, with a price of £50 on him. He was eventually arrested and sent to the Gatehouse prison. After performing ably at his trial, he was executed at Tyburn in June with four other Jesuits, whom he led in an act of contrition; they refused a last-minute offer of a royal pardon if they revealed what they knew of the Plot.[52] They were beatified among the English Martyrs in 1929. Peter Giffard (alias Walker) was in Staffordshire by 1661 and was rector of the college at the time of the frenzy. He was in Stafford gaol in 1681, and the Jesuit Provincial then recorded that 'Father Walker has certainly declared what belongs to the College of St Chad, all of which is fallen into other hands'.[53] Robert Petre was arrested in 1679 and put in Stafford gaol. Having been remanded to London, he was one of the first three Jesuits to be released in June 1680.[54] Richard Vavasour, on whom the proclamation of 1679 placed a price of £50, was in custody by February 1681, but by then the frenzy was abating; he went to Flanders, dying at Nieuport in 1683.[55]

Another Jesuit with a brief Staffordshire connection was William Ireland, who was arrested in September 1678.[56] At

Stephen Dugdale.

his trial for involvement in the Plot, he refuted the accusation that he had been in London in August and at the beginning of September with an alibi showing that he had left London for Staffordshire on 3 August and Wolverhampton for London on 13 September. On leaving London Fr Ireland went to Lord Aston's estate at Standon in Hertfordshire. On 5 September he went with Lord Aston and his wife to St Albans where they were joined by Aston's sister Elizabeth, Lady Southcote, her husband Sir John, and two sons. They all went on to Tixall via Northampton and Coventry. On 15 August, accompanied by the dowager Lady Aston, they went to St Winifred's Well in North Wales, returning to Tixall the next day. Fr Ireland then went to Chester. He was at the Boscobel gathering towards the end of August, going from there via Black Ladies to Wolverhampton. Charles Giffard saw him in Wolverhampton about 26 August and again on 7 and 9 September when he was planning to return to London; while at Wolverhampton he stayed at the house of Jane Harwell, a widow, in Goat Street (now North Street). He went fishing with Walter Heveningham at Aston on 31 August when he caught a pike a yard long. The next day, 1 September, he hunted buck with Richard Gerard in the park at Hilderstone, and he was at nearby Milwich on 2 September. Fr Ireland was however found guilty and suffered at Tyburn in January 1679; the King at first delayed the execution and then ordered that Fr Ireland should be hanged until dead instead of being cut down and drawn while alive. He too was beatified in 1929.

❧

Staffordshire produced a sub-plot, with the part of Oates being taken by Stephen Dugdale, Lord Aston's bailiff.[57] Dugdale stated that he was about forty years of age and had been in the Astons' service for about fifteen years. He was brought up a Protestant until converted to Catholicism about the age of twenty by a priest called Knight; on Knight's death he passed into the care of Fr Evers at Tixall. He claimed to have become deeply trusted by the Jesuits, who called him honest Stephen.

Items from 'A Representation of the Popish Plott in 29 figures . . .'.

The third Lord Aston succeeded his father in April 1678, and in mid-November, having discovered that Dugdale was embezzling his money, Lord Aston suspended him. Dugdale was in financial difficulties; his debts included one of 100 guineas which he had lost to Sir John Crewe at a foot race and for which on his own admission he had been 'clapt up in Stafford'. On the night of his suspension he went to a public house in Tixall with his pockets full of documents which he proceeded to burn. He then went into hiding at Rolleston at the home of the Protestant John Bond, between whose niece and Dugdale there had 'long been a purpose of marriage'. He returned to the area in December and was taken into custody at Haywood by the watch. He was examined at Stafford by two magistrates, and having cleared himself of all knowledge of the Plot, he took the oaths of allegiance and supremacy and was discharged.

William Southall of Penkridge, however, one of the county coroners and a man who was making money out of priest hunting, had other plans for Dugdale. He had known Dugdale as 'a kind of governor' in Lord Aston's household and now dangled the informer's reward before him. Dugdale proceeded to make depositions and statements, at first locally and then in London, that led to the condemnation of Lord Stafford as well as of Fr Ireland. Stafford had already been arrested with four other Catholic lords on the strength of Oates's evidence, sent to the Tower and impeached. Dugdale now unfolded a tale of the comings and goings of Jesuits at Tixall, conversations overheard, and letters concerned with the restoration of Catholicism. He claimed that within the past two years the Jesuits had involved him in their plans against the King which had been laid over six years before. Lord Stafford, while staying at Tixall in September, had summoned Dugdale to his room and told him of 'a design on hand' with a reward of £500 if he would go to London and assist in the plot. Dugdale was puzzled and asked Fr Evers to explain. The Jesuit told him that the plan was to kill the King and the Duke of Monmouth, Charles's illegitimate son, and said that if Dugdale helped, the Pope would grant him a pardon and canonize him. Dugdale stated that he was involved in the collection of money from the local gentry to finance the plan on the pretext that it was for the college at St Omer. He further claimed that Lord Stafford, while staying in Stafford in September, had come over to Tixall and had told Dugdale that

> it was a great trouble that we could not have the liberty to say our prayers but in such a hid manner but speedily he hoped there would be a reformation to the Romish religion and if there was a good success we should have our freedom.

Though not implausible, that was hardly treasonable: Charles himself had promised as much at Moseley in 1651. Dugdale also stated that he had overheard Stafford talking to Lord Aston in such a way that Aston must have had some idea of what was proposed. While Ireland was the mastermind in London, Evers was the leader in Stafford, with John Gavan and several secular priests as his assistants. Dugdale was due to be summoned to London for a briefing, but in the meantime Oates had revealed all.

Dugdale was escorted to London by two royal messengers, staying the first night at Rolleston with the Bond family. On 8 January 1679 he appeared before the King and the Committee of Examinations. The King sent to Lord Stafford saying that he been convinced of his guilt but would pardon him if he would confess, an offer which Stafford refused. Dugdale was hesitant about positively implicating Lord Aston, who was, however, sent to the Tower and remained there until June 1685.[58] Tixall Hall was searched twice but no incriminating papers were found. Four of the gentry who had been at Boscobel were summoned before the Committee of Examinations. They admitted patronising priests but denied all knowledge of the Plot and were allowed to go home. In May, however, Walter Heveningham and Sir James Simeon were arrested and were still in prison in June 1680. At the same time Richard Gerard, sent from Stafford gaol to the Gatehouse in London to be a witness on behalf of the five Catholic lords in the Tower, was accused by Dugdale of complicity in the Plot; he strongly denied this, stressed the innocence of the Boscobel meeting, and explained that the only money given by him to the Jesuits was £25 a year for the education of each of his three sons at St Omer. He was transferred to Newgate, where he died in March 1680.[59] Walter Fowler, however, was not accused by Dugdale, who claimed on the contrary that Fr Evers had told him that Mr Fowler was excommunicated, or due to be, for refusing to take part in the Plot.

After more than two years in the Tower Lord Stafford was tried by his peers in Westminster Hall at the end of 1680, with places screened off where the King and the Queen could listen to the proceedings. He was chosen from among the five Catholic peers in the Tower probably because he seemed the least likely to run an effective defence. He reached his sixty-eighth birthday on the day when the trial started (30 November), and despite deafness and impaired eyesight he had to conduct his own defence. Dugdale was among the chief witnesses against him. He was found guilty of treason by fifty-five votes to thirty-one and attainted, and his Stafford barony thereby became forfeit. At the suit of the Lords the King agreed that he should be beheaded and not hanged, drawn and quartered, and he was executed on Tower Green on 29 December.

He was beatified in 1929, though until his final days he had hardly shown heroic virtue. The diarist John Evelyn commented that 'Lord Stafford was not a man beloved, especially of his own family'; on the other hand his confessor, the Benedictine Maurus Corker, described him as 'ever held to be of a generous disposition, very charitable, devout, addicted to sobriety, inoffensive in his words, and a lover of justice'. He was by nature short-tempered, and his irascibility was aggravated by ill health, law suits brought by two of his nephews over his mother's will, and disappointment with the restored monarchy; he bore grudges, notably against the Jesuits for what he regarded as a failure to support him in the law suit. He was, however, devoted to his wife and children, and his last days were spent in writing letters to them as well as in prayer and the preparation of his speech from the scaffold. He regarded his judicial murder as martyrdom:

> I conceive this sentence is fallen upon me upon account of the religion I am of; if I had numbers of lives, I would lose them all, rather than forsake that Church, that I am of; and which I am well assured that it maintains nothing but what is warranted by the Word of God.

It can be said that nothing in his life became him like the leaving of it.[60]

༺ঌ

Not surprisingly the Plot frenzy produced the fullest list of Staffordshire Catholics so far drawn up.[61] It was submitted at the beginning of 1681 by the deputy clerk of the peace, Zachary Babington, in answer to a request from Sir Walter Bagot, one of the county MPs. Based on a list of convicted recusants drawn up by the sheriff late in 1678 with additions by Babington to July 1680, it contains 1,548 names, though Babington admitted that 'some nine or ten Quakers may have slipped into the number'. It shows concentrations similar to those in earlier lists.

It ends with a list of priests, those arrested in Staffordshire under a warrant of December 1678 and those still at large two years later. The nine arrested included the Jesuits William Atkins and the deceased Francis Cotton and also 'Edward Peters', probably an error for the Jesuit Robert Petre. Francis Leveson, deceased, may have been the Franciscan of that name who died in prison and was declared Venerable in 1886.[62] Of the remaining five, two can be identified as secular priests: William Manley, whose Staffordshire connection is unclear, was living in London in 1683,[63] and Gregory Farmer, who died in Stafford gaol under sentence of death in 1685[64] and according to the list 'appertained to Lord Stafford'. The 'Mr Lacon' may have been either Edward

Lacon, who was born in Shropshire, studied at St Omer and the English College in Rome, was sent to England in 1643 and died in 1679, or Richard Lacon, who grew up in Shropshire, studied at the English College, Rome, and left for England in 1668.[65] Sampson Smith and William Higgins have not been identified. A tenth name was omitted from the list, that of the secular Andrew Bromwich arrested in 1679.

Of the eight priests still at large, three were the Jesuits, Richard Vavasour, Francis Evers and Edward Leveson mentioned above. The rest were seculars. Francis Towers was a Londoner educated at St Omer and the English College who left for England in 1669; his Staffordshire connection is not clear.[66] 'Mr Fitzherbert' was probably Robert Fitzherbert, born 1629, the son of Francis Fitzherbert of Tissington in Derbyshire; having studied at the English College in Lisbon and been sent to England in 1653, he spent most of the remainder of his life at Paynsley with his Draycott relatives. He died there in 1701, having been Archdeacon of Staffordshire from 1682 until at least 1694.[67] Valentine Harcourt was born in 1611, the son of Humphrey Harcourt of Ranton and Bridget, daughter of Francis Biddulph of Biddulph, and entered the English College, Rome, in 1629, leaving for England in 1634. He worked in Oxfordshire, Warwickshire and Worcestershire. It is not clear that he was in fact at large: he was in Shrewsbury gaol in December 1678 and was sent to London to be examined the following January. He was living in Shropshire in 1684 and died evidently in 1690.[68] John Bradsheet (given as 'Mr Broadstreet') was educated at St Omer and the English College at Valladolid and was sent to England in 1659. He was with the Howards at Hoar Cross in 1673 and was included in the proclamation of January 1679 with a price of £50 on him. He died in Staffordshire in 1689.[69]

There were also the two Fitter brothers, Francis and Daniel, sons of Thomas and Margaret (or Margery) Fitter of Wolverhampton; a daughter Joan was the mother of Andrew Bromwich. Francis was born at Wolverhampton in 1622 and studied at Lisbon. He was sent to England in 1647, settling with another sister and her husband Andrew Cross at Oulton in Norbury in western Staffordshire. He fled abroad during the Plot frenzy but returned to Oulton. He succeeded his nephew Andrew Bromwich in the Oscott mission in 1702 but died in Shropshire in 1710. By 1666 he was a member of the Chapter established in 1623, and he was Archdeacon of Staffordshire from 1666 or 1667 until his resignation in 1682. Daniel's name is missing from Babington's list, but he too went abroad during the Plot frenzy. Born in 1628, he studied at Lisbon like his brother but was sent to finish his studies in Paris. On the way he was badly hurt when his ship was attacked by Dutch pirates and a powder keg exploded. He left for England in 1654 and became chaplain to the Fowlers at St Thomas, dying there in 1700. He was buried in the chancel of Baswich church, described by William Fowler in a family memorial plaque as his 'virtuous friend'. He was a member of the Chapter and vicar general for Staffordshire from 1687 until at least 1694.[70]

❧

By 1681 the frenzy was dying down, and it was followed by reaction. Stephen Dugdale died in London in 1683, discredited, evidently suffering from alcoholism and venereal disease, and claiming to have seen ghosts of his victims.[71] With the accession of James II in 1685 Catholic hopes ran high once more, but James mishandled the situation and his reign lasted less than four years.

Viscount Stafford's widow, as Baroness Stafford in her own right, was summoned to James's coronation. In 1688, twenty-four years after her husband's failure to secure the revival of the Stafford earldom, she was created Countess of Stafford for life and her son Earl of Stafford; at the same time the new Earl changed the family name to Stafford-Howard. At the beginning of the reign a Bill was passed by the Lords declaring that the testimony on which Lord Stafford had been convicted was false but it failed to pass the Commons. In October 1688 a Bill to reverse his attainder was passed by the

Lords but got no further because of the ensuing political upheaval; his Stafford barony remained forfeit until 1824–5.[72]

The most enduring benefit for the English Catholic community was the restoration of bishops in the form of vicars apostolic. James and the Chapter wanted a bishop in ordinary – a bishop with a diocese and full jurisdiction – but because of the still abnormal situation in England Rome would allow only a vicar apostolic – a titular bishop with no diocese and holding office at the Pope's pleasure. Dr John Leyburn arrived in October 1685 with the title of Bishop of Adrumetum. For lack of a bishop the sacrament of Confirmation had not been administered since the 1620s, and in 1687 Leyburn made a tour of the North and Midlands and confirmed over 20,000 candidates. On 2 October he confirmed 219 in the chapel at Stafford, recently built by Daniel Fitter, which was used as a centre on this occasion not only for the immediate vicinity but for a wide area mainly to the north and west of the town. Leyburn confirmed another five at St Thomas and went on to Wolverhampton where he confirmed thirty-seven. On 7 October he confirmed 499 at Edgbaston over the Warwickshire boundary, presumably including a number from south Staffordshire.[73]

In 1687 King James petitioned Rome for three more vicars apostolic, and in 1688 England was divided into four districts, each with a vicar apostolic. Staffordshire was included in the Midland District, stretching from the Welsh border to East Anglia, with Bonaventure Giffard as its vicar apostolic. James had specifically asked for him, and in April he was consecrated Bishop of Madaura in the newly built royal chapel in Whitehall Palace in the presence of the King and Queen; the papal nuncio officiated, assisted by Bishop Leyburn and an Irish bishop. Bonaventure was born in 1642, a younger son of Andrew Giffard of Cock Street, Wolverhampton (brother of Peter of Chillington and killed in the Civil War), and Catherine, daughter of Sir Walter Leveson of Wolverhampton; two of his brothers, Augustine and Andrew, also became priests. Having studied at the English College in Douai and later in Paris, he came to England in 1678, but in 1679 with the Plot

Bonaventure Giffard, Vicar Apostolic of the Midland District 1688–1703 and of the London District 1703–34.

frenzy at its height he left for France. Returning in 1681, he was made secretary to the Chapter and Archdeacon of Essex and in 1687 was appointed vicar general of the eastern vicariate, one of four created by Leyburn that year. He was also appointed a royal chaplain and preacher. Shortly before his consecration James imposed him as president on Magdalen College, Oxford, which the King intended to turn into a Catholic seminary; Bonaventure's brother Andrew was later appointed a fellow.[74]

Whereas the income of the Jesuit College of St Chad was sufficient for only three priests in 1685,[75] the secular clergy were becoming increasingly organised. In line with the Chapter's directive for the establishment of local funds, a Common Purse for a Staffordshire district covering Staffordshire, Worcestershire, Derbyshire and Shropshire had been established by 1676 with Daniel Fitter in charge; by 1680 he and Francis Fitter had made it up to £200. Its aim was the relief of priests in want, who had shown themselves 'true clergy men' by acknowledging the Dean and Chapter. Funds were raised by members' legacies and gifts from the laity.[76] In 1686 nineteen secular priests working in the county drew up twenty-two articles of association after choosing a superior. The articles, which began with a promise of obedience to the bishop placed over them by God, were concerned mostly with the organisation of pastoral work, including meetings of the brethren. They also provided for mutual support in sickness, danger and death, and the superior was empowered to organise a collection among the brethren if any one of them was in want. A treasurer and assistant were chosen to take charge of the common purse of the county and to account to an annual meeting of the brethren; every brother was to pay ten or twenty shillings into the purse if he could afford it. It was also agreed that 'we endeavour for youths of our own county to be sent to colleges that a succession may follow us in the mission'. Finally every brother was to leave some of his books to maintain 'a public library or two in the county'.[77] This appears to have been the creation of the Staffordshire branch of the Institute of Secular Clergy Living in Common, which

The Deanery, Wolverhampton, in 1837.

originated in Bavaria; the only other English branch was that
for London. Like the Staffordshire Common Purse, the
Staffordshire district of the Institute covered Staffordshire,
Worcestershire, Derbyshire and Shropshire. Six of its nine
original members were Staffordshire clergy, and Daniel Fitter
was elected first provincial president and procurator.[78]

Two public chapels were opened in Staffordshire during
James's reign. Daniel Fitter bought land in Foregate Street in
Stafford in December 1684 and later more in Eastgate Street.
By 1687 he had opened a chapel and a school for poor
Catholics evidently on the Eastgate Street plot.[79] In Wolver-
hampton six Jesuits were living in the Deanery Hall in Horse
Fair (later Wulfruna Street) north-east of St Peter's church by
1688. They had a large and much frequented chapel there and
a school where nearly fifty boys were taught, some twelve of
them boarders.[80]

A description of Walter Fowler's private chapel at St
Thomas survives from the period 1684–8 and shows it gener-
ously furnished.[81] There were several sets of vestments – one
green, three white, three red, one purple, two black, and one
calico, with antependia and veils to match; there were also a
cope and a mitre. Altar furnishings included an old carpet for
daily use, a new carpet for great feasts, a black carpet, cush-
ions in the various liturgical colours, red and black curtains,
hangings, two black covers for a hearse and 'two cloths with
death heads for the cross on the hearse'. Linen included altar
cloths, a surplice, two girdles, three albs, four amices, and
napkins and towels. Among the numerous candlesticks were
six of silver and six of pewter. Other precious metalware
included a silver cross, a little gold cross, a gilt chalice and
paten, 'one silver cup for the communicants', a silver bell, a
silver pax and a silver plate for the cruets. Wooden fittings
included the altar table (with an altar stone), two credence
tables, a great chair, six great forms and two little ones, a
tabernacle, several presses, and 'one triangular frame for
Tenebrae'. Besides an altar piece, there were pictures of 'Our
Saviour and Our Lady, Our Lady with Our Saviour in her
arms, Our Saviour taken down from the Cross' and various

saints. There were also items belonging to Gertrude Fowler, Walter's aunt, including a silver cup for Communion, white, red and black vestments, and 'two sets of flowers being the best used on great feasts and the ordinary ones on weekdays with earthen pots'.

Typical of the high-handedness which cost James his throne was his interference in borough affairs at Stafford.[82] Following the surrender of the borough charter at the end of Charles's reign, James granted a new one in 1685, which gave him the right to remove officers and members of the corporation. In 1687 he filled a vacancy among the aldermen by appointing a Catholic, Dr Benjamin Thornburgh. Later that year Thornburgh was elected mayor, and James dispensed him from taking the oaths of allegiance and supremacy. In May 1688 James dismissed several aldermen and burgesses along with the high steward, the recorder and the town clerk and nominated the replacements. There was some resistance, and in October James backed down, reinstating those whom he had dismissed and restoring the old charter.

It was too late. In November the Protestant William of Orange landed with an army on the shore of Torbay. In December James fled the country, leaving the way open for William and his Protestant wife, James's daughter Mary.

Notes

1   The following account of Charles II's escape is based on T. Blount, *Boscobel* (1822 edn.), supplemented by other contemporary (though conflicting) accounts printed in W. Matthews (ed.), *Charles II's Escape from Worcester* (Berkeley and Los Angeles, 1966), pp. 85 sqq. See also R. Ollard, *The Escape of Charles II after the Battle of Worcester* (1966).

2   *S.H.C.* new ser. v, pp. 168–72. The house was so named from the adjoining remains of a medieval priory of Augustinian canonesses which, like Black Ladies, had come into the hands of the Giffards after the Dissolution.

3   *Oxford D.N.B.* x, p. 137.

4   A. H. Chatwin, 'The Catholic Underhills of Northycote Farm

in Bushbury, Staffordshire', *Mid. Cath. Hist.* ix (2002–3),
p. 6 (the quotation being from Fr Huddleston's account in
Matthews (ed.), *Charles II's Escape*).

5　Humphrey, in his petition of 1673 (below, p. 132), provided a
variation of the quip: 'His horse carried a very great trade, for
he carried the price of three kingdoms on his back.'

6　Matthews (ed.), *Charles II's Escape*, p. 119.

7　M. Hodgetts, *Secret Hiding-places* (Dublin, 1989), p. 203; A.
Fraser, *King Charles II* (1979), p. 117.

8　Matthews (ed.), *Charles II's Escape*, p. 119.

9　Blount, *Boscobel*, pp. 9–10.

10　L. J. Bird, 'Recusant Epitaphs in the Midlands', *Mid. Cath.
Hist.* vi (1998), pp. 7–8, with the translation by Michael
Hodgetts on p. 17.

11　*S.H.C.* new ser. v (1902), pp. 178–9.

12　*Calendar of Committee for Advance of Money*, iii, p. 1415.

13　*Calendar of Committee for Compounding*, iii, pp. 1876–7.

14　*S.H.C.* 1915, pp. 327–8.

15　*Cal. S.P. Dom. 1654*, p. 307.

16　D. A. Johnson and D. G. Vaisey (eds), *Staffordshire in the
Great Rebellion* (Staffordshire County Council, 1964 edn), pp.
38–40; *V.C.H. Staffs.* iv, p. 147.

17　M. W. Greenslade, *Saint Chad of Lichfield and Birmingham*
(Archdiocese of Birmingham Historical Commission, publication number 10, 1996), pp. 16, 26–8.

18　M. W. Greenslade, 'List of Staffordshire Recusants 1657',
S.H.C. 4th ser. ii (1958), pp. 71 sqq.

19　*V.C.H. Staffs.* viii, pp. 116, 271–2.

20　J. F. Champ, 'The Franciscan Mission in Birmingham
1657–1824', *Recusant History*, xxi (1) (1992), pp. 40–1.

21　Father Thaddeus [Francis Hermans], *The Franciscans in
England 1600–1850* (1898), pp. 89, 176.

22　R. M. Kidson, 'The Gentry of Staffordshire, 1662–3', *S.H.C.*
4th ser. ii, pp. 7, 14–15, 22, 38–9.

23　*V.C.H. Staffs.* xx, pp. 165, 171.

24　*S.H.C.* new ser. v, pp. 178–9.

25　Ibid., pp. 181–8.

26　*Oxford D.N.B.* x, p. 138; D. Horowitz, *Brewood* (Brewood,
1992 edn), pp. 136, 150, 154–5, 374; Blount, *Boscobel*, pp.
85–6. For Ironmonger see also *S.H.C.* v (2), p. 186.

27　Blount, *Boscobel*, pp. 78–81.

28 *Oxford D.N.B.* xxviii, pp. 562–3; *Complete Peerage*, v, p. 365.

29 *Cal. S.P. Dom. 1665–1666*, pp. 415, 504, 530, 573.

30 *Calendar of Treasury Books*, vii (2), p. 754.

31 For the next two paras. see J. A. C. Baker, 'The Pendrill Pensions', *Staffordshire History*, xx (Autumn 1994).

32 Blount, *Boscobel*, pp. 88–9.

33 *Cal. S.P. Dom. from 1672 to 1675*, pp. 496–7, 516.

34 *Calendar of Treasury Books*, iv, pp. 757–9.

35 *Cal. S.P. Dom. from 1671 to 1672*, p. 150; *Calendar of Treasury Books*, iv, p. 838.

36 The copy of the grant formerly at Chillington is now in the Giffard collection in S.R.O., D. 590/499a.

37 *Complete Peerage*, v, pp. 190–1; J. M. Robinson, *The Staffords* (2002), p. 68.

38 *Cal. S.P. Dom. from 1675 to 1676*, pp. 51–3. He was described as a Roman Catholic in the list of Staffordshire gentry compiled in 1662–3, and his sister was the wife of the Catholic Walter Fowler of St Thomas: *S.H.C.* 4th ser. ii, pp. 14–15, 38. It was stated in 1679 that he was reputed a Protestant but was said to have died a Catholic: *The Journals of the House of Lords*, xii, p. 579.

39 *Cal. S.P. Dom. from 1675 to 1676*, p. 87.

40 *Calendar of Treasury Books*, iv, p. 756.

41 Foley, *English Province S.J.*, vii (1882), pp. lxxxviii, xci, xciv, cl.

42 For this para. see *The Journals of the House of Lords*, xii, p. 579; J. Kenyon, *The Popish Plot* (1972), pp. 141, 143; *Cal. S.P. Dom. from 1680 to 1681*, p. 167; W. F. Carter, 'Notes on some Staffordshire Families', *S.H.C.* 1925, pp. 43–4; W.S.L., S.MS. 312, evidence of 23 Jan. For the other Jesuit present, William Ireland, see below, p. 141.

43 Alias Clare. His real name was Eure.

44 Alias Williams and Spencer.

45 Alias Parker and Giffard.

46 Kenyon, *Popish Plot*, p. 166.

47 *S.H.C.* new ser. v, p. 187; A. Fea, *The Flight of the King* (1897), pp. 329–4. The two lists of names differ.

48 Kenyon, pp. 178–9; *V.C.H. Staffs.*, iii (1970), p. 106.

49 For Atkins see *Staffs. Cath. Hist.* iii, pp. 5–6; T. M. McCoog, *English and Welsh Jesuits 1555–1650 Part 1* (*C.R.S.* lxxiv,

1994), p. 108. For Bromwich see B. Penny, *Maryvale* (Arch-diocese of Birmingham Historical Commission, publication no. 1, 1985), p. 1; *V.C.H. Staffs.* iii, p. 106, note 90. On the taking of the oaths see Kenyon, pp. 229–32.

50 Kenyon, p. 141; *Cal. S.P. Dom. 1680 to 1681*, p. 167.

51 *Staffs. Cath. Hist.* iii, p. 8.

52 Kenyon, pp. 141–2, 159, 161–2, 180; Foley, *English Province S.J.* v (1879), pp. 454–5.

53 *Staffs. Cath. Hist.,* iii, p. 10.

54 Ibid., pp. 13–14 (which has him still in gaol in London in 1682); Kenyon, p. 201. According to G. Holt, *The English Jesuits 1650–1829* (*C.R.S.* lxx, 1984), p. 192, he was in Stafford gaol 1678–82 and in prison in London in 1683.

55 Kenyon, p. 141; *Cal. S.P. Dom. from 1680 to 1681*, p. 167; *C.R.S.* lxx, p. 254 (which, however, has him in Ghent 1679–82).

56 Alias Ironmonger. For this para. see Kenyon, pp. 44, 127, 141, 144, 166, 209, 253; *Staffs. Cath. Hist.* iii, pp. 11–12; Foley, *English Province S.J.* v, pp. 117–19, 137–8; T. and A. Clifford, *A Topographical and Historical Description of the Parish of Tixall in the County of Stafford* (Paris, 1817), pp. 152, 269 (which, however, cites the statement by Lord Aston and his nephew that Fr Ireland was back at Tixall on 8 September and left with Sir John Southcote for Surrey on 9 September).

57 For this section see S. A. H. Burne, *The Trial of William Howard, Viscount Howard* (Stafford, 1964; copy in W.S.L.); Kenyon, pp. 138–44; S. N. D. [Rose Meeres], *Sir William Howard Viscount Stafford 1612–1680* (1929), especially chapter ix; W.S.L., S.MS. 312 (statements by Dugdale with allied papers).

58 *Complete Peerage*, i, p. 286.

59 *The Journals of the House of Lords*, xii, pp. 578–9.

60 Robinson, *The Staffords*, pp. 66–75; *Complete Peerage*, v, p. 191, note g.

61 D. Fowkes and M. W. Greenslade, 'A List of Staffordshire Recusants 1678–80', *Staffs. Cath. Hist.,* xxiv (1990), pp. 1 sqq.

62 Kenyon, p. 272. Two members of the Willenhall branch of the family about this time were named Francis: *S.H.C.* v (2), p. 203.

63 Anstruther, *Seminary Priests*, ii, p. 209.

64 Ibid., p. 371.

65   Ibid., p. 181; ibid. iii, p. 125–6.

66   Ibid., iii, pp. 231–2.

67   Ibid., ii, p. 111.

68   Ibid., p. 144.

69   Ibid., p. 35; Kenyon, p. 141.

70   M. B. Rowlands, 'The Allegiances and Loyalties of three Catholic Priests in the late Seventeenth Century', *Midland History*, xxv (2000), pp. 78 sqq.; Anstruther, *Seminary Priests*, ii, pp. 109–10; iii, p. 98; *Mid. Cath. Hist.* vi, p. 9.

71   *Oxford D.N.B.* xvii, p. 152.

72   *Complete Peerage*, pp. 191–2; Robinson, *The Staffords*, pp. 75–6; below, p. 233.

73   M. Greenslade, 'Bishop Leyburn at Stafford and Wolver-hampton', *Staffs. Cath. Hist.* ii, pp. 19–26; J. A. Hilton and others (eds), *Bishop Leyburn's Confirmation Register of 1687* (Wigan, 1997), pp. 234–40, 306. The figure of 422 for Stafford includes three names which had been crossed out. For an analysis of the area covered by the Stafford confirmation see M. B. Rowlands, 'Surviving the Times, 1625–90', *English Catholics of Parish and Town 1558–1778*, ed. M. B. Rowlands (C.R.S. Monograph Series v, 1999), pp. 71–2. For the chapel at Stafford see below, p. 153.

74   J. A. Williams, '"Our Patriarch": Bishop Bonaventure Giffard, 1642–1734', *Recusant History*, xxvi (3) (2003), pp. 426 sqq.; Anstruther, *Seminary Priests*, ii, pp. 65–9; G. P. Mander and N. W. Tildesley, *A History of Wolverhampton to the early Nineteenth Century* (Wolverhampton, 1960), p. 62.

75   Foley, *English Province S.J.* vii, p. cli.

76   *V.C.H. Staffs.* iii, p. 107; *Midland History*, xxv, p. 81.

77   M. Greenslade, 'The Association of the Staffordshire Clergy, 1686', *Staffs. Cath. Hist.* ii, pp. 13–18.

78   R. H. Turner, 'Clergy Funds and Episcopal Control – Was John Stanford Maligned?', *Recusant History*, xxvii (1) (2004), p. 52; M. Rowlands, 'Catholics in Staffordshire from the Revolution to the Relief Acts 1688–1791' (Birmingham University M.A. thesis, 1965), pp. 44–7; *V.C.H. Staffs.* iii, p. 110, n. 39.

79   *Midland History*, xxv, p. 84.

80   Foley, *English Province S.J.* v, p. 450; Mander and Tildesley, *Wolverhampton*, pp. 96, 103, and endpaper map.

81   B.A.A., CF2 (formerly C110).

82   *V.C.H. Staffs.* vi, p. 225.

5

THE GROWTH OF
TOLERATION: 1688–1791

The flight of James II brought an end to prospects of a restoration of Catholicism. Yet the century that followed saw a
growth of toleration, culminating in the Catholic Relief Act of
1791. Initially, however, there was renewed persecution.
Catholics were excluded from the Toleration Act of 1689.
Under an Act of 1700 saying Mass became a crime punishable
by life imprisonment, the Elizabethan treason law having
become difficult to enforce, although it remained on the
Statute Book until 1844; Catholic schoolmasters became
subject to the same penalty. Catholics were also barred from
inheriting and buying land. Such measures were, however,
mainly a threat hanging over Catholics, and the main persecution was financial. Under the Land Tax Act of 1692 all
papists aged sixteen and over who had not taken the oaths of
supremacy and allegiance were subject to double land tax. An
Act of 1715 obliged all Catholics to register their estates with
the clerk of the peace, and an Act of 1723 levied a special tax
on those estates.

Soon after the landing of William of Orange in November
1688 mobs proceeded to wreck Catholic chapels. The chapel
and school at Stafford disappeared. At Wolverhampton the
mob destroyed the altar, altar rails and fine pulpit in the Jesuit
chapel or put them to profane uses and the greater part of the
well stocked library was burned in the market place. Benches,
the reading desk, chairs and ornamental woodwork from the

school along with all the household furniture were plundered by the mob or seized by commissioners sent in. Chalices, vestments and ornaments on the altar, however, were saved. A man was accidentally killed during the disturbance. The superior and another of the priests fled to Lancashire, but a third was captured; after a year in Stafford gaol he was sent to London under a writ of *habeas corpus* and discharged.[1] There is a tradition that the Biddulphs' tenants at Rushton Grange near Burslem fled their home, leaving it to be ransacked by a mob from Burslem and its neighbourhood. This is a further indication that it may have been a Mass centre before the eighteenth century.[2]

Bishop Giffard tried to escape abroad in December 1688 but was caught in Kent and imprisoned in Newgate. He was released in 1690 and probably then based himself on his family's home in Cock Street, Wolverhampton.[3]

Lord Aston remained loyal to James II, and in 1689 he was deprived of the lord lieutenancy of Staffordshire which he had held since 1687.[4] Henry Stafford-Howard, the new Earl of Stafford, joined James in France along with his brothers Francis and John. He eventually left Paris for Brussels, and being in straitened circumstances, he began overtures to William III. In 1699 he received a royal pardon and returned to England, but a few years later he went back to Brussels. Meantime, however, he was with James II at his death in 1701, and he was a witness to the King's will. The Earl died in 1719; he was buried in Westminster Abbey, where his mother had also been buried in 1694. He had been separated from his wife, daughter of the Comte de Gramont, since 1695, less than two years after their marriage. In his will he described her as 'the worst of women', leaving her 'forty-five brass halfpence which will buy her a pullet to her supper'.[5]

As part of an unsuccessful attempt to expropriate Catholic landowners an inquisition at Wolverhampton in 1690 'discovered' that Lord Stafford and his mother had conveyed Stafford Castle and lands worth £400 a year to Cardinal Howard and others in trust for the Congregation de Propaganda Fide in Rome, which was to celebrate 4,000 Masses a year for fifty-one years for Viscount Stafford's soul and then to begin a process for his canonization. At the same time it was claimed with equal improbability that Francis Harcourt was holding Ranton in trust for the Jesuits of St Omer and that Walter Fowler had mortgaged the St Thomas estate and property in Stafford to the Provincial of the English Dominicans.[6] In 1694 further allegations were made that there had been a meeting at Paynsley in 1691 attended by Sir William Gerard, Sir Richard Fleetwood and his sons, Thomas Giffard of Wolverhampton, William Coyney of Weston Coyney and others. Their plan was stated to have been to raise the Midlands and North Wales for James II, with Lord Stafford bringing officers' commissions. It is likely, however, that Thomas Brome Whorwood of Sandwell in West Bromwich, a crypto-Catholic, was the Colonel Whorwood who in 1694 received a commission to raise a cavalry regiment as part of a Jacobite plot. In March 1696 instructions were given for a search of gentry houses, and in August Sir James Simeon of Aston and Sir Robert Howard of Hoar Cross were ordered to the Fleet prison; Philip Draycott went abroad and died in Germany in 1698.[7]

Staffordshire Catholics in fact showed little sign of Jacobite sympathies at any time, even in 1745 when Prince Charles Edward Stuart marched through the north-east of the county on his way to Derby and back. All the same, it is perhaps surprising that in 1716, despite the Jacobite rising of the year before, the King in Council confirmed the Order in Council of 1679 exempting those who had helped Charles II after the battle of Worcester from recusancy proceedings and repeated a similar Order of 1709. George I was acting on a petition from thirty-three men and women, including Penderels and Giffards, claiming descent from those named in 1679.[8]

☙

Bonaventure Giffard was appointed Vicar Apostolic of the London District in 1703. His successor in the Midland District was George Witham, the English clergy's agent in Rome; he had been nominated Bishop of Marcopolis at the wish of

George Witham, Vicar Apostolic of the Midland District 1703–16 and of the Northern District 1716–25.

James II's widow Mary of Modena and was consecrated in 1703, initially intended for London. The Fowlers provided him with a home at St Thomas, where he used the alias Markham. He had several young priests helping him in order to give them experience of mission work. One of these, Richard Hitchmough, apostatised and worked for the commissioners appointed after the Jacobite rising of 1715 to seize the property of those implicated and also property 'given for superstitious usages'. Reporting on plate in Catholic houses, he submitted a list which provides a further picture of the provision made for the chapel at St Thomas:

> One large massy silver chalice, one paten, one other silver chalice and paten double gilt with gold, two large silver crucibles, one large silver plate for the said crucibles to stand upon, two large silver thuribles, six large silver candlesticks and a large silver crucifix, one other silver crucifix carried in procession on Maundy Thursday, and a large silver ciborium double gilt within with gold, in which was kept the consecrated Host – all which plate this deponent has used when officiating at the altar.

The second chalice and paten listed were presumably the 'big silver-gilt chalice with a silver-gilt paten to it' which Francis Fitter had noted in an addition to the earlier description of the chapel furnishings; it was bought by Daniel Fitter, though added only after his death in 1700, and was intended by him for use in the chapel during the lifetime of William Fowler and then for transfer to the Staffordshire clergy generally.[9]

Witham was translated to the Northern District in 1716 and was succeeded in the Midland vicariate by John Stonor, who based himself in London and his family home at Stonor in Oxfordshire – the only Midland vicar not to live in Staffordshire. In 1752 he consecrated his friend John Hornyold as his coadjutor with the title of Bishop of Philomelia. Hornyold had been chaplain since 1739 to Mary, widow of Thomas Giffard of Chillington, at Longbirch, the Giffard dower house on the Chillington estate. She died in 1753, but Hornyold continued

Longbirch in 1838.

to live at Longbirch. He succeeded Stonor as Midland Vicar Apostolic in 1756, and Longbirch remained the residence of the vicars until 1804. Soon after becoming coadjutor Hornyold had rebuilt Oscott House as a residence for future vicars apostolic, but with the death of Mary Giffard Longbirch became available on a permanent basis. Hornyold died there in 1778 and was buried in the chancel of Brewood parish church, with a memorial inscription. In his will of 1768 he left his gold watch to his nephew, Anthony Clough, chaplain at Chillington from 1758 to 1791, a gold guinea and 'the silver crucifix that hangs at my bed's head' to Thomas Giffard of Chillington, five guineas to the poor of Brewood parish and the residue of his estate to Thomas Talbot, his coadjutor. Talbot had been consecrated with the title Bishop of Acon in 1766 and having succeeded Hornyold, continued as Midland Vicar Apostolic until his death in 1795. Both he and Hornyold enlarged the farm attached to the house, Talbot in particular having a business sense: he was also involved in the Wolverhampton land market and in turnpike trusts.[10]

~

The Jesuit superior at Wolverhampton returned from Lancashire after only six months, and by 1690 there were four fathers in St Chad's college. Their numbers thereafter varied between four and three and consisted of three at the time of the suppression of the Society in 1773. In the 1690s and the early years of the eighteenth century they depended on the alms of the faithful and their own private means, having lost all their title deeds and other documents in what they described as 'the evil times'. In 1710 they had some 260 Catholics under their charge.[11] Robert Collingwood, rector of the college from 1703 to 1734, lived variously at Black Ladies (where he was chaplain from 1694) and Boscobel and was buried in the chapel at Black Ladies in 1740.[12] Four other Staffordshire houses regularly had Jesuit chaplains for much of the eighteenth century:[13] Aston near Stone (the Simeon family); Gerrard's Bromley (Gerards and Fleetwoods) followed after its demolition about 1750 by the nearby Rudge;[14] Moseley (the Whitgreaves); and Swynnerton (the Fitzherberts). At Moseley two of the chaplains were sons of the house, James Whitgreave 1738–50 (also rector of St Chad's College from 1743) and his brother Thomas *c*.1752–1757; both died in harness and were buried at the parish church in Bushbury.[15] The Jesuit John Hardesty served at Tixall from 1741 until 1752 when he died at Daventry in Nothamptonshire on his way to take up the rectorship at St Omer.[16] Francis Fleetwood, the priest at Paynsley from 1732 to 1735, joined the Jesuits in the latter year and was at Swynnerton in 1746.[17]

The Franciscan Laurence Loraine, alias Thomas Hall, who was active in the Midlands for half a century from 1720, served part of Staffordshire. A list of his converts dated 1737 included Uttoxeter, Anslow in Rolleston, Bellamour in Colton, and Pipe Hall. In 1767 he was living in the parish of St Michael, Lichfield, as a member of the household of Miss Teresa Wakeman, a Catholic described as 'a young lady of fortune'.[18] There was a Franciscan, Francis Copley, at Hoar Cross in 1758.[19] A Benedictine died at Tixall in 1703, and two served at Swynnerton between 1782 and 1787.[20]

There were nine secular priests working in the county in 1692[21] and at least ten in 1702. The Institute aroused hostility, including that of Bishop Giffard, and the Staffordshire branch was dissolved in 1701 or 1702; the agreement was drawn up by Giffard and signed by nineteen priests, ten of them from Staffordshire. The funds of the branch seem to have been divided between a Common Fund set up by Bishop Giffard for the Midland District and the existing Common Purse covering Staffordshire, Worcestershire, Derbyshire and Shropshire. Some of the Common Purse assets, however, remained under the control of Francis Fitter, and on his death in 1710 that money became a separate fund for priests of the four counties who were in need. It became known as the Johnson Fund after the death of John Johnson, chaplain at Chillington and its first administrator, in 1739. The clergy were jealous of their control of these two funds independently of the vicars apostolic, even though they were guilty of mismanagement. There was particular conflict under Bishop Stonor, who tried to extend his limited control of the Common Fund to the other two also. In 1743 Peter Giffard and his chaplain Thomas Brockholes, as trustees of the Common Purse, threatened to take the bishop to law for detention of a £200 bond; Brockholes described Stonor's reply as 'Billingsgate language'. A compromise over control was reached under Bishop Hornyold in 1760, and administration of the funds became more orderly. By 1794 the capital of the Common Fund was over £21,500, of the Common Purse over £10,000 and of the Johnson Fund £2,500.

༺ઌ

Some details survive of the provision made by the gentry for the support of their chaplains. Robert Fitzherbert served as chaplain to the Draycotts at Paynsley for most of his life after arriving in England in 1653, and he died there in 1701. Meanwhile Philip Draycott, who died childless in 1698, left Paynsley to his sister's son Marmaduke Langdale (Baron Langdale from 1718). The heir lived in Yorkshire, and Philip in his will of 1697 also made provision for the continuance of the Paynsley mission. He settled £15 a year 'for the perpetual maintenance of a secular priest to assist the family of Paynsley and the tenants and neighbourhood of Draycott and Paynsley' and to say two Masses a week for Philip's soul. When the fund was established in 1706, the trustees stipulated that the priest was to live at Paynsley if the owner required or else in the neighbourhood; the nomination of future priests was vested in Langdale and his heirs.[22] Fitzherbert's successor, Edward Coyney, mentioned in 1721 that his chapel was at one time at Leeshouses, north-west of Paynsley.[23] In 1729 George Leyburne, newly arrived as the priest, listed his income as Philip Draycott's £15 and £5 from Philip's widow Dorothy for a weekly Mass for the soul of her second husband, Sir William Goring. There was a further £6 a year which Philip had paid and which continued without any obligations attached. Leyburne's residence was at Leeshouses. He commented just after his arrival that the people there 'seem to be good, civil, obliging folks enough and keep a very sufficient table, for which, with washing, fire and candle and strong drink, I'm to pay £12 per annum'.[24]

William Fowler paid Thomas Berington, chaplain at St Thomas from 1711 to 1720, a salary of £20.[25] In 1727 Peter Giffard was paying the priest at Chillington, Edward Dicconson, 'a voluntary pension of £20 per annum besides the keeping of a horse and washing of his linen'. Dicconson also received £3 6s. 8d. from an endowment settled by an earlier Giffard for three priests to say one Mass each a week; Peter paid the rest of the income to John Johnson, at Longbirch since 1718, and Philip Hickin at Oscott.[26] Edward Weld, having rebuilt Pipe Hall about 1770, made provision for a resident priest, with Weld paying a stipend of £15 a year and the tenant providing board. When John Kirk was appointed priest there in 1788, Weld's brother and successor Thomas increased the stipend to £20, but Kirk had 'to find his washing and supply the altar'; the tenant still provided board.[27]

༄

The eighteenth century, however, saw a move towards the establishment of missions no longer dependent on the gentry. Daniel Fitter (d. 1700) gave £600 to provide £30 a year for the support of a chaplain at St Thomas 'approved of by the bishop and one of the Institute if may be'. He also left £400 to provide £20 a year for a priest not 'confined to any gentleman's house':

> I would have him table in some convenient place in the county that he may be ready to help any poor whom other priests cannot help; as also if any priest die in the county this priest may supply his place and residence till another priest come to supply the place.

He again expressed a wish that if possible a member of the

Institute should be appointed.[28] Bishop Giffard (d. 1734) left £30 a year for a second priest at Wolverhampton serving the outlying areas of Sedgley, Gornalwood, Dudley and Bilston.[29]

In his will of 1701 Thomas Purcell of Wolverhampton, a member of the Catholic Purcell family of Yieldfields Hall, Bloxwich, endowed an itinerant chantry priest.[30] He left £160 'to the Roman Catholic clergy of England', the interest to be used from his death until 'the end of the world' to support a priest spending two nights a month at Yieldfields. On the first morning he was to say Mass for Thomas's soul and on the second for the soul of Thomas's wife, Joan; before each Mass the priest was to turn from the altar to face the congregation and ask them to pray for the donors, though without naming them. While at Yieldfields he was to instruct and catechise the people of the house and also poor Catholics of the neighbourhood and administer the Sacraments to them. In addition the priest, in whatever place he was during the same month, was to say a Mass for Thomas's father and mother and a Mass for the souls in Purgatory, at the same time commemorating Thomas and Joan. On the assumption that the interest would be at 5 per cent (£8), the priest was to receive £5 for himself and pay the remaining £3 to the people with whom he lodged for his horse and food; if for safety or convenience he came on foot – 'as many formerly have done' – he was to distribute what he saved among the most needy of his congregation. If because of persecution or for any other reason he could not safely come to Yieldfields, he was to use some other place in the neighbourhood. If that proved impossible he was to say the four Masses wherever he happened to be, keeping £5 for himself and distributing the rest to his most needy penitents on or near the feast of St Thomas the Apostle (21 December). If persecution became so severe that no priest was available and the congregation dwindled to nothing – 'of which in my days I have seen very sad examples in many places' – the superior of the clergy was to 'appoint one or two priests of their college beyond the seas to say and celebrate the four Masses'. Finally Purcell, who clearly tried to think of every contingency, noted: 'I desire that this writing may be kept in some box or trunk to keep it from rats and mice and to preserve it from wearing out.' He has had his wish: it is now safely among the Birmingham Archdiocesan Archives.

A mission was started by Andrew Bromwich centring on his family home at Oscott House.[31] The sale of the Perry Hall estate by the Stanfords in 1659 left the Bromwich family as the main Catholic family in the area, with Andrew as its head by 1678.[32] On his release from gaol in 1688 he returned to Oscott and served an area covering much of south-east Staffordshire. He died in 1702 and was buried in the family vault in Handsworth parish church. His legacies in his public will included £50 to his housekeeper Juliana Dorrington 'for her great pains and care of my dear mother and myself in our illness'. He also made an unofficial will designed to secure the mission which he had founded. He left the whole of the Oscott House estate 'for the maintenance of a secular priest belonging to Staffordshire to live at my house in Oscott where I now inhabit', a point to which he returned: 'it is strictly required by me, Andrew Bromwich, that what priest soever helps here after my death, that this house be the chief place of his residence, especially upon Sundays and holydays'. Besides caring for the poor Catholics of the Handsworth area the priest was also to say four Masses a week, one each for the souls of Andrew's father William, his mother Joan and his sister Elizabeth after her death and for Andrew's own soul. Legacies included £20 for twenty secular priests and £5 for poor Catholics of Handsworth parish, in addition to £5 left in the public will for the poor in general at the rate of 2d. each.

Bromwich assigned the nomination of the priest at Oscott to the superior of the Staffordshire secular clergy along with his two executors and their assigns. He expressed a preference, however, for Philip Hickin, who 'hath been very helping to me in my weakness'. Bromwich's uncle, the aged Francis Fitter, served the mission briefly, possibly while sorting out his nephew's affairs as one of the executors, but Hickin then took over soon after Bromwich's death. He was receiving a stipend of £15 in 1704 and remained at Oscott until his death in 1732.

A survey of Oscott House in 1732 shows a well furnished chapel. There were two silver chalices, a ciborium, a lamp, a silver pax and a silver spoon. The vestments consisted of 'two suits of white, one satin and one damask, two red suits, one of satin laid with silver and gold lace and the other with red lace, one suit of purple, two suits of black'. There were three albs, one laced and one with point lace, five amices, two surplices and three girdles. There were eight candlesticks and an ample supply of linen. The furnishings included a pulpit, two credence tables and a crucifix. There was a painting of the Resurrection in a gilt frame over the altar, and there was also a picture of Our Lady in a gilt frame. Besides the altar there were two altar stones, presumably used for Mass in other parts of the mission.

A house in Tup Street (later North Street), Wolverhampton, was described in 1729 as 'the house where time out of mind the Roman Catholicks have been used to meet for their devotions'.[33] It belonged to Edward Giffard and was leased from 1712 by Elizabeth Giffard. In 1723 the administrator of the Common Fund bought the house with a view to rebuilding it as a chapel and priest's house, although work was delayed until after Elizabeth's death in 1727. Peter Giffard of Chillington acted as front man, and in 1728 he bought a second house in Tup Street from Edward Giffard, reconveying it to Edward Dicconson, his chaplain at Chillington, and Thomas Brockholes, the newly arrived priest at Wolverhampton. Work began the same year. It seems to have been briefly suspended when Brockholes was driven from the town by informers who laid information that he was a priest; on Sunday 4 May the first house was searched. A month later, however, Mass was said there by Francis Dodd, the priest at Chillington. Work on what was described as 'the new great house and chapel' was finished in 1733, but furnishing was not complete until 1737. The cost of building came to £1,069 2s. 2½d. Bishop Giffard contributed £500, Mary Giffard of Longbirch 100 guineas, Peter Giffard £100 and Edward Dicconson £76 12s. 5d.

The building is a striking brick house, with Peter Giffard's initials on the rainwater heads. Its local attribution to the

Giffard House, Wolverhampton.

design of Francis Smith of Warwick has been dismissed on the grounds that he no longer had close connections with the town. Rather it is seen as the work of local craftsmen under Giffard supervision; the chief carpenter, Thomas Evans, is credited with its most striking feature, a main staircase which has one flight passing over another without intermediate support.[34] It was known as the Great House and was registered under that name in 1791,[35] but it came to be called Giffard House. The chapel was built as part of the house, discreetly tucked away at the back. Too big for just two priests, the house was also used for a time as a 'boarding house for respectable Catholics, who might choose to live retired, and enjoy the comforts of religion without going out of the house'.[36]

A mission was established in the county town after the closure of the long-established gentry mission at St Thomas in the 1730s. William Fowler died in 1717, and St Thomas passed through the female line. By William's will of 1712 it came to Thomas Belasyse, Viscount Fauconberg, on his marriage to Fowler's great-niece in 1726. A will of 1715 dividing the Fowler estates between the heirs of his two sisters came to light, and although Fauconberg disputed that will, the House of Lords in 1733 ordered him to surrender half the estates. He conformed to the Established Church in 1737 and sold St Thomas to Sarah, Duchess of Marlborough, in 1738. Meanwhile he refused to continue to pay the interest on Daniel Fitter's bequest for the maintenance of a chaplain at St Thomas. Simon Berington, the last resident chaplain, left in 1733. On 29 April 1739 the Baswich parish register recorded 'the first baptism from Snt Thomas since the Reformation'.[37]

A chapel appears to have been opened in a house in Stafford under the auspices of Lord Stafford.[38] The mission may have been served from 1740 by Richard Palin, who moved from Chillington to Dearnsdale, a farm three miles west of the town; his father John was one of the three pupils of John Huddleston at Moseley when Charles II was there in 1651. Richard was buried in the parish churchyard at Bradley beside his brother and sister in 1750, noted in the register as aged eighty and 'the last of that family, a Popish Priest'.[39] In 1754 his cousin Elizabeth Ryder of Grove Park in Warwickshire, one of his two heirs, settled an annual charge on the farm for a priest to say Mass once a month in the neighbourhood and on Sunday once every two months at Dearnsdale; the charge was 'to be paid for ever to the world's end, or restoration of the Catholic Religion in the kingdom'. It was probably no coincidence that the same year Thomas Wilson, the Astons' chaplain at Tixall since 1738, moved to Stafford, where he remained until his death in 1766. Within the next three years Mary, Comtesse de Rohan-Chabot, eldest daughter of the second Earl of Stafford, established a fund for the priest at Stafford, but Stafford may next have been served from Tixall by George Beeston, the chaplain there from 1763 to 1797. The first of Stafford's regular line of priests was Thomas Barnaby, who was at the Rudge in Ashley in 1779 but died in 1783 at Stafford. There is a tradition that he said Mass in the garret of a house on the Green in Forebridge. He was succeeded in 1784 by John Corne, a native of Betley who came to Stafford from Cobridge in the Potteries and rented a house in Tipping Street with his chapel in the garden.

In 1788 Corne was given a ninety-nine-year lease of half an acre on the Wolverhampton road in the Forebridge suburb of Stafford by John Berington of Winsley House in Hope-under-Dinmore, Herefordshire, and his eldest son. It was part of the land attached to the Augustinian friary in Forebridge which had passed in 1610 to the Beringtons from the Stanfords of Perry Hall along with the Rowley Hall estate south-west of the town.[40] There Corne built a house for the priest with a small chapel, some 34 feet by 18 feet, hidden behind it. The chapel was opened in July 1791, with Charles Berington, another son of John, coming over from Oscott to preach. It was dedicated to St Austin in memory of the Augustinian friars who followed the rule of St Augustine of Hippo. Confusion arose when the second church was built in 1862 with St Augustine of Canterbury depicted in one of the sanctuary windows.

While at Cobridge John Corne built a chapel for the rapidly developing Potteries area in place of the chapel at the nearby

Rushton Grange. The mission received its first resident priest, Thomas Flynn, in 1760, though he lived in Burslem. As well as saying Mass at Rushton Grange, he went once a month to Chesterton Hall north-west of Newcastle-under-Lyme, the home of the Macclesfield family since the sale of Maer Hall in 1693; in the 1750s it had been served from Paynsley. In 1773 Bishop Talbot confirmed thirty-five people, mostly teenagers, in the Rushton Grange chapel. When Flynn left for Hoar Cross in 1779, he was succeeded by Corne, who in 1780 began to build a chapel at Cobridge on the hilltop east of Rushton Grange. The subscribers included the Biddulphs and Elizabeth Macclesfield, who inherited Chesterton in 1779 and contributed £300. Local potters also subscribed – the Bagnall, Blackwell, Bucknall and Warburton families – along with Thomas Dadford, the agent of the Grand Trunk Canal Company. The chapel, 21 feet by 15 feet, was opened in 1781 with accommodation for seventy. A house for the priest was built to the west. It may have been designed by Dadford, who was an architect as well as a canal engineer.[41]

❧

The clergy were also responsible for a new venture in education, of national importance but based in Staffordshire. Although the practice was illegal from 1585, the gentry normally sent their sons abroad, mainly to the secular college at Douai or the Jesuit college at St Omer; in Staffordshire the Astons, the Giffards and the Macclesfields favoured Douai, the Gerards and the Simeons St Omer. There were also a few schools in England, but they tended to be expensive and short-lived. For daughters there was a wide choice of convents abroad and the schools at York and Hammersmith run by the Ladies of the Institute of the Blessed Virgin Mary.[42] In 1773 there was a girls' boarding school with some day pupils at Oscott House, which had moved there from Harvington in Worcestershire; it was run by the priest's housekeeper, and the vicar of Handsworth that year reported having seen about a dozen pupils when he called on the housekeeper's sister, an

Sedgley Park School *c*.1797.

Anglican.[43] At the other end of the scale there were five schools in Staffordshire in 1767 run by women described as schoolmistresses, one in Alrewas, one in Colwich and three in Wolverhampton; of the mistress at Colwich, a convert of seven or eight years' standing like her labourer husband, it was stated that 'she has taught a little school but has promised she will not any longer'. The establishments were probably dame schools without any particular Catholic ethos.[44] There remained a need for a school for the sons of the middle classes, including students for the priesthood. In 1753 Bishop Hornyold, supported by Bishop Stonor, had plans for a school for middle-class boys first at Oscott House and in 1754 at Longbirch; Stonor suggested fees under £12 a year and a basic curriculum. The plans came to nothing for fear of opposition from the Franciscans, who ran a small school at Edgbaston, from the gentry and from the county justices.[45]

Richard Challoner, Vicar Apostolic of the London District, entrusted the foundation of a secondary school for middle-class boys, technically illegal, to Richard Errington, one of his chaplains.[46] After two false starts in Buckinghamshire and Wales a start was made in 1762 under the newly ordained John Hurst at Betley in north-west Staffordshire in the house of a convert, James Corne (father of John, the priest who built the chapels at Cobridge and Stafford).[47] In 1763 Hurst with another master and fifteen boys moved to Park Hall in Sedgley south of Wolverhampton. It was rented from Lord Ward (that year created Viscount Dudley and Ward) through the influence of Thomas Giffard of Chillington, who stood as guarantor for the rent. By 1767 there were ninety-seven boys and five assistant masters under the presidency of Hugh Kendal (1763–81). The annual pension was twelve guineas, but there were also parlour boarders paying £20 a year and taking their meals in with the masters. Pupils came as young as seven or eight and usually left when between thirteen and fifteen; they included church students who went on to colleges abroad to complete their studies for the priesthood. The curriculum by the early nineteenth century concentrated on the basics, with geometry, book keeping and land surveying for those going into

John Philip Kemble as Hamlet.

commerce; a minority took French and even fewer Latin and Greek.

The school's importance was not confined to the Midlands: during Kendal's presidency over half of the pupils came from London and the south of England. At least seventy-three future priests attended the school between 1762 and 1781. Other early pupils included John Philip Kemble, son of the actor Roger Kemble. He was sent there in 1767 to study for the priesthood and went on to Douai in 1771. He left in 1775 to become an actor, making his debut at Wolverhampton with a touring company in 1776. He was probably recommended to the company by his sister Sarah, the wife of William Siddons.[48] Success meant that the first of many extensions to the buildings soon became necessary. The premises continued to be held on a yearly tenancy, but Errington was the owner of the school until his death in 1768; it then passed to the vicars apostolic of the Midland District and their successors. The school, which became known as Sedgley Park, moved to Cotton in North Staffordshire in 1873, remaining there until its closure in 1987.

༄

The eighteenth century saw a marked rise in the number of Staffordshire Catholics. In 1706 the Privy Council ordered a return by the parish clergy of papists and reputed papists 'with their respective qualities, estates and places of abode': the 'several instances of the very great boldness and presumption of the Romish priests and papists in this kingdom' required that 'a more watchful eye should be had over them for the future'.[49] For Staffordshire over 1,200 persons were returned, including children. The main concentrations were Brewood (133, including Thomas Giffard of Chillington and his family); Bushbury (65, including Thomas Whitgreave and his family); Colton (39, including John Aston's household of 10 at Bellamour); Draycott (47, including Edward Coyney, the priest at Paynsley; Marmaduke Langdale was 'not yet resident at his house at Paynsley but married and expected ere long to come and to live

C. A. Buckler, from a drawing by F. C. H.

G. & C. Waite, Lith.

SEDGLEY PARK CHAPEL.

The Chapel at Sedgley Park School, built in 1800–1.

amongst us') with 17 in Checkley, mainly at Upper Tean, and 8 at Leigh; Handsworth (54); Sedgley (105); Swynnerton (27, including the bailiff of Jane, the widow of Basil Fitzherbert who was living in London, and Thomas Adams, the resident priest); Tamworth and its out-townships including one in Warwickshire (some 55, including Mrs Comberford of Comberford with 3 grandchildren and 3 servants); Walsall (29); Wolverhampton (192) and its chapelries of Bilston (17), Wednesfield (10) and Willenhall (10); and Yoxall (30, with the Howards stated as not then resident at Hoar Cross).

In 1767, following an outcry in the press accusing the clergy of failing to curb the spread of popery, the House of Lords ordered the Anglican bishops to organise a return from every parish of resident papists, with details of sex, age, occupation and length of residence. A more thorough list than that of 1706 resulted, although it also seems clear that numbers had risen. For the Anglican archdeaconry of Stafford (virtually Staffordshire) 2,964 were returned, half as many again as the whole of the rest of the Lichfield and Coventry diocese.[50] In 1773 Bishop Hornyold had given Rome a figure of 1,760;[51] that figure, however, included only communicants, whereas the 1767 figures include children down to infants.

The earlier centres continued, with greatly increased figures. Brewood remained the largest rural centre, with 389 Catholics, including Thomas Giffard, father and son, at Chillington, with Anthony Clough, their chaplain, and Bishop Hornyold at Longbirch with another priest, Philip Perry. Bushbury had 117, including Francis Whitgreave at Moseley with his two sons and a Jesuit chaplain, Thomas Howard; there were another 64 in neighbouring Shareshill. Draycott had 156, with Edward Grannan as resident priest, although the Langdales were not resident;[52] there were a further 3 at Checkley, 11 at Leigh and 9 at Gratwich, which in 1773 had 17 visited by Grannan 'but seldom'.[53] In Handsworth, by then an industrial village where the metal trades vied with agricultural pursuits, there were 132 Catholics, with Pierce Parry the priest at Oscott. The Sedgley figure, 253, was inflated by the presence of the boarding school, with 97 boys under the

Swynnerton Hall.

president and five assistants plus six maidservants. Stone had 132, with Sir Edward Simeon's steward living in Aston Hall; the chapel there was served by James Fox, a Jesuit living at Gerrard's Bromley in Eccleshall, a parish which itself had 47 Catholics. Swynnerton's 100 were headed by Thomas Fitzherbert and his family and their Jesuit chaplain, Robert Cole,[54] and Tixall's 44 by Thomas Clifford and his family and their chaplain George Beeston. Yoxall had 47, including the widow of Thomas Talbot and her family at Hoar Cross. Even the closure of the mission at St Thomas in the 1730s seems not to have been a disaster: 41 Catholics were listed at neighbouring Baswich, where 24 were recorded in 1706.

The growing towns had an increased number of Catholics. Stafford had 84, as against 14 listed in 1706. Tamworth had 46 and Walsall 110. Wolverhampton had 491, a large number of them engaged in the metal trades; there were a further 13 in Bilston chapelry, 5 in Wednesfield and 16 in Willenhall. The nascent Potteries towns were still a string of growing villages containing 133 Catholics, 24 of them potters with one pot merchant.

෴

Despite financial persecution there is evidence of prosperity among some Catholic families. At St Thomas the Fowlers, having turned the west range of the cloister into their house after they had acquired the priory site, rebuilt it in the late seventeenth century.[55] In the later 1720s Thomas Fitzherbert, using Francis Smith of Warwick as his architect, reconstructed the house at Swynnerton which his grandfather had rebuilt on a new site apparently in the early 1660s; further work was carried out to the designs of other architects later in the century.[56] Lord Aston started to rebuild his house of 1555 at Tixall, but by his death in 1750 he had completed only a quadrangle containing offices and some bedrooms. His son-in-law Thomas Clifford built a new house on to the quadrangle, completing the shell in 1782 and finishing the house just before his death in 1787.[57]

The Giffards appear to have been by far the wealthiest Catholic family in Staffordshire. In 1715–16 Thomas Giffard registered estates worth just over £2,110 a year, with the Fowlers as the next wealthiest at £1,489.[58] Although the Giffards are estimated to have spent some £9,000 extra in land tax between 1692 and 1851 because of the double tax on Catholics, they were exempted from the special levy on Catholics in 1723 along with other descendants of those involved in Charles II's escape in 1651.[59] For much of the century they were rebuilding and landscaping at Chillington.

Peter Giffard of the Black Ladies branch succeeded his cousin at Chillington in 1718 and soon set about the first stage of rebuilding the Tudor house which had replaced its medieval predecessor probably in the 1540s. Part of the south side of the quadrangle was rebuilt as a three-storey brick range, probably by Francis Smith of Warwick, perhaps completing work begun by his brother William; the rainwater heads carry the date 1724 and the initials PGB, those of Peter and his second wife Barbara (Throckmorton). A grand staircase was inserted in this wing. Peter also built new kitchens and a large quadrangle containing stables and farm buildings with a dovecot in the centre. He laid out formal gardens and erected an arched stone screen in front of the bowling green with wrought-iron gates bearing his initials. He created a new approach to the house by laying out the Upper Avenue, described in 1727 as lately made by him.[60]

His house had a chapel, originally perhaps in the attic at the south end of the east wing to the left of the gatehouse but by the 1780s at the north end of the ground floor of the wing.[61] Richard Hitchmough, reporting after the Jacobite rising of 1715, stated that he had seen at Chillington a large gold chalice and paten, six large silver candlesticks, a large silver crucifix, and a large silver ciborium double gilt within with gold, with a cover and a cross on the top.[62] There was a register of baptisms, marriages and confirmations from 1721. Bishop Stonor confirmed in the chapel four times between 1721 and 1731, and candidates came from a wide area: in 1731 there were twenty-two from the Chillington congregation, seven from Black Ladies and Boscobel, three from Longbirch, twenty-three from Wolverhampton, three from Moseley, three from Yoxall and two from Linley in Shropshire.[63]

In 1745, a year before his death, Peter provides a glimpse of Catholic practice. He recorded a resolve to go to Confession and Communion every three or four weeks. The formula for his examination of conscience begins with 'What guard do you keep upon your thoughts, words, actions and senses?' and includes 'What are the obligations of your state, and how far do you correspond with them?' and 'Will the present method of your life and actions conduct you to a happy eternity?' Peter secured a certificate from his Anglican medical adviser, Richard Wilkes of Willenhall, on the strength of which his chaplain excused him from fasting; instead he had to give alms to the poor and recite the penitential psalms and Lenten prayers every fast day.[64] Another example of religious practice is recorded in the Chillington register in 1733: 'Baptised in his mother's womb by Mr Altery, the man midwife, John, son of Peter Giffard, Esq., and Helena Roberts his wife. The child was born dead.'[65]

Peter was succeeded by his son Peter, who died in 1748 with his half-brother Thomas, a fifteen-year-old schoolboy still at Douai, as his heir.[66] After coming of age Thomas employed Lancelot ('Capability') Brown and James Paine to create a new park, obliterating the village of Chillington. The work, evidently carried out by 1761, included a sixty-six-acre lake with bridges, which Paine described as 'confessedly one of the finest pieces of water, within an inclosure, that this kingdom produces'. A Classical and a Gothic temple were built beside the lake in 1772. Thomas also planned to rebuild the house. Brown was probably the author of one unsigned plan, and in 1772 Robert Adam submitted two plans, one for a new house apparently near the lake and the other incorporating the wing of 1724. Thomas, who set up a London residence in 1774,[67] died in 1776 before any work was carried out.[68]

His son and heir Thomas was aged only twelve. He set out on the Grand Tour in 1782, his tutor being Charles Berington,

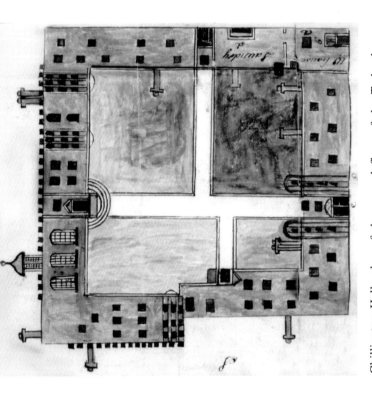

Chillington Hall: plan of the ground floor of the Tudor house, with the 1724 wing on the south (top left).

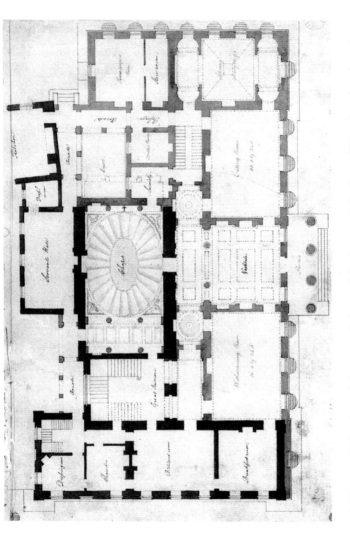

Chillington Hall: plan of the ground floor of the house of the late 1780s, showing the saloon as the chapel with a sacristy attached.

Thomas Giffard the younger *c*.1784.

the future Midland Vicar Apostolic, who had refused the presidency of St Gregory's seminary in Paris in order to accompany him. Like his father in 1766, Thomas had his portrait painted in Rome by Pompeo Batoni. He appears there as a dandy, and on his return in 1785 he was noted as a young man of large patrimony, which he was rapidly dissipating. One of the ways in which he did so was to set about the rebuilding of Chillington to the design of the young John Soane; this was possibly on the recommendation of Sir Henry Bridgeman, Thomas's neighbour at Weston-under-Lizard, for whose brother-in-law Soane was then carrying out work. Soane submitted a design for a completely new house, but it was decided to incorporate the 1724 wing. Work was in progress by 1786 and was brought to a somewhat hasty conclusion probably as a result of Thomas's marriage in 1788. A notable feature is the saloon on the site of the Tudor great hall, which was originally intended to be a chapel.[69]

That change of plan is perhaps symptomatic of the weakening of the link between the Giffards and the Catholic Church. Thomas broke with family tradition by marrying a non-Catholic, Charlotte Courtenay, daughter of Viscount Courtenay, and of the twelve children only the eldest son, Thomas William, was brought up a Catholic, being baptised at the Portuguese embassy chapel in London. The number of Catholic servants also dwindled. Soane's further plan for a free-standing chapel was rejected, but perhaps for financial reasons. Instead the chapel at Black Ladies, which had apparently been closed for nearly half a century, was opened for public worship. In 1791 Thomas presented it with a set of plate, eight silver candlesticks and a crucifix. He also fitted up the part of Black Ladies which had been occupied by an agent as quarters for Anthony Clough, chaplain at Chillington since 1758. Clough, however, quarrelled with Thomas over his marriage and his extravagance – Thomas had put his estates in commission in 1790 to avoid bankruptcy – and left Black Ladies in 1791; he died in 1793, evidently at Oscott, and was buried in the chancel of Brewood church. He was succeeded by John Roe, who remained there until his death in 1838. A traveller passing one Sunday in July 1792 found 'the Catholic service then performing'.[70]

In a letter of November 1791 Clough expressed his doubt 'whether Mr Giffard will be able to live at Chillington on his present income. He had better go to some retired place – live in a saving manner until he has paid off his debts, and then return to Chillington and appear like the Lord of that Ancient Place.' Thomas in fact went to Rouen and left his Catholic steward Matthew Ellison to tackle the problems, largely by selling timber from the estate and raising rents. Thomas was back in time to make his Easter Communion at Black Ladies in 1793, accompanied by several émigrés. He died in 1823, having received the last rites and with debts of £7,760.[71]

His heir Thomas William likewise remained a Catholic, although he too married a non-Catholic. He supported the building of a Catholic church in Brewood in 1843–4, but with the opening of the new church the chapels at Black Ladies and Longbirch were closed and Giffard patronage ended. The family's 300-year recusant tradition ended in 1861 when Thomas William died, fortified by the last rites, and was succeeded by his non-Catholic brother Walter.[72]

❧

Toleration — and tolerance — slowly made headway. The Giffards felt it safe to show their chapels on their estate maps. One of Black Ladies made about 1700 depicts the chapel as a side wing surmounted by a dome with a cross. Another of Chillington in the early eighteenth century shows a cross on the gable end to the left of the gatehouse on the entrance front, probably an indication of the site of the chapel.[73] In Wolverhampton, on the other hand, the chapel at the Great House was tucked away at the back. In the mid-eighteenth century, it was later recalled, Catholics going there 'were obliged to steal our way in small parties, or rather singly, and by different and circuitous routes, to avoid observation, and the consequences, which often attended detection'.[74] In 1754 the Catholics of Wolverhampton were eager to contribute towards

Chillington Hall from the north-east in 1843.

The Chapel at Black Ladies in 1837.

the building cost of St John's Anglican church partly because they depended on their Protestant neighbours for trade but also because 'if troublesome times should come again 'twill keep the mob from molesting our chapel, breaking the windows, etc.'[75] In 1765, however, Bishop Hornyold felt able to employ Italian plasterers to decorate the chapel, 'so that it was considered to be, and with reason, the most handsome chapel in this or any neighbouring county'.[76] It was described in 1767 as 'a Mass-house open, and publickly resorted to'.[77]

The chapel at Cobridge too was discreet. It was built well away from the main road and made to appear as much as possible part of the priest's house. Work was temporarily stopped in 1780 for fear of an outbreak following the Gordon Riots in London, although in the event there were no outbreaks in Staffordshire.[78] St Austin's at Stafford on the main Wolverhampton road on what was then the edge of the town was built on to the back of the priest's house, a three-storey brick building.[79]

Viscount Dudley and Ward showed less caution when he allowed Park Hall in Sedgley to be used for an illegal school from 1763. Bishop Talbot later recalled how Lord Dudley and Ward gave 'the strongest assurances' that the school should not be disturbed, declaring that 'his word should be as good as a lease'. He appears to have defended his action when challenged in the House of Lords, at the same time paying tribute to Hugh Kendal, the president of the school, and he is said to have dined at Park Hall with Thomas Giffard and Bishop Hornyold. He died in 1774, leaving the house to his younger son and future heir, William Ward. The new owner promptly wrote to Kendal, declaring that as he was 'so lucky as to have so good and worthy a man as Mr Kendal for my tenant at Sedgley Park, he may depend upon my giving him no trouble' and promising rather to give him every support. During the Gordon Riots of 1780 William Ward reluctantly wrote requiring the departure of the school, but he soon withdrew the requirement, declaring that 'nothing but the unavoidable reality of the time could possibly have induced me to have done it'. He warned, however, that on the least suspicion of further disturbances the boys must be sent away at once, 'or Lord Dudley's and my houses both in Town and Country will most certainly be burnt'. On Kendal's death in 1781 his successor and nephew Thomas Southworth wrote to Ward, asking that the school be allowed to continue at the Park. Ward replied cautiously, saying that he had asked his agent to look into the state of the school but promising that if it did have to leave he would do 'everything that is proper and right'. In the event the school continued at Sedgley.[80]

Burials reflect the influence of Catholic gentry, at least as far as their own families were concerned. Mention has already been made of the Erdeswick tombs of 1596 and 1601 in the chancel of Sandon church, the earlier-seventeenth-century Giffard tombs in the chancel of Brewood church and the memorial to Thomas Whitgreave (d. 1702) in Bushbury church. The chancel of Baswich church was the burial place of the Fowlers. The tomb of Brian Fowler (d. 1587) was situated there until its removal to the north transept when the church was rebuilt in 1739. In 1700 William Fowler erected a tablet in memory of his grandmother, father and mother and numerous other relatives, 'whose bodies ly buried in this chancel'; also included was his 'virtuous friend' Daniel Fitter, the family's long-standing chaplain who died that year.[81] Sir Philip Draycott (d. 1559) was buried, in accordance with his will, in the chancel of the parish church of Draycott-in-the-Moors. His grandson and heir John (d. 1604) and John's grandson and heir Richard (d. 1662) had table tombs in the family chapel in the church; Richard's tomb contains the figure of his eldest son Philip kneeling in prayer with a rosary hanging from his belt.[82] At Draycott indeed even humbler Catholics, estimated at around one-third of the population, received special mention in the parish register between 1679 and 1752 when it came to burials: they were noted as popish recusants, and their burial place was normally recorded as on the north side of the church; the burial of their missioner, Edward Coyney, on the north side in 1722 was recorded as that of a popish priest. In the returns for the bishop's visitation in 1752 the churchwardens stated initially that they had not presented the names of any popish recusants 'but if my Lord will not oust them we will present them at your next visitation'; later in the same year ten heads of families were presented. [83] At Brewood it was presumably through Giffard influence that two of the vicars apostolic who lived at Long-birch were buried in the chancel of the church in the later eighteenth century, as well as a former Giffard chaplain.[84] In 1797 the Cliffords' chaplain George Beeston, was buried in Tixall churchyard with a headstone openly proclaiming him 'Chaplain to the Family of *Tixall Hall* and Minister to the *Catholic* Congregation There during Thirty five Years'.[85]

The attitude of Anglican incumbents towards recusants varied. John Middleton at Stone reported to his bishop in 1767 that he found James Fox (the Jesuit at Gerrard's Bromley who also served Aston Hall) not 'so impudent as some others, especially that at Burslem'.[86] He was referring to Thomas Flynn, the priest with whom he had clashed over a convert won by Middleton at Hanley: 'The priest took great pains to recover his disciple, both by cajoling and terrifying. But I threatened to convict him (which I believe I could have done) and this made him extremely cautious ever after.' Middleton also lamented the two ways in which Catholic numbers were maintained:

1. By the farmers tampering with and perverting Protestant servants. These practices I have heard of – and threat-ened to prosecute them. But how far that would be proper and prudent, or whether the magistrates would choose to act, I know not.
2. Whenever a Protestant and a Papist intermarry, the Church of England is generally a loser: for whether it be the man or the woman that is the Papist, the children are all baptized into the Church of Rome.

At West Bromwich in 1767, in addition to fifteen named Catholics, the incumbent reported to the bishop that there were five men and one woman who sometime since thro' the prejudices of education and family connections were Papists. But as they have for some years been convinced of their errors, now attend the worship of the Church of England and assure me that they have not the least thought of ever joining with the Roman Catholicks again, I conclude your Lordship will not think it necessary that their names should be inscribed.[87]

At Handsworth in 1773 things were more easy-going.[88] The incumbent reported no conversions to Catholicism in the five years and more that he had been there:

The priest, whose name is Pierre [Pierce] Parry, a middle-aged man, disclaims making any attempt of that kind. I several times visited a sick gentlewoman at his house, of our communion, sister to his housekeeper; when I cautioned him, as I have done since, not to rouse a sleeping Act of Parliament, so severe as to that particular ... I never heard of a bishop's coming hither, and Mr Parry tells me he has not been visited a long while. He appears to be a sleek Aristippus, inoffensive, easy, indolent; so that he has been known sometimes to forget that it was a fish-day; a circumstance I must not tell to *his* bishop though I may to *my own*.

The marriage of Thomas Whitgreave in 1780 was an occasion for even more relaxed Catholic-Anglican relations. On 21 June the Catholic chaplain from Moseley officiated at a ceremony in Thomas's home at nearby Saredon in Shareshill. The next day, to comply with the law, the wedding party went to the Anglican church at Bushbury where the curate performed a second ceremony. He accompanied the party back to Saredon for dinner, after which the chaplain, the curate and the groom's father left together for home.[89]

The Independent minister at Walsall in the later 1780s, whose view of the whole state of religion in the town was highly jaundiced, declared that he saw there 'as much papists as those at Rome'.[90] A visitor to Moseley in 1792 saw 'a sneaking priest glide by me' and commented: 'of what should they fear now?'[91]

⁂

In 1778 a Catholic Relief Act was passed, repealing the Act of 1700; an oath of allegiance was attached. It resulted from the efforts of the Catholic Committee, a lay initiative which was instrumental in securing a second Relief Bill in 1789. Anxious to convince their non-Catholic fellow countrymen that they had nothing to fear from Catholics, the Committee devised an oath swearing allegiance to the house of Hanover and repudiating papal deposing power and spiritual jurisdiction which interfered with the kingdom's constitution. The vicars apostolic condemned the oath, but Bishop Talbot and his brother James in the London District declined to publish the condemnation in the interests of Catholic unity.

The Staffordshire clergy now became involved as champions of the oath.[92] Talbot's coadjutor Charles Berington, consecrated Bishop of Hierocaesarea at Longbirch in 1786, had been a member of the Committee since 1788 and published his support of the oath in November 1789. In January 1790 Anthony Clough, the priest at Chillington, eager to support Bishops Talbot and Berington, asked Joseph Berington at Oscott to draw up an address to Talbot supporting the oath and went on to secure the signatures of all fifteen Staffordshire clergy to the address. It was sent to Talbot and also printed and circulated. In February Talbot accepted the oath, though refusing to make his acceptance public, again in the interests of unity; in May he was elected to the Committee.

In the event a simple oath of allegiance already used in the Irish Relief Act of 1779 was included in the English Relief Act when it was passed in 1791, but the clash of views continued in a pamphlet war. The views of the Staffordshire clergy were dubbed the Staffordshire Creed and declared heretical by its principal opponent, Charles Walmesley, Vicar of the Western District. Those views were in essence opposition to absolutism in the Church, whether exercised by the Pope or the vicars apostolic – Cisalpine as opposed to Ultramontane. John Carter of Wolverhampton, the last of the Staffordshire Creed clergy and a die-hard to the end, summed up his position in his will of 1802:[93]

> I loved my people and taught them with undeviating fidelity the saving and orthodox doctrines of the one holy Catholic and Apostolic Church ... Various motives have been assigned for declining to subscribe certain formulas. Truth will be alive when I am dead. It is, was and ever will be simply this. I conscientiously, *Domine tu scisti*, refused to sign away the canonical liberties of the Christian clergy and obliquely to wound the reputation of two beloved superiors.

The 1791 Act restored freedom of worship to Catholics, provided their chapels were registered. Immediately thirteen were registered in Staffordshire.[94] Six were gentry chapels: Longbirch (Bishop Talbot and his chaplain Edward Eyre); Black Ladies (John Roe); Moseley (Thomas Stone); Hoar Cross (Thomas Flynn); Swynnerton (John Howell); and Tixall (George Beeston). George Maire, the Jesuit who had moved from Swynnerton to Aston Hall after the suppression of his Order in 1773, remained at Aston until his death in 1796,[95] but he did not register the chapel. The remaining seven chapels were all clergy controlled: Ashley (served by the priest at Swynnerton); Cobridge (William Hartley); Cresswell (James Tasker, who had built or acquired a house there soon after taking over the Paynsley mission in 1779 and opened a chapel in an adjoining farm building);[96] Oscott (Joseph Berington); Sedgley Park (Thomas Southworth, who at the same time was recorded as a Roman Catholic schoolmaster under the Act); Stafford, St Austin's (John Corne); and Wolverhampton, the Great House (John Carter).

The way was now open for full-scale emancipation.

Notes

1 Foley, *English Province S.J.* v, p. 420; M. B. Rowlands, 'Surviving the Times, 1625–90', *English Catholics of Town and Parish 1558–1778* (C.R.S. Monograph Series, v, 1999), ed. M. B. Rowlands, p. 73; *Staffs. Cath. Hist.* iii, p. 14.

2 J. Ward, *The Borough of Stoke-upon-Trent* (1843), p. 280; below, pp. 174–5. For the 1647 evidence see above, p. 127.

3 J. A. Williams, '"Our Patriarch": Bishop Bonaventure Giffard, 1642–1734', *Recusant History*, xxvi (3) (2003), pp. 438–9.

4 *Complete Peerage*, i, p. 288.

5 Ibid., xii (2), pp. 192–3; *V.C.H. Staffs.* v, p. 87; J. M. Robinson, *The Staffords* (Chichester, 2002), p. 76.

6 *Calendar of Treasury Books January 1603 to March 1696*, x (2), pp. 590–2; P. A. Hopkins, 'The Commission for Superstitious Lands of 1690', *Recusant History*, xv (4) (1980), pp. 268–9 (with thanks to Dr Hopkins for drawing my attention to this article).

7 M. Rowlands, 'Catholics in Staffordshire from the Revolution to the Relief Acts 1688–1791' (Birmingham University M.A. thesis, 1965; copy in W.S.L.), p. 133; P. Bailey, *Painsley: A History of Cresswell's Roman Catholic Community 1570–2000* (Market Rasen, 2005), p. 23. The details about Colonel Whorwood have been supplied by Dr Hopkins.

8 A. Fea, *The Flight of the King* (1897), pp. 329–30.

9 J. Gillow, *St. Thomas's Priory* (no date, mid- to later 1890s), pp. 53 sqq.; Anstruther, *Seminary Priests*, iii, pp. 103, 251–2; E. E. Estcourt and J. O Payne (eds), *The English Catholic Nonjurors* (preface dated 1885), pp. 348–9; M. Rowlands, 'An Inventory of the Chapel of St. Thomas', *Staffs. Cath. Hist.* ii (1962), p. 31.

10 Anstruther, *Seminary Priests*, iii, pp. 211–12; iv, pp. 66–7, 142–3, 270–1; J. Hicks Smith, *Brewood* (Wolverhampton, 1874), p. 24; *V.C.H. Staffs.* iii, p. 110; v (1959), p. 38; B. Penny, *Maryvale* (Archdiocese of Birmingham Historical Commission, publication number 1, 1985), p. 5; M. Rowlands, 'The Staffordshire Clergy', *Recusant History*, ix (5) (1968), p. 227.

11 Foley, *English Province S.J.* v, pp. 420–1; vii (1882), pp. clii sqq.

12 G. Holt, *The English Jesuits 1650–1829* (*C.R.S.* lxx, 1984), p. 63.

13 Ibid. (index under the four places); T. B. Trappes-Lomax, *Swynnerton* (*Staffs. Cath. Hist.* ix, 1967–8), pp. 8–11.

14 See also M. J. Bailey, 'Ashley', *Staffs. Cath. Hist.* iv (1963–4), pp. 33, 42.

15 *C.R.S.* lxx, p. 265.

16 Ibid., p. 111.

17 Ibid., p. 93.

18 Justin McLoughlin, 'The Converts of Laurence Loraine', *Staffs. Cath. Hist.* xv (1975), pp. 17–18.

19 Father Thaddeus [Francis Hermans], *The Franciscans in England 1600–1850* (1898), p. 157.

20 F. Roberts, 'Staffordshire Benedictine Monks', *Staffs. Cath. Hist.* i (1961), p. 14.

21 *V.C.H. Staffs.* iii, p. 110. For the rest of this para. see *Recusant History*, ix (5), pp. 223–6; R. H. Turner, 'Clergy Funds and Episcopal Control – Was John Stanford Maligned?', *Recusant History*, xvii (1) (2004), pp. 51 sqq.

22 B.A.A., A163; Anstruther, *Seminary Priests*, ii, p. 111; *Complete Peerage*, vii, p. 431. Fitzherbert was Archdeacon of Staffordshire from 1682 until at least 1694. There was also a clerical tutor for Philip in the 1660s, Francis Gage; they were together from 1667 to 1675, and in 1676 Gage was appointed president of Douai: Anstruther, ii, p. 120.

23 B.A.A., C359.

24 B.A.A., A203; W. F Carter, 'Notes on Staffordshire Families', *S.H.C.* 1925, p. 142.

25 B.A.A., A173; Anstruther, *Seminary Priests*, iv, p. 12.

26 B.A.A., A184; Anstruther, *Seminary Priests*, iii, p. 118; iv, pp. 49, 98.

27 *V.C.H. Staffs.* xiv, p. 222.

28 B.A.A., A522, A533, A550.

29 *V.C.H. Staffs.* iii, p. 110.

30 M. W. Greenslade, 'Yieldfields Hall 1701 and West Bromwich 1877: two Black Country documents', *Staffs. Cath. Hist.* xv (1975), pp. 1–6.

31 For the next three paragraphs see Penny, *Maryvale*, pp. 1–5; F. Grady, 'Andrew Bromwich', *Staffs. Cath. Hist.* ii (1962), pp. 9–12; J. F. Champ, 'The Seminary Priests of Old Oscott, 1687–1794', *Opening the Scrolls* (Downside Abbey, 1987),

ed. D. A. Bellenger, pp. 135 sqq.

32 In the return of popish recusants in 1678 the Perry Barr list is headed by Andrew Bromwich, gentleman, followed by his mother Joan, a widow: D. Fowkes and M. W. Greenslade, 'A List of Staffordshire Recusants 1678–80', *Staffs. Cath. Hist.* xxiv (1990), p. 3.

33 B.A.A., A70a. For the rest of this para. see M. Rowlands, 'The Building of a Public Mass House in Wolverhampton, 1723–4', *Staffs. Cath. Hist.* i (1961), pp. 24 sqq.; G. P. Mander and N. W. Tildesley, *A History of Wolverhampton until the early Nineteenth Century* (Wolverhampton, 1960), pp. 127–9.

34 A. Gomme, *Smith of Warwick* (Stamford, 2000), pp. 398–9.

35 Below, p. 198.

36 *Staffs. Cath. Hist.* xiv, p. 306.

37 Gillow, *St. Thomas's Priory*, pp. 69–77; Anstruther, *Seminary Priests*, iii, p. 12; *Berkswich w. Walton Parish Register* (Staffordshire Parish Registers Society, 1905), pp. 78, 95; *Complete Peerage*, v, p. 266; R. Longden, 'The Fowlers of St. Thomas, near Stafford, 1543–1738' (dissertation for the Keele University M.A. in Local History, 2004; copy in W.S.L.), pp. 36–9; B.A.A., A533.

38 For the next two paragraphs see Gillow, *St Thomas's Priory*, pp. 78 sqq.; M. W. Greenslade, *Saint Austin's, Stafford* (Archdiocese of Birmingham Historical Commission, publication number 8, 2004 edn), pp. 11–12.

39 *Bradley Parish Registers* (Staffs. Par. Regs. Soc. 1989), pp. 145–6.

40 *V.C.H. Staffs.* v, p. 90. Forebridge was then still part of Castle Church parish, being transferred to Stafford borough in 1835: ibid., vi, p. 185.

41 Ibid., iii, p. 109; M. Greenslade, *A Brief History of the Catholic Church in Stoke-on-Trent* (1960), p. 18; M. Rowlands, 'Staffordshire Papists in 1767' (Part II), *Staffs. Cath. Hist.* vii (1965), p. 30; F. Roberts, 'The Confirmation Register 1768–93 of Thomas Talbot, Vicar Apostolic of the Midland Region', ibid., xii (1972), pp. 17–18; ibid., xiv, p. 661; T. Dunn, 'Pedigree & History of the Macclesfield Family . . .' (1995; copy in W.S.L.), pp. 237, 243. For Dadford see H. Colvin, *A Biographical Dictionary of British Architects 1600–1840* (1995 edn), p. 287; he designed a new chapel at

Sedgley Park school (below, pp. 177, 179) built in 1800–1.

42 M. Rowlands, 'Catholics in Staffs.' pp. 195–6, 200, 206. For
the Jesuit schools at Wednesfield and Wolverhampton in the
seventeenth century see above pp. 83, 153. For the three
daughters of Viscount Stafford with the Augustinian nuns at
Louvain in 1653 see above, p. 85.

43 Penny, *Maryvale*, pp. 5–6.

44 M. Rowlands, 'Staffordshire Papists in 1767', *Staffs. Cath.
Hist.* vi (1965), pp. 4, 8, 27, and vii (1965), pp. 30, 32, 42;
M. W. Greenslade, *The 1767 Return of Staffordshire Papists*
(*Staffs. Cath. Hist.* xvii, 1977), pp. 3, 16, 47–8, 57. For a
dame school in Draycott-in-the-Moors run by a suspected recusant in 1625 see P. G. Adams, 'The Survival and Continuity
of Roman Catholicism in the Parish of Draycott-in-the-Moors
and the Painsley Mission' (dissertation for the Keele University M.A. in Local History, 2004), pp. 47, 53. For the school
at Stafford under James II see above, p. 153.

45 M. Rowlands, 'The Education and Piety of Catholics in
Staffordshire in the 18th Century', *Recusant History*, x (2)
(1969), pp. 72–3.

46 F. Roberts, *A History of Sedgley Park and Cotton College*
[1986], chapters i to v; M. W. Greenslade, 'Cotton College,
formerly Sedgley Park School', *V.C.H. Staffs.* vi, pp. 156–8;
J. Kirk, *Biographies of English Catholics in the Eighteenth
Century*, ed. J. H. Pollen and E. Burton (1909), p. 102.

47 For Hurst and for the Corne family see Anstruther, *Seminary
Priests*, iv, pp. 73–4, 149.

48 *Oxford D.N.B.* xxxi, pp. 155–6; l, pp. 515–16.

49 M. W. Greenslade, *Staffordshire Papists in 1705 and 1706*
(*Staffs. Cath. Hist.* xiii, 1973). There had been a similar return
in 1705; in the case of three Staffordshire parishes (Baswich,
Sedgley and Wombourne) there is a return only for 1705 and
those figures have been used here. In several cases the number
of children is not specified so that an exact total is not possible.

50 The two versions of the returns for the Archdeaconry of
Stafford are printed in *Staffs. Cath. Hist.* vi and vii (1965),
and xvii (1977), the latter being more detailed (although with
Weston-under-Lizard listed under Salop Archdeaconry). For
the archdeaconries of Coventry, Derby and Salop see *Mid.
Cath. Hist.* v–vii.

51 *Staffs. Cath. Hist.* vi, p. 2.
52 Lord Langdale was stated in 1731 to have settled at Paynsley: Anstruther, *Seminary Priests,* iv, p. 182.
53 *Staffs. Cath. Hist.* vii, pp. 34–5. Gratwich was returned in 1706 as having no Catholics.
54 For Cole see *C.R.S.* lxx, p. 63.
55 J. C. Dickinson, 'The Priory of St. Thomas by Stafford', *Old Stafford Society Transactions*, 1963–5, pp. 7–8; N. Pevsner, *The Buildings of England: Staffordshire* (Harmondsworth, 1974), p. 247.
56 Gomme, *Smith of Warwick*, pp. 77, 172–3, 520 and colour plate 8; *Staffs. Cath. Hist.* ix, p. 4.
57 T. and A. Clifford, *A Topographical and Historical Description of the Parish of Tixall in the County of Stafford* (Paris, 1817), p. 70; above, p. 92. One of the window sills in the Tudor house built by Sir Edward Aston bore the inscription 'William Yates made this house MDLV': S. Erdeswick, *A Survey of Staffordshire* (1844 edn), pp. 68–9. The gatehouse, which still stands, was built by Sir Edward's son, Sir Walter (succ. 1568, d. 1589): ibid., 70; J. C. Wedgwood, *Staffordshire Parliamentary History*, i (*S.H.C.* 1917–18), p. 329.
58 P. J. Doyle, 'The Giffards of Chillington, a Catholic landed family, 1642–1861' (Durham University M.A. thesis, 1968; copy in W.S.L.), pp. 123–5.
59 M. Rowlands, 'Staffordshire Papists and the Levy of 1723', *Staffs. Cath. Hist.* ii (1962), p. 35; M. Rowlands, 'The Iron Age of Double Taxes', ibid., iii (1963), p. 45.
60 A. Oswald, 'Chillington Hall, Staffordshire', *Country Life*, 13 and 20 Feb. 1948; Gomme, *Smith of Warwick*, pp. 20, 78, 157–8, 216–17, 298, 301, 521; *V.C.H. Staffs.* v, p. 29. Mr John Giffard has mentioned to me an uncatalogued agreement of 1724 with William Smith, in S.R.O., D590; William died in 1724, and Francis finished work begun by his brother elsewhere: Gomme, pp. 26–7.
61 Above, p. 46; P. Dean, *Sir John Soane and the Country Estate* (Aldershot, 1999), p. 42.
62 Estcourt and Payne (eds), *English Catholic Nonjurors*, p. 349.
63 *Roman Catholic Registers* (Staffs. Par. Regs. Soc. 1958–9), pp. 15 sqq.; M. Rowlands, 'Catholic Registers of the Chillington Area 1771–95', *Staffs. Cath. Hist.* xv (1975), pp. 21 sqq.

64   M. Rowlands, 'The Education and Piety of Catholics in Staffordshire in the 18th Century', *Recusant History*, x (2) (1969), pp. 67, 70–1, 78.

65   *Roman Catholic Registers*, p. 34.

66   Doyle, 'The Giffards', pp. 154, 477–8. For Clough see also Anstruther, *Seminary Priests,* iv, p. 66; *Notes and Collections relating to Brewood* (Wolverhampton, 1860), p. 22.

67   Ibid., p. 291.

68   *V.C.H. Staffs.* v, p. 29; P. Dean, 'Chillington, Staffordshire', *Country Life*, 30 Sept. 1999; S.R.O, D590/368.

69   Dean, *Soane*, pp. 40 sqq.; *V.C.H. Staffs.* v, pp. 29–30.

70   P. J. Doyle, 'Catholics of the Cisalpine School: Thomas Giffard 1764–1823 and William Giffard 1789–1861', *Staffs. Cath. Hist.* xii (1972), pp. 28 sqq.; *Staffs. Cath. Hist.* xiv, p. 302; Anstruther, *Seminary Priests*, iv, p. 231; C. Bruyn Andrews (ed.), *The Torrington Diaries* (New York and London, 1970 reprint), iii, p. 142.

71   Doyle, 'The Giffards', pp. 296–8, 300–1, 339. Ellison left in 1802 to enter the service of the future Duke of Norfolk at Glossop in Derbyshire.

72   *Staffs. Cath. Hist.* xii, pp. 36 sqq.; below, p. 223.

73   S.R.O., D590/360 above, p. 46.

74   *Staffs. Cath. Hist.* xiv, p. 306.

75   B.A.A., C363.

76   *Staffs. Cath. Hist.* xiv, p. 306.

77   Ibid., xvii, p. 54.

78   S. Holmes, 'The Leith Papers: the writings of Thomas Mathias Leith, pastor of Cobridge Roman Catholic mission, Stoke upon Trent, 1851–1873' (Keele University M.Litt. dissertation, 1994; copy in B.A.A.), p. 70. This contains a transcript of T. M. Leith's 'Records of the Mission of St. Peter, Cobridge', the whereabouts of which were unknown in 2004.

79   M. W. Greenslade, *Saint Austin's* (2004 edn), photograph on inside front cover and plan on p. 31.

80   F. C. Husenbeth, *The History of Sedgley Park School, Staffordshire* (1856), pp. 14–15; W. Buscot, *The History of Cotton College* (1940), pp. 33–5, 43–7; Roberts, *Sedgley Park and Cotton College*, p. 21.

81   Longden, 'The Fowlers', p. 10; *Mid. Cath. Hist.* vi, pp. 8–9; above, p. 148.

82 S. A. Jeavons, *The Monumental Effigies of Staffordshire* (Oxford, 1935), part I, p. 15, part III, pp 32–3; above, p. 28.

83 S.R.O., D3455/1/1; W.S.L., transcript of the Draycott parish register; Adams, 'Roman Catholicism in the Parish of Draycott-in-the-Moors', pp. 50–2, 70.

84 Above, pp. 165, 189; below, p. 207.

85 *Mid. Cath. Hist.* vi, p. 10.

86 *Staffs. Cath. Hist.* xvii, p. 40

87 Ibid., vii, p. 29.

88 Ibid., vi, p. 39.

89 *V.C.H. Staffs.* iii, p. 109.

90 Ibid., xvii, p. 240.

91 Bruyn Andrews (ed.), *The Torrington Diaries*, iii, p. 145.

92 M. Rowlands, 'The Staffordshire Clergy', *Recusant History*, ix (5) (1968), pp. 228 sqq.

93 Anstruther, *Seminary Priests*, iv, p. 56.

94 B. Donaldson, *The Registrations of Dissenting Chapels and Meeting Houses in Staffordshire, 1689–1852* (*S.H.C.* 4th ser. iii, 1960), pp. 131–3; S.R.O., Q/SO 20, ff. 81v.–82v.

95 *C.R.S.* lxx, p. 157.

96 *Staffs. Cath. Hist.* xiv, p. 660; Bailey, *Painsley: Cresswell's Roman Catholic Community*, pp. 33–6; *Roman Catholic Registers*, p. 141. He started a baptismal register in 1780. Both house and chapel still stand to the west of the present church of 1816.

6

EMANCIPATION: 1791–1850

With the grant of freedom of worship in 1791, pressure mounted for the restitution of civil rights to Catholics. The process culminated in the Act of Catholic Emancipation in 1829, enabling Catholics to vote, sit in the Lords and Commons and hold most public offices. Meanwhile the increasing size of the Catholic population, much of it consisting of Irish immigrants, led to new pastoral needs. In 1840 Rome doubled the number of vicars apostolic to eight, with Staffordshire included in a new Central District. In 1850 the vicars were replaced by a hierarchy of territorial bishops; Staffordshire became part of the new Diocese of Birmingham (an Archdiocese from 1911).

Thomas Talbot, the Midland Vicar Apostolic, died of apoplexy in 1795 while taking the waters near Bristol accompanied by his coadjutor Charles Berington. He was buried in Bristol, but Berington, whose Cisalpine views were unacceptable to the Vicar of the Western District, was not allowed to officiate at the Requiem. Although Berington succeeded Talbot in the Midland District, Rome delayed the grant of his full faculties pending some retraction of his Cisalpine views. In 1797 a formula was agreed, and Berington signed it in October at a meeting with the Vicars of the London and Northern Districts at the Swan in Wolverhampton. There was delay in the despatch of the faculties, and three days after their arrival in London Berington was dead: riding home from

Sedgley Park on the evening of 8 June 1798 he died of apoplexy on the roadside between Wolverhampton and Longbirch. He was buried in the chancel of Brewood church, commemorated in a wall tablet.[1] He had no coadjutor, and it was not until 1801 that Gregory Stapleton, the last president of St Omer, was appointed as his successor, consecrated, like Berington, as Bishop of Hierocaesarea. It fell to Stapleton to settle the remnants of the Staffordshire clergy dispute. Most of the original clergy had left the county or died, and Stapleton secured a retraction of errors from Thomas Southworth, James Tasker, John Kirk and John Roe and a partial one from John Carter. Stapleton died in 1802 at St Omer, having gone to France as one of a group seeking restitution of property belonging to the former English colleges.[2]

Again there was no coadjutor, and Stapleton was succeeded by the Ultramontane apologist John Milner, who was consecrated Bishop of Castabala in his chapel at Winchester in 1803. He found Longbirch altogether unsuitable as a residence:

> The expense of keeping a *gentleman's farm* (as is unavoidable in the situation of a bishop) and entertaining all visitors with their horses must make it a loosing [*sic*] concern to any bishop who has not a plentiful fortune of his own, not to speak of the remoteness of the situation, and the difficulty of procuring letters, victuals etc.

He therefore moved to the Great House at Wolverhampton. He died in 1826 and was buried in the orchard behind the house. He was succeeded by his coadjutor Thomas Walsh, consecrated Bishop of Cambysopolis in 1825. Milner left £1,000 for a new church at Wolverhampton, and the church of St Peter and St Paul was completed in 1828, incorporating the existing chapel as a transept. It was designed by Joseph Ireland at first in a Perpendicular style which he changed to Greek Revival. Milner's body was moved to a tomb in the crypt. A Gothic memorial brass on the south wall of the nave designed by A. W. N. Pugin was originally exhibited at the

John Milner, Vicar Apostolic of the Midland District 1803–26, in 1816.

Great Exhibition of 1851 as a brass for a priest in Mass vestments under a canopy containing the figure of Christ flanked by St Peter and St Paul.[3] Walsh, created Vicar Apostolic of the new Central District in 1840, ended the vicars' longstanding Staffordshire connection. He moved his church and residence to Birmingham, opening St Chad's in 1841 with the new Bishop's House facing it.

 ✑

New chapels continued to be opened and existing ones enlarged or rebuilt, largely to serve the rapidly growing urban population. The first after 1791 was at Sedgley. John Placidus Perry, a native of Bilston, was appointed as the second priest at Wolverhampton about 1786 and said Mass in rotation at Yieldfields, in a house adjoining the Red Lion in Sedgley and in a house at Gornalwood. The two latter centres were replaced by St George's chapel in Sedgley, 31 feet by 21 feet, which Perry opened on St George's Day (23 April) 1792. He lodged with a nearby farmer until the completion of a priest's house two years later. He remained at Sedgley until his death in 1819, requesting in his will to be buried in St George's. The will also mentioned an annuity of £13 10s. due to Elizabeth Harris on '£180 which she delivered to me and was spent on the organ'. Perry was succeeded by Thomas Tysan, who had come as his assistant in 1812 and remained until his death in 1867. Tysan opened a larger chapel in 1823. He used the materials from the old chapel to build a presbytery, described in 1834 as 'small, unfinished, and uncomfortable'. A school was built in 1837.[4]

In the mid-1790s a rural chapel was built at Wood Lane in Yoxall. It replaced the Mass centre at the nearby Hoar Cross Hall established by John Wells, who died in 1648. The estate passed through the Howards to the Talbots, and Charles Talbot, Earl of Shrewsbury, demolished the Hall in 1794 and sold the estate in 1795. He reserved land on the Lichfield–Ashbourne road where he built and endowed the chapel of St Francis de Sales. Thomas Flynn, the last chaplain

John Kirk.

at the Hall, was the first priest of the new chapel.[5]

Lichfield was served from the mission at Pipe Hall until 1800 when Thomas Weld sold the Hall to a non-Catholic and the chapel there was closed.[6] Weld gave the vestments, chalice and furnishings to T. H. Clifford of Tixall along with £200. Having collected a further £480 Clifford bought a house in the centre of Lichfield tenanted by a Catholic baker. Two rooms on the first floor were formed into a chapel, and a parlour and bedroom were made available for a resident priest. John Kirk was appointed to the mission by Bishop Stapleton in 1801 at a stipend of £60 a year. He had been chaplain at Pipe Hall from 1788 until sacked by Weld in 1792 as one of the clergy of the Staffordshire Creed, and was President of Sedgley Park from 1793 and secretary and chaplain to Bishop Berington at Longbirch from 1797. He found his Lichfield quarters cramped and disliked having to eat with the baker's family. In addition the sanctuary of the chapel was directly over the baker's oven and the heat was almost unbearable. In 1802 Kirk issued an appeal for subscriptions to provide a new chapel. A brick building in a simple Gothic style dedicated to Saints Peter and Paul was opened in 1803 on the London road on the southern outskirts of the city. As elsewhere it was made to look like a dwelling house by being under the same roof as the adjoining priest's house. An organ and a gallery were installed in 1823. In 1834 Kirk felt it safe to build an entrance front with a turret; at the same time he added a sanctuary, for which A. W. N. Pugin provided a screen in 1841.[7] With the improvements of 1834 the dedication was altered to Holy Cross. A school was built in 1844,[8] although before that Kirk had secured money to pay for the schooling of a few Catholic children. Initially the mission had sixty adult communicants,[9] and numbers were soon increased by French prisoners of war. In 1841 the core congregation at Lichfield was between seventy-five and eighty, but travellers to London, presumably Irish, increased Sunday Mass attendance to about ninety. By mid-century there was a large number of Irish in the Sandford Street part of the city.

Kirk was by inclination a scholar, and his pastoral style was cautious and conciliatory. He sent a copy of the 1802 appeal to the Anglican bishop, stressing the spirit of toleration that had produced the 1791 Act and declaring 'that instead of disturbing the faith of others, my great concern has ever been to preach the great truths of the Gospel to those of my own flock'. He was given the run of the cathedral library, with his name appearing frequently in the borrowers' book between 1803 and 1830. Because of a stammer he did not preach. He could be outspoken and abrupt, and when he died in 1851 at the age of ninety-one one obituarist stated that he was highly respected but not regarded with affection.

In 1801 Kirk took over responsibility for the Tamworth area, which had previously been served by the priest at Oscott. There was evidently a chapel in the Comberfords' house at Comberford until the mid-eighteenth century, when the estate was sold. Mass was then said at Coton in the house of a weaver named Crowley and by 1767 in the house of a basket maker named Birch. That year there were forty-six Catholics in the Tamworth area. After the transfer to Lichfield Kirk said Mass at Coton on the first Sunday of every month. The house was eventually sold to a Protestant and in 1815 the Birches built a room, 24 feet by 12 feet, in the garden of another house, part of which was also used. When that house was let to a Protestant about 1820 the room alone was used, but it soon became hemmed in 'by cottages, and nuisances, even up to the chapel door'. A resident priest, James Kelly, was appointed in 1826, and Kirk bought land off Aldergate in Tamworth on which a chapel dedicated to St John the Baptist was built in 1828–9. It was designed by Joseph Potter of Lichfield in a plain Grecian style and had a house for the priest attached on the north side; schools were built to the south-west. The cost of the land, chapel and house was £2,294, and collections raised £2,176 19s. 6d. An altarpiece depicting the healing at the pool of Bethsaida and formerly part of the collection of Lucien Bonaparte was bought in Rome by Lord Shrewsbury, who presented it to the chapel along with an organ. The Easter communicants numbered eighty in 1833.

About 1800 John Perry, the out-priest at Wolverhampton, used money left for the establishment of a mission in the Bloxwich area of Walsall to buy a house and shop in Harden Lane. He enlarged the shop and opened it as a chapel able to hold seventy to eighty people, replacing the Yieldfields mission. A French émigré priest, Jacques Normand, was appointed as resident assistant, and in 1804 he was replaced by another émigré, Louis Bertrand. Francis Martyn, ordained two years before from Old Oscott,[10] took over in 1807. By 1808 numbers were well over 100, and that year a new chapel dedicated to St Thomas the Apostle and incorporating the old chapel, was opened with a capacity of 300. In 1819 Martyn hired the assembly room at the Dragon in High Street, Walsall, holding morning and evening services there every Sunday as well as in Bloxwich. In 1825 he began building St Mary's on the Mount to the Grecian design of Joseph Ireland. The site was given by Joseph Cox and his wife, and Joseph Bagnall, a Walsall tanner and a member of the congregation, was a major contributor towards the building cost. The chapel was opened in 1827, along with a presbytery. Martyn moved there, and Bloxwich became a separate mission in 1829. A day and Sunday school for boys and girls was opened nearby in the early 1830s. In 1834 there were 150 communicants at Bloxwich and some 400 at Walsall.[11]

With the separation of Bloxwich Martyn was able to start work in West Bromwich, where he quickly made a number of converts. A Nonconformist chapel was rented as a Mass centre, and a house was bought for a resident priest. St Michael and the Holy Angels, designed by Joseph Ireland, was opened off the London–Chester road in 1832; over a third of the cost was met by its priest, George Spencer, youngest son of the 2nd Earl Spencer and a convert formerly in Anglican orders. In 1833 110 people were confirmed there, 70 of them converts. By 1834 there were 120 communicants, and there was also a school.[12] Spencer bought a site in Dudley in 1837 where the church of Our Blessed Lady and St Thomas of Canterbury was built in 1839–40 to the design of A. W. N. Pugin.[13]

Francis Martyn.

St Mary's, Walsall, *c*.1920.

George Spencer (from 1846 the Passionist Fr Ignatius).

Robert Richmond, chaplain to the Benedictine nuns who settled at Caverswall Castle in 1811, built a chapel in the castle which was consecrated in 1813 and used by local Catholics as well by the nuns. He opened a girls' school in Caverswall village in 1812 and one for boys in 1815. An observer stated in 1817 that Richmond had problems:

> The priest, who is a man of very agreeable manners, has taken much pains to convert several of the peasantry of the parish to the principles of Catholicism. His success, however, has not been commensurate to his zeal; when he has anything to bestow upon them they are mean and willing enough to receive it, but he has discovered that the majority of his converts come to the chapel in Caverswall Castle more for the hope of gain than the hope of salvation.

In 1812 he extended his efforts to the nearby south-eastern end of the Potteries, starting a Mass centre in a house at Normacot. In 1819 he opened a chapel dedicated to St Gregory in the Greendock area of Longton (then still known as Lane End). Later the same year he returned to Longbirch, where he had been sent after ordination in 1808, and St Gregory's was served from Caverswall and Cresswell until 1822 when Edward Daniel was appointed resident priest. By 1834 he had installed an organ and opened a school; in 1835 he added a tower to the chapel and built a presbytery; in 1850 he added a Lady chapel. He founded a mission at Stoke in 1838, with a Mass centre in a house in Whieldon Road. He moved it to a joiner's shop in Liverpool Road in 1841, and in 1843 he opened a chapel in Back Glebe Street dedicated to St Peter's Chains (the medieval parish church being dedicated to St Peter ad Vincula). Daniel continued to serve Stoke from Longton until 1850 when a resident priest was appointed.[14]

At Newcastle-under-Lyme in the early nineteenth century Mass was said in a room in the Shakespeare Hotel in Brunswick Street by the priests at Ashley and Cobridge. The mission was served from about 1826 by Edward Daniel and was taken over in 1829 by James Egan, who moved there

Holy Trinity, Newcastle-under-Lyme, in 1840.

from Ashley. In 1834 he opened Holy Trinity, built to his own striking design and partly at his own expense. The west front, for which vitreous bricks were used, is covered with arcaded panels, and the whole building is surmounted by turrets and embattled parapets. It stands in full view on the main road south from the town – there was no question of hiding this church discreetly behind a priest's house. In fact the south aisle was used as the priest's residence until a presbytery was built to the north in 1849; the north aisle was used as a school until 1864. It was probably no coincidence that in 1834 two preachers touring under the auspices of the Reformation Society held a public meeting in the town in 1834 to denounce the Church of Rome.[15]

The émigré Louis Gerard, after arriving at Cobridge in 1813,[16] said Mass in Leek for the French prisoners of war held there until 1814 and for the Irish working as silk weavers. He used a room in Pickwood Road and later the garret of a house in King Street belonging to William Ward, a solicitor. James Jeffries, appointed to Cheadle in 1827, soon started to say Mass in Leek, with a congregation of fifteen or sixteen. He used to arrive on Sunday evening, stay the night with Henry Bermingham in London Road and say Mass on Monday morning. He built a chapel dedicated to St Mary on the corner of Fountain Street and Portland Street in 1828–9. He added a presbytery in 1830, and a resident priest, Samuel Whitaker, was appointed in 1832. The total cost was some £1,050. There was a Sunday school by 1834 and a day school was opened in 1845. Numbers went down in the 1830s when most of the Irish working in the mills left for Manchester and Macclesfield.[17]

The Cheadle mission was founded by William Wareing soon after his arrival as assistant priest at Cresswell in 1819. He used an upper room in a house in Charles Street, which quickly proved too small. The Earl of Shrewsbury, who attended Mass there when his chaplain at Alton was away, bought a building which had been used as a militia armoury during the recent war, along with the adjoining adjutant's house. Wareing, who took over at Cresswell in 1823, said

Mass in the armoury on Sundays and some weekdays. The newly ordained James Jeffries was appointed as resident priest in 1827 with the adjutant's house as his presbytery. He had been trained at the seminary established at Cresswell by Wareing's predecessor Thomas Baddeley when he built a new chapel there in 1816, and while a student Jeffries had run catechism classes at Cheadle. He was succeeded in 1833 by Francis Fairfax, also newly ordained; he too had been a student at Cresswell, although he had gone on to Oscott in 1829. By 1835 there were some ninety communicants. Fairfax remained until 1847 and was thus involved in the building of the church of St Giles.[18]

Another mission founded from Cresswell was that at Uttoxeter. In the early 1830s John Dunne, after conducting two Sunday services at Cresswell, went on to Uttoxeter where he used the stables of the Blue Bell inn for an evening service and a lecture and for Mass on Monday morning. Responsibility for Uttoxeter was taken over by George Morgan, who went to live with Dunne in 1835. He proceeded to collect money from various sources, including the sale of his own estate, to enable him to build a church and house and moved to Uttoxeter in 1838. St Mary's, designed by A. W. N. Pugin, was opened in 1839.[19]

Bilston was still part of the Wolverhampton mission when it was hit by the cholera epidemic of 1832, and the two priests at Wolverhampton, Francis Mostyn and Patrick O'Sullivan, worked among the victims. As a result of their devotion a petition signed by over 300 local people, including non-Catholics, was sent to Bishop Walsh requesting a church and a priest for Bilston. Walsh made an appeal in his Lenten pastoral letter in 1833. Holy Trinity church, built in Oxford Street at a cost of £1,800, was opened in 1834 with Francis Mostyn as its first priest. The congregation grew as a result of the influx of Irish into the local industries, and the church was enlarged in 1844.[20]

Wood Lane had an urban extension from the 1830s when James Jeffries, having moved there from Cheadle in 1833, started to say Mass in Burton-upon-Trent, first in a malthouse and later in a cottage, evidently for a mainly Irish congregation. His request to the Marquess of Anglesey in 1839 for land as the site of a school-chapel to serve a congregation of about forty, was refused because numbers were considered too small. In 1843 he was saying Mass once a month at 8 a.m. for a congregation which had risen to nearly 120 as a result of further Irish immigration. He described the premises as 'so objectionable' that some people felt 'a repugnance to attend', but a further request to the Marquess was again turned down. On 31 March 1851 Mass attendance was 160, and the following year the next priest was able to build a school-chapel and a presbytery.[21]

In 1836 Thomas Green, the priest at Tixall, began to hold Sunday evening services in Rugeley, apparently using a house in Nine-foot Row, an alley behind Albion Street. In 1839 he started a Sunday Mass. He bought land for a church in 1842, and in 1846 John Grenside was appointed resident priest. Mass was transferred to the school built by subscription in 1847. The church of SS Joseph and Etheldreda, built to the design of Charles Hansom, was begun in 1849 and opened in 1851, with a presbytery to the south.[22]

In 1842 Blessed Dominic Barberi, an Italian Passionist, feeling a call to work for the conversion of England, established a Passionist community at Aston Hall.[23] He proceeded to visit nearby Stone several times a week, and on the first Sunday of Advent, 27 November, he started to say Mass in a room in the Crown hotel.[24] In the afternoon he followed Vespers with a catechism class, and in the evening he ran a course of lectures on points of controversy. Initially he was jeered at and pelted. Protestant clergy began house-to-house visits with the object, he wrote, of persuading the people not to come near him. He persevered, and by December 1843 he had eighty-six converts; he had reservations, however, about some of them, considering them more concerned with 'material aid rather than the salvation of their souls'. Thousands attended the Corpus Christi processions which he started in the grounds of Aston Hall in 1844, half of them non-Catholics. In 1849 thousands watched his funeral procession on its way from Stone to Aston.

Detail from the Whitgreave memorial window in the Church of SS Joseph and Etheldreda, Rugeley, showing the principal contributors to the building of the church, Joseph Whitgreave and his sister Etheldreda.

Fr Dominic moved the Mass centre to a room in Elmhurst, the home of James Beech in what is now Margaret Street. Beech also gave land in Newcastle Street as the site for a chapel. A. W. N. Pugin submitted a design costing £1,000, but on Wiseman's advice the scheme was scaled down to a school-chapel costing £500. Fr Dominic laid the foundation stone in July 1843, and by November £150 had been subscribed, including £50 from Wiseman and £40 raised by the local congregation. Dedicated to St Anne, the chapel was opened on 22 April 1844; the school was opened the next day, St George's Day, with twenty-four pupils and two schoolmistresses. The east window by William Wailes of Newcastle-upon-Tyne shows St Anne holding Our Lady as a child. The cost was £600, which was cleared within a year. Fr Dominic wrote that 'my hope is that the little building at Stone will be the grain of mustard seed which, blessed by God, will become a great tree'; in the event it became part of the Dominican convent begun in 1852. Mass was transferred to the convent in 1853, and a new church was opened in 1854. St Anne's remained in use as a school until replaced by new buildings in 1870.

At Brewood the chapels at Black Ladies and Longbirch on the Chillington estate were replaced by a church built on the western edge of the village in 1843–4. St Mary's forms part of an ensemble also containing a presbytery and school and designed by A. W. N. Pugin. The cost was £2,010 and contributors included Lord Shrewsbury, Bishop Wiseman and George Spencer; Pugin and Henry Whitgreave of Moseley gave money for windows. Thomas Giffard provided the stone and indirectly contributed to the building fund by buying church land in Brewood so that the proceeds from the sale could go towards the building costs. The church was consecrated on 13 June by Wiseman with at least thirteen priests assisting. The founder and first priest was William Richmond, Robert Richmond's nephew; he had served two spells at Longbirch before returning there in 1838 after retiring as vice-president of Oscott. He died a week after the opening and was succeeded by his nephew Henry Richmond, who served there until his death in 1848. Both were buried in the churchyard and are commemorated by floor slabs in the chancel. At the end of each aisle is a medieval statue of the Virgin and Child. That in the south aisle is probably fifteenth-century Flemish, perhaps a gift by Pugin, and nearby is a seventeenth-century crucifix from Black Ladies; the statue in the north aisle is said to have come from the former Augustinian nunnery of White Ladies near Boscobel in Shropshire via Black Ladies.[25]

In 1845 Charles Mousley built a chapel in his garden at Haunton in Clifton Campville for the sole use of his family. Mass was occasionally said there, evidently by the priest at Tamworth, who stated in 1852 that 'there is duty done there about seven times in the year' with a congregation of about ten.[26]

❧

Clergy numbers received a boost with the arrival in England from 1791 of émigré priests fleeing the French Revolution. Their plight touched a chord in the English, who now feared revolution more than Catholicism. A relief fund was organised, and Staffordshire contributors included the Marquess of Stafford (£100), the Bishop of Lichfield and Coventry (£40), and the people of the admittedly Catholic Wolverhampton (£90 15s.).[27] Employment was found. Louis Martin de Laistre came to Staffordshire about 1794 as tutor to the children of the rector of Mucklestone. When he took over the mission at nearby Ashley in 1796, he also found a welcome from the rector there, William Anwyl; in his will of 1810 he begged Anwyl

> to accept of my books, of six silver forks for himself and of my golden watch for his amiable little son – Tom Anwyl. His compliance with this my last request will complete his long uncommon kindness to me, which I never could repay and the recollection of which overpowers now my feelings.[28]

At Bloxwich on the other hand Jacques Normand, the first resident priest *c*.1800–1804, had to face considerable hostility; his successor Louis Bertrand, another émigré (1804–7), had an easier ride.[29]

While at Mucklestone de Laistre said Mass in the house of a Catholic farmer at Napley Heath. At the end of 1795 Thomas Howell decided to give up the mission at Ashley, and in February 1796 John Darley of Dairy House wrote to Bishop Milner on behalf of the congregation requesting the appointment of de Laistre and adding a list of nine men who were willing to subscribe a total of £13 4s.; he himself headed the list with a contribution of £5 5s. De Laistre was duly appointed. Mary Cartledge, a local widow, lent him the money to start a farm, and with the proceeds of that and from French lessons he was able to support himself. He died in 1813, leaving his house to Mary Cartledge on condition that she allowed free access to the chapel and recommending the bishop to keep the chapel in good repair.[30]

An émigré may have served Bellamour in Colton where Mary, the widow of Sir Walter Blount, built a second house *c*.1796 and opened the chapel to the Catholics of the area; her younger son Edward continued to do so until he sold the property in 1824. His nephew, Sir Edward Blount, recalled being taught French *c*.1800 by Nicholas Malvoisin, who was living nearby at Rugeley. By 1806, however, Bellamour was served from Tixall.[31] That too had an émigré from 1810 when Henri le Sage, great-nephew of Alain René Lesage, author of *Gil Blas*, went as chaplain to the Cliffords. He remained at Tixall until his death in 1821 and was buried in the parish churchyard. He also served at Stafford during an interregnum there in 1813.[32]

The Cobridge mission was served by Louis Gerard from 1813 to 1842. Born in 1760, he arrived in England with his family in 1794, having been brought from Toulon by the English fleet. He was ordained at Wolverhampton in 1809 by Bishop Milner, changing his name on Milner's advice from Giraud to Gerard, 'a good old English name, sir, that people can pronounce'. His predecessor had lengthened the church

The Benedictine Nuns at Caverswall Castle in 1817.

about 1812, and in 1816–17 Gerard added a nave at right angles to the existing chapel, which became a south transept. He also installed a gallery and in 1820 an organ. He built a school in 1821–2 and enlarged his house in 1831. He left Cobridge to serve as chaplain to the Dominican nuns at Atherstone in Warwickshire and in 1852 went to Woodchester in Gloucestershire where he was professed as a Dominican the following year. He died there in 1856.[33]

The refugees also included religious communities. The first in Staffordshire, representing the permanent return of the religious Orders to the county, was a community of English Benedictine nuns from Ghent, where they had been founded in 1624 from the English Benedictine convent at Brussels. Arriving in England in 1794, they settled in Preston in Lancashire in 1795. In 1811 they moved to Caverswall Castle in North Staffordshire, leased for them by Walter Hill Coyney of nearby Weston Coyney whose wife was a Catholic. The community numbered sixteen. They opened a boarding school for girls and also taught in the girls' school established in Caverswall village by their chaplain in 1812. The following description of the community and their school appeared in 1817:

> The nuns are sufficiently active in the good work of instructing young ladies in the principles of their faith, and they have at present about thirty pupils in progress. Their discipline is sufficiently strict; the pupils wear an uniform of buff-coloured cotton; they are not suffered to ramble beyond the bounds of the gravel walk which surrounds the moat, and two or three small fields; they walk two and two, like other boarding-school girls, and in their half-hour's exercise along the walk in the garden, are required, as a religious duty, to utter their ave-marias and pater-nosters in a low voice. The nuns themselves may be termed the Black Ladies. Their dress is entirely sable, with long thick black

veils thrown over the right shoulder. Their demeanour is grave, and they generally walk with some book in their hands. Their countenances are pleasing and pensive; and if a man approaches them, they turn away as if they feared the imputation of vanity, or were in danger of weakening their principles by gratifying the eye of curiosity.

The community moved to Oulton near Stone in 1853.[34]

The English Franciscans who fled to England from Douai tried various ways of providing for their novices. In 1818 they established a noviciate at Aston Hall near Stone, where there was already a Franciscan in 1817. In 1823 there were only two novices and the noviciate was closed. Franciscans, however, continued to serve the Aston mission until 1839.[35]

The community of English Benedictine nuns who had been in Paris since 1652 came to England in 1795 and settled at Marnhull in Dorset the same year. They went to Cannington in Somerset in 1807, establishing the Perpetual Adoration of the Blessed Sacrament there in 1829. They moved to Staffordshire in 1836, having bought Mount Pavilion in Colwich in 1835 on the recommendation of Bishop Walsh. This was a shooting box converted from a mid-eighteenth-century house by Robert Shirley, Viscount Tamworth, eldest son of Earl Ferrers, and it had been on the market since his death in 1824. The money needed for the purchase was provided by a novice, Sister Teresa Gertrude Tempest, who brought a large fortune with her. A chapel was formed by turning the entrance hall into the choir and a boudoir into a sanctuary. The three windows over the altar are said to have been an early design by A. W. N. Pugin, who is also credited with the reredos; the cost was met mainly by Lord Clifford of Chudleigh and Joseph Weld of Lulworth in Dorset. Clifford further provided two silver lamps to burn before the Blessed Sacrament. The choir was blessed by the vicar general, Henry Weedall in 1837, and the chapel was opened to the public.[36]

Non-émigré Orders too settled in Staffordshire. Bridgettine nuns from Lisbon opened a convent in Cobridge Cottage in 1822. In 1829 they moved to Aston, remaining until 1837;

paintings of St Helen, St Edward the Confessor, St Lucius and St Edith, which they had brought from Lisbon, were given to the chapel opened at Leek in 1829.[37] In 1842, after being served by a secular, Benjamin Hulme, from 1839, Aston was taken over by Passionists under Blessed Dominic Barberi in 1842. He began building St Michael's church there in 1847, and the first service was his own funeral in 1849; the church was officially opened on the feast of St Michael, 29 September 1850. In 1854 it was decided that the Aston Hall community should move to Cotton Hall in North Staffordshire, which the Order had taken over in 1850, holding the first chapter of the Anglo-Belgian province there in 1851. Cotton proved too costly and most of the community left in 1855; the last two members followed the next year.[38]

Cotton Hall had been bought by Lord Shrewsbury in 1843 and let in 1845 to a convert clergyman, John Campbell Smith. He brought his chaplain, John Kennedy, with him and opened a chapel in the house. In 1846 Lord Shrewsbury established the convert Frederick Faber and his Brothers of the Will of God at Cotton. As Faber was not ordained until 1847, John Kennedy remained at Cotton, but meanwhile Faber set about evangelising the area. A temporary chapel was opened in farm buildings and a day school and a night school were established; numerous converts were made. It was at Cotton that Faber wrote the hymn 'Faith of Our Fathers'. A church dedicated to St Wilfrid – Faber had taken the name Brother Wilfrid – was built to the design of A. W. N. Pugin, who stated that it would have 'the only perfect chancel in England and with an east window he could die for'. The foundations were blessed on the feast of St Wilfrid, 23 October, 1846, and the church was opened on Easter Tuesday 1848. Bishop Nicholas Wiseman, Walsh's coadjutor, sang the Mass and John Henry Newman preached. Lord Shrewsbury contributed £2,300. A school was built at the expense of Lady Shrewsbury, and the Earl gave an endowment of £65 a year.[39]

Earlier the same year Faber and his community had joined Newman's Oratorians. In 1846 Newman and a group of other converts had moved to Old Oscott to spend time considering

St Mary's Convent, Handsworth, in 1842.

their vocation, and he gave the place its present name of Maryvale. Later the same year Bishop Wiseman sent Newman to Rome for a year's study, and in 1847 he was ordained priest there. He decided to join the Oratorians, as Wiseman had suggested, and he carried out his noviciate training in Rome before returning to Maryvale. There in 1848 he established the first English Oratory but moved to Cotton later the same year. The Oratorian mission, however, was to urban areas, and the papal brief of 1847 establishing the first English oratory had specified Birmingham. In 1849 Newman moved to Birmingham and Faber to London. The same year Maryvale was taken over by the Oblates of Mary Immaculate as a noviciate and a house of studies in theology. It met with the strong approval of Bishop Eugène de Mazenod, who had founded the Congregation in 1816 and visited Maryvale in 1850. Soon, however, he realised that it was too expensive to run, and the Oblates left in 1851.[40]

Maryvale then passed to the Sisters of Mercy. Their first convent in the Midlands was built in Hunter's Road, Handsworth, in 1840–1. It was founded by John Hardman, a button maker and medallist, whose house stood on the opposite side of the road. Besides providing the site he gave the buildings and furnishings at a cost of £5,535, and Lord Shrewsbury gave £2,000; both were commemorated in the east window of the chapel where they were shown kneeling on either side of the Virgin attended by their patron saints, St John the Evangelist and St John the Baptist. St Mary's convent was designed by A. W. N. Pugin, who claimed that Handsworth and his Mercy convent in Liverpool were 'the first regular conventual buildings erected in this country since the change of religion'. He added a second cloister and chapel in 1846–7. The convent chapel was open to the public until the present church of St Francis was built nearby in 1894. The nuns ran a girls' boarding school and an orphanage and in 1844 opened a house of mercy for unemployed servant girls. Two of John Hardman's daughters by his second wife joined the convent: Juliana later became superior, while her elder sister Mary was superior of the orphanage which the nuns

The Chapel at Tixall in 1841.

opened at Maryvale in 1851. After John's death in 1844 his widow by his third marriage went to live in the convent for the rest of her life.[41] In 1849 the nuns opened a convent and school in Giffard House in Wolverhampton.[42]

☙

Although control of missions by the gentry and nobility was dwindling, they continued their support. Mary, daughter and heir of the last Lord Langdale (d. 1778) who married Lord Stourton in 1775, paid for the chapel opened at Cresswell in 1816, and she and her family were still the principal supporters of the Cresswell mission in the 1830s.[43] The 15th Earl of Shrewsbury provided the chapel at Wood Lane after the demolition of Hoar Cross in 1794 and bought premises for the Cheadle mission in the early 1820s.[44] At Stafford St Austin's was rebuilt in 1817–18 by the Jerninghams of Costessey in Norfolk, who had inherited the Stafford Castle estate in 1769 (and were to secure the revival of the Stafford barony in 1824): Sir George Jerningham and his brother Edward paid for the rebuilding, which Edward also designed.[45] Sir Thomas Clifford built a new chapel at Tixall in 1827–8 to the design of Joseph Ireland at a cost of nearly £19,000; when the Tixall estate was sold to the Protestant Earl Talbot of neighbouring Ingestre in 1845, the chapel was moved stone by stone to land in Great Haywood reserved from the sale.[46] Lord Camoys, having inherited Rushton Grange, was contributing to the support of the Cobridge mission by 1842.[47] Thomas Giffard gave the stone for the church built at Brewood in 1843–4 and indirectly contributed towards the building costs.[48] The Earl of Arundel and Surrey, son and heir of the Duke of Norfolk, gave £100 towards Dominic Barberi's church opened at Aston in 1849, and his arms were placed above the high altar.[49] The principal contributors to the church opened at Rugeley in 1851 were Joseph Whitgreave of Heron Court, built opposite the same year, and his sister Etheldreda, who became a nun at Princethorpe in Warwickshire; hence the dedication of the church to Saints Joseph and Etheldreda. The Marquess of

Anglesey, the Protestant lord of Rugeley manor, gave the stone for the church and presbytery.[50]

The most generous patron in the county was John Talbot, the 16th Earl of Shrewsbury, who succeeded his uncle at Alton in 1827. His first contribution was £130 towards the chapel and house at Leek (1828–30).[51] In 1833 he replaced the domestic chapel at Alton Towers by a much larger building, which, like its predecessor, served the local Catholics as well as the family.[52] He also built two schools in Alton and another at Oakamoor by the mid 1830s; 180 children were then receiving what one commentator considered 'such education as is suitable to their station in life'.[53] With the establishment of his protégé Augustus Welby Northmore Pugin as the apologist of the Catholic revival, Lord Shrewsbury became more closely involved.[54] In Staffordshire he subscribed to or paid entirely for most of Pugin's ecclesiastical buildings as well as donating furnishings. He died in November 1852 two months after Pugin's death in September. His heir was his second cousin Bertram Talbot, who died in 1856 aged twenty-three, unmarried and the last of the senior and Catholic line. After two lawsuits the title and the estates passed in 1858 and 1859 to Henry Chetwynd-Talbot, third Earl Talbot, of Ingestre, representing a junior and Protestant line.[55]

Poverty, however, was a mark of many of the new missions. Success itself brought problems: numbers increased with conversions, Irish immigration and the general growth in population, and with the increase there were new needs which the generally poor congregations could not easily pay for. Thus at Cobridge increased numbers meant the enlargement of the chapel in 1816–17, and that produced a debt of £200. At one Sunday Mass Louis Gerard had the vestments brought on to the sanctuary and proceeded to tear them to ribbons as a disgrace to the mission. He gave French lessons to earn money and stated that 'I sold my library to save my life'. He enjoyed a small annuity left by Joseph Bucknall in 1789, and as confessor to Lord Shrewsbury he received £40 a year. In 1834 a committee fixed seat rents at 4s. each a year; those who did not rent were expected to make an offering as they

entered the church. Lord Camoys as owner of Rushton Grange
was contributing four guineas a year to the mission by 1842.
The total income that year was £120, but there was a debt of
£95. In 1827 and 1833 bazaars – still a rare means of raising
money – were held to help towards the costs of the school and
work on the presbytery. Gerard's successor in 1842, the Franciscan Roger O'Higgin, introduced an offertory collection and
improved the seat rents. An 'influx of Irish', described as
recent in 1851, increased the problems as they were 'mostly
very destitute'. Thomas Leith, who took over the mission in
1851, found on his arrival that 'in a few years more the house
would have been uninhabitable', with altar furnishings and
vestments to match: 'the place was becoming a byword in the
neighbourhood'. Repairs and refurnishing cost between £600
and £700.[56]

By 1810 Kirk was supplementing his stipend at Lichfield
by taking private pupils. In 1841 he described his congregation as very poor, the only exceptions being a farmer, an
innkeeper, one or two small tradesmen and Lady Fitzgerald,
a widow living at Maple Hayes near Pipe Hall.[57] The mission
started at Lane End in 1819 was poor, as was its daughter
mission started at Stoke in 1838. Mother Margaret Hallahan,
the Dominican nun who established a convent at the Foley in
Fenton in 1851 before moving to Stone in 1853, described the
area as 'a complete range of dust hills. The people say it is
the fag-end of the Potteries; I think it is the fag-end of the
world.' She was greatly distressed when she visited the chapel
which had been opened at Stoke in 1843: 'We went yesterday
to the chapel at Stoke, and oh, I cannot tell you what I have
felt since. A total want of all things. Our Lord and God in a
pewter ciborium. We must do something for the place.'[58] The
Rugeley mission was described in 1847 as 'paralysed with
poverty'.[59] At Walsall in 1851 the priest stated that there was
an 8 a.m. Mass on Sundays 'for poor people who from want
of proper clothes do not like to appear out of doors at a later
period of the day'. The average attendance at the Mass was
350, which accounted for half the total morning attendance.[60]

It was not only the urban missions that had problems. After

the death of Louis de Laistre in 1813 the Ashley mission lived from hand to mouth.[61] It was too poor to support a resident priest and was served from Swynnerton and Cobridge. The Swynnerton priest sent Bishop Milner a note of what he found there:

> The chapel left by the Rev. Louis Martin de Laistre for the use of the Catholick congregation at Ashley contains an altar, tabernacle and crucifix with two very old wooden candlesticks. In the area there are a few old seats. To the place belong a small chalice with paten, of silver formerly gilt, and another chalice and paten of an inferior composition, looking much like pewter ... There are a few vestments of divers colours but of little value. The best is a new one apparently intended to serve for all colours. Of chapel linen I found very little, an alb, two or three corporals and purificators and an old cassock.

An appeal in 1820 said of the mission that it was 'not able to support a priest – salary only £5 per annum ... occasional visit of neighbouring priest, but that only on a weekday and the chapel is in a bad state of repair'. Enough was evidently raised which, combined with local subscriptions, enabled a new chapel to be opened in 1823. A further appeal in 1824 declared that 'a little more assistance will enable us to support a pastor and our joy will be complete'. James Egan was appointed as resident priest in 1825 at a salary of £20 a year and with a house described in another appeal of 1826 as 'small, damp and out of repair'. In 1824 the mission was given a house and garden in the Forebridge suburb of Stafford from Mary Frith, and by her will of the same year the Comtesse de Front left it £500. Mary Frith, who was living in Ashley in 1834 and had died by 1841, evidently left the money which was used to buy a ciborium, a silver thurible, boat and spoon, an alb and surplice for the priest and surplices for the acolytes.

In 1848, during an interregnum at Ashley, the priest at Swynnerton reported on the mission to the bishop. The chapel was in need of repair and had lately had to be 'buttressed by a large triangular prop' to make it safe for the congregation; in addition the gable over the chancel arch had become unsafe. The house 'was scarcely habitable, it is so damp from the repeated influx of rain'. The congregation was estimated at just over 100; at nearby Market Drayton there was a small Irish community to whom the last priest had given much attention but with little hope of success. The income was 18d. a week from the congregation and a further £46 a year; out of this all expenses had to be met, including those of the school.

☘

Catholic immigration was not confined to the clergy. Lay émigrés were among those making their Easter Communion at Black Ladies in 1793. As mentioned above, Catholic numbers at Leek and Lichfield were increased by French prisoners of war in the early nineteenth century.[62]

Staffordshire was already experiencing Irish immigration at the end of the eighteenth century. Irish names began to appear in the Catholic baptismal register at Wolverhampton, and one entry in 1811 noted: 'all Irish people'. The Communion list for Black Ladies recorded 'an Hibernian' on Christmas Day 1795, and an Irishman from nearby Four Ashes was among the Easter communicants at Longbirch in 1798.[63]

In the early nineteenth century there were a number of Irish working in Leek as silk weavers, but most of them moved to Manchester and Macclesfield in the 1830s.[64] Irish immigrants had settled in the Potteries by 1828 when Louis Gerard, in an appeal on behalf of his Cobridge mission, declared: 'I plead for the English and the Irish.'[65] By 1851 the Irish element in the Cobridge congregation had seen a further increase, described as recent.[66] At Bilston the local industries attracted an influx of Irish around 1840.[67] About the same time Irish travelling from Liverpool to London increased the numbers attending Sunday Mass at Lichfield, and by 1851 there was a large Irish community in the Sandford Street part of the city.[68]

By then too there was a concentration of Irish in the Blue Lane area of central Walsall.[69]

☙

In 1793 Joseph Berington, the most extreme exponent of the Staffordshire Creed, left Oscott to become chaplain to Sir John Throckmorton at Buckland in Berkshire.[70] The following year Bishop Talbot established a school and seminary in the large house under the presidency of Dr John Bew, former president of St Gregory's in Paris. A board of lay governors was responsible for the general running of the college; the vicar apostolic was in charge of all religious matters, including the nomination of the president where, however, the board had the right of veto. Far from being seen as a rival the scheme received the encouragement of John Kirk, President of Sedgley Park. Talbot's three fellow vicars apostolic, however, were hostile, fearing Cisalpine influence. John Milner, the future Midland Vicar Apostolic then still at Winchester, criticised the whole idea of educating lay boys with seminarians: 'There must be fiddling, dancing, drawing, sporting etc., or else the College will not take', he wrote in 1794. He also predicted that the 'Cisalpine school will have the means of doing irreparable mischief'.

The aim as set out in the prospectus was to meet the needs of all Catholic youth, 'those who are born to independence, those who are designed for the learned professions, and those who are destined for business'. The plan of studies was to be broader than that of the foreign colleges and would comprise 'those branches of education which are either generally useful or peculiarly necessary'. Fees were £30 a year, to include board, washing and lodging. Each pupil had to bring 'two pairs of sheets and a knife, silver fork and silver spoon'. Vacations consisted of a fortnight at Christmas and a month at midsummer. The first student to be ordained was Francis Martyn, also the first priest to be educated entirely in England since the Elizabethan Reformation: born in 1782, he was at Sedgley Park from 1790 to 1796, then went on to Oscott and was ordained at Wolverhampton in 1805.

In 1800 Bew extended the building, but numbers were insufficient to make the college pay. In 1808, with thirty lay and seven church students, the board offered it to the vicar apostolic, John Milner, provided that he also took over the £600 debt. Eager to rescue the college from Cisalpine influence, Milner accepted the offer, cleared the debt and reorganised the regime with the vice-president, Thomas Potts, promoted to the presidency. On 15 August, the feast of the Assumption, Milner placed the college under Our Lady's patronage, naming it St Mary's College. As part of the reorganisation he separated the church students from the lay boys as far as possible, building a three-storey block to include accommodation for them in 1809, substituting a period of meditation for military drill, encouraging spiritual reading and introducing weekly conferences. Further building in 1816 included a colonnade across the frontage, and in 1819 a small wing was built for Milner's own occupation.

In 1809 Milner enlarged the chapel by turning the sacristy behind the altar into the sanctuary and building a sacristy to the side. Above the new sacristy he built an oratory which in 1814 became the first public shrine to the Sacred Heart in England. When in Rome that year Milner secured an indult for the shrine from Pius VII and brought back a stained-glass panel depicting the Sacred Heart which he installed at the east end; the cracks can still be seen where it was broken on the journey. Milner issued a pastoral in 1820 encouraging visits to the shrine and the establishment of local Associations of the Sacred Heart. Several were formed, committing members to frequent Communion and monthly visits to the shrine. Milner also started to assemble the students there, leading prayers himself, and the devotion became popular with them.

Numbers at the college increased and the accommodation became inadequate, especially when the 1809 block became unsafe and had to be demolished. Money too was a problem. Writing to the Cardinal Prefect of Propaganda in 1818 Milner stated that 'the little College and Seminary at Oscott ... having no funds, nor other support, except what I myself can

St Mary's College, Old Oscott (later Maryvale).

procure for it, is incapable of raising more than half the number of priests who are wanted in the Midland District'.[71] Thomas Walsh, vice-president from 1808, president from 1819 and Milner's successor as vicar apostolic in 1826, bought land nearby just over the county boundary in Warwickshire in 1835, and a new St Mary's College was opened there in 1838. Old Oscott then became a preparatory school for New Oscott.

⌘

New Oscott provided a base for the leading architect of the Catholic revival, Augustus Welby Northmore Pugin.[72] He was appointed Professor of Ecclesiastical Antiquities at the college in 1837, and he established a museum for the instruction of the ordinands; he also took in hand the decoration and furnishing of the chapel, consecrated in 1838. Oscott became a platform for the propagation of Pugin's architectural programme for the Catholic revival – for replacing the pagan Classical style of church building by a return to the Christian High Gothic coupled with medieval liturgy and furnishings. Walsh commissioned churches in line with Pugin's ideas, helping to make the transition from chapel to church architecture, with St Chad's Cathedral (1839–41) as the biggest commission. He earned a tribute from Pugin in 1839 as 'the only bishop in England who has really advanced the dignity of religion. Dr Walsh found the churches in his district worse than barns; he will leave them sumptuous erections. The greater part of the vestments were filthy rags, and he has replaced them with silk and gold.'[73]

Pugin's main patron, however, was John, Earl of Shrewsbury. Pugin met him in 1836[74] and began corresponding with him; by the autumn of 1837 Pugin was visiting the Earl's home at Alton Towers. He may well have been introduced to the Earl by his chaplain, Dr Daniel Rock, an enthusiastic reader of Pugin's *Contrasts* (1836). By 1838 Lord Shrewsbury was declaring that 'in consequence of the lamentable failure of most of our modern chapels I have come to the resolution to

Lord Shrewsbury, John Hardman junior, and A. W. N. Pugin, depicted in a window at St Mary's Convent, Handsworth.

subscribe to no buildings which are not erected under the designs and superintendence of Mr Pugin'.[75] He also arranged introductions to potential patrons, often at gatherings at Alton Towers.

In addition Pugin had a fruitful association with the Hardman family of Handsworth. John Hardman senior, maker of buttons and medals in Birmingham, was a promoter of the new St Chad's, and Pugin, having dined at Handsworth in May 1837,[76] sent him drawings for the new church in June. At Pugin's instigation Hardman's eldest surviving son, also John, set up the firm of John Hardman & Co. in 1838 to meet the increasing demand for metal fittings in new churches. With the opening of new premises in 1845 the firm added stained glass to its products, again at Pugin's instigation. Pugin's eldest daughter Anne married the younger John's nephew, John Hardman Powell. Another connection was Herbert Minton, a pottery manufacturer of Stoke-upon-Trent, who produced encaustic tiles to Pugin's design and later tableware and decorative ceramics also. After stained glass the rediscovered medieval encaustic tile was for Pugin the most important decorative item. He was in contact with Minton by the summer of 1840, over the production of tiles for the Handsworth convent.

One of the first of all Pugin's churches was St Mary's at Uttoxeter, begun in 1838 and opened in August 1839.[77] He claimed that it 'may truly be described as the first Catholic structure erected in this country in strict accordance with the rules of ancient ecclesiastical architecture since the days of the pretended Reformation'. Though much altered since, it was a brick structure consisting of an aisleless nave and chancel with a double bellcote instead of a tower; there was also a presbytery. The interior contained all that Pugin thought was required for the celebration of the medieval Sarum rite. The stone font with a locking cover would, he hoped, herald a restoration of fonts – 'old bottles and jugs are but sorry substitutes for fonts'. Instead of a screen there was an arched rood beam surmounted by a crucifix. The stone altar had a reredos with side panels that could be closed for Lent and two large

St Mary's Catholic Church, Uttoxeter, in 1839.

St John's Hospital, Alton, as planned in 1842.

candlesticks instead of the big six. On the south side of the chancel there were sedilia and a sacrarium for washing the vessels and on the north side an Easter sepulchre. At the opening in August 1839 Bishop Walsh presided, wearing cloth of gold vestments designed by Pugin; fourteen priests wore voluminous medieval-style surplices, with others in rich copes. Lord Shrewsbury was a major benefactor; the only significant stone carving in the church was the lion's head from the Shrewsbury arms over the interior of the west door. He and the Countess were present at the opening, along with their son-in-law and daughter, the Prince and Princess Doria-Pamphilj Landi. Dr Rock sang the Mass, supported by the Alton Towers choir.

Not surprisingly Pugin was soon at work on Alton Towers itself, including the transformation of the interior of the chapel and of its furnishings in 1839–40 and 1849–51. The chapel was the scene of the reception into the Catholic Church of his second wife Louisa in 1839. In Alton village on the opposite side of the Churnet gorge he designed the hospital of St John the Baptist. A hospital in the medieval sense – almshouses with a chapel and other communal buildings and with a resident warden – it was situated within the precinct of the ruined Alton Castle on the edge of the village. Pugin described the site as 'one of the most beautiful and suitable for such an edifice which can well be imagined'. The project was paid for by Lord Shrewsbury and took its name from his patron saint. It was conceived as more than just a medieval hospital: with its chapel, school and guildhall it was intended to provide a service to the local community embodying the social values of medieval Catholicism. Pugin informed the Earl in a letter written on Christmas Day 1841: 'Nobody now *dies* a Protestant at Alton if they do not all live Catholics.' A pamphlet war ensued between the vicar of Alton and Lord Shrewsbury over a charge of Catholic proselytism.

Pugin completed drawings in 1839 for a building on three sides of an open quadrangle. Using local stone, work began in 1840 on the left-hand (north) side, which consisted of St John's school-chapel and the warden's house. The altar of the chapel was consecrated by Bishop Walsh in July 1842 – the whole building was consecrated as a parish church in 1930 – and was intended as a church for those of the area who had hitherto attended the chapel at the Towers: the average Mass attendance at St John's was 300 by 1850–1, with an additional 104 Sunday scholars. St John's is a simple sandstone building, consisting of nave, chancel and bellcote, with a Blessed Sacrament chapel on the north side of the chancel. It had a fine wooden rood screen which was removed about 1967 at the insistence of Archbishop Dwyer, but the crucifix survives suspended from the ceiling. A burial ground was opened to the east of the chapel in 1843; it has a wooden Calvary under a tiled gable, claimed to be only the second since the Reformation (the first being at Grace Dieu in Leicestershire). On either side of the altar are the tombs of the 16th and 17th earls; each has a Hardman memorial brass, a tradition which Pugin had been instrumental in reviving.

Pugin saw the building as more than a church. He regarded the nave as primarily a schoolroom. It could be closed off from the chancel but opened up for additional space for worshippers as required; the benches could be turned into desks by raising a hinged flap. The floor was of timber in the interests of warmth, while the rest of the chapel was floored with Minton tiles. The statue over the entrance was not of the patron, St John the Baptist, but of St Nicholas, the patron of children. A cottage in the village had been adapted as a house for the schoolmaster by the end of 1841. Pugin also made special provision for another aspect of the school: 'I have arranged the privies for the schools', he informed Lord Shrewsbury that year, 'in a most picturesque manner. You descend to them by steps cut [out of] the side of the rock & they are hid amongst the trees.'[78]

Work on the remaining hospital buildings was suspended in 1843 in favour of the northern part of the site where Pugin desiged a new castle to the east of the medieval ruins. It may ultimately have been intended as a dower house for the Countess in the event of her being widowed, and one wing may first have been planned as a residence for the Earl's cousin and

heir, Bertram. The Earl planned to use another part of it as a
residence for retired priests – to Pugin's horror: he was thoroughly disappointed at the suspension of work on the hospital
for which he had a similar plan, and a mock castle for priests
he regarded as a violation of all his principles; the idea was
dropped. Work proceeded slowly. The first part to be begun
was the castle chapel, built over the crypt of the medieval
chapel; the roof is covered with coloured tiles ordered from
Herbert Minton in 1848 and is reminiscent of the Hôtel Dieu
at Beaune which Pugin had presumably visited when in the
area the previous year. Structural work on the castle was
evidently completed by the spring of 1852, though interior
work remained to be done.

Meanwhile work had been resumed on the hospital. The
east range was the almshouse, originally intended for twelve
poor brethren. After a discussion in December 1841 with
Nicholas Wiseman, Walsh's coadjutor, Pugin changed the
scheme to a college of six 'decayed priests'; Wiseman had
mentioned the existence of an annual £64 endowment each for
retired North Staffordshire priests, then living in farmhouses
scattered throughout the region. The almshouse range was to
consist of a hall, chambers and a library for the six chaplains;
the poor brethren were to be moved to the south range, with
a single kitchen serving both communities. Drawings of the
almshouse made in 1849 show the more elaborate style
adopted in place of the simpler original. The south range,
drawings for which were sent to Lord Shrewsbury in 1847,
consisted mainly of a guildhall intended to be used for social
gatherings and for the school, and in October 1849 Pugin
reported to his wife 'strange doings here at S John's. Balls in
the Guildhall, dancing till two in the morning'. By 1851 it
housed a mechanics' institution and the boys' school.[79] In
March 1852, however, Lord Shrewsbury wrote to Pugin that
he was wanting 'to finish the Hospital as a residence ...
Surely the masonry will all be done this summer & autumn.'
On Pugin's death that year the work was taken over by his son
Edward. In the event no decayed priests or poor brethren were
ever housed there, and the hospital became a Mercy convent.

In the late 1990s the archdiocese converted the castle and hospital into a residential youth centre.

Pugin was also at work on Catholic buildings elsewhere in Staffordshire. In 1840 he designed the convent of the Sisters of Mercy at Handsworth opened in 1841, with further buildings in 1844 and 1846–7. In 1843–4 he designed St Mary's in Brewood with presbytery and school attached. St Wilfrid's at Cotton was opened in 1848.[80]

Pugin's masterpiece was the church of St Giles, Cheadle, which he described to Lord Shrewsbury in 1841 as 'Cheadle, *perfect* Cheadle, Cheadle my consolation in all my afflictions'. Dedicated like the existing Anglican church to the patron of the ancient parish and built mostly of local stone, it was intended as the supreme realisation of Pugin's ideals, 'a perfect revival of an English parish church of the time of Edward I'. Besides a nave and chancel it has aisles ending in a Lady chapel and a Blessed Sacrament chapel, a tower with a 200-foot spire, north and south porches and a wooden rood screen. The chancel with its Easter Sepulchre on the north side and sedilia and sacrarium on the south was intended as a setting for the medieval Sarum liturgy. An organ loft on the north side with exterior access represented Pugin's successful answer to Lord Shrewsbury's proposal in 1842 for a west gallery; the idea horrified Pugin as 'a protestantism' which would ruin 'all the sublime effect of the tower arch'. The metalwork, mostly by Hardmans, is more extensive than in any other Pugin church. It originally included four brass coronae which lit the nave but were replaced in the 1960s by wrought-iron versions; in the chancel there is also a fifteenth-century corona from Flanders. The decoration of the interior is a blaze of colour, red, gold, and blue, from floor and wall tiles (by Minton), stained glass (by Wailes), and painted surfaces. The original scheme for the church was, in Pugin's words, 'for a plain parochial country church'. It became more elaborate as Lord Shrewsbury increased the funds available: a budget of £5,000 rose to a final one of £40,000. Pugin also had general reservations about the use of painting and in the case of Cheadle blamed Lord Shrewsbury:

St Giles's, Cheadle, in 1847.

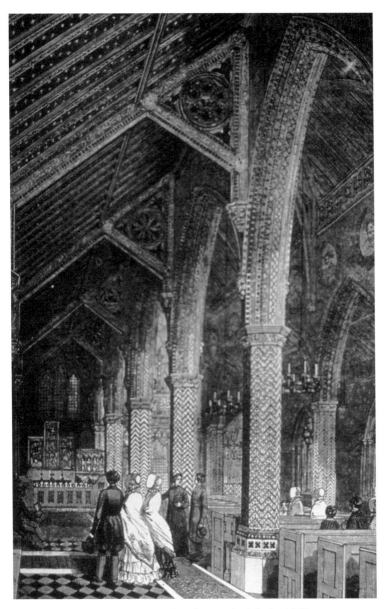

St Giles's, Cheadle: the north aisle in 1847.

It was quite an afterthought of its noble founder to cover it with coloured enrichment; hence there is a great anomaly between the simplicity of its walls and mouldings and the intricacy of its detail, but all this is the result of a chain of circumstances over which I had no control, yet I have no doubt that many people imagine it is the ne plus ultra of my ideas on church decoration, and that I designed it on a carte blanche, when in truth it was planned to meet a very limited outlay. Had we commenced on the same scale as we ended, a truly fine building might have been produced.[81]

Cheadle was no longer perfect.

Lord Shrewsbury had bought the site in 1837, and work had begun in 1841. The church was consecrated by Bishop Wiseman at a private ceremony on 31 August 1846. The next day, the feast of St Giles, Bishop Walsh presided at a Mass sung by Wiseman. The procession consisted of some twenty priests in medieval surplices with at least another forty in full vestments, eight bishops and two archbishops; the bishops included William Wareing, founder of the Cheadle mission and from 1840 Vicar Apostolic of the Eastern District (and Bishop of Northampton 1850–8). Pugin's work further included a presbytery, a school, and a convent adapted from an eighteenth-century building in 1848–9.

Pugin also designed individual items in buildings not his own, including the three windows and the reredos in the choir at Colwich (1837), a screen and other furnishings at Holy Cross, Lichfield (1841), an Annunciation window at Cresswell given in memory of Lady Stourton (1841), and a font with a pinnacled canopy (by 1841) and two coronae at St Austin's, Stafford. He extended such work to Anglican churches. He designed a memorial window in the north aisle of St Mary's, Stafford, commissioned by the mother of John Masfen, who died aged nineteen in 1846; Masfen produced a fine set of drawings of Gilbert Scott's recent restoration of St Mary's, described by Pugin as 'the best restoration which has been effected in modern times'. Pugin designed encaustic tiles for the church built at Leigh by the Bagots in 1845–6 and restored the chancel of the Bagots' parish church at Blithfield in 1851.

It was Pugin who designed the final resting place of St Chad after the relics had spent three centuries wandering through Catholic Staffordshire. Having passed into the custody of the Fitzherberts at Swynnerton in the mid-eighteenth century, the relics were evidently taken to Aston Hall in Stone soon after Basil Fitzherbert's death in 1797 when his widow and the heir, a minor, moved there. The whereabouts of the relics soon became forgotten, but a parcel of six bones was discovered under the altar of the chapel in the Hall, still in the box of 1665, by Benjamin Hulme soon after his arrival as priest at Aston in 1839. St Chad's in Birmingham was then being built to Pugin's design. The bones were taken to Oscott, and Bishop Walsh satisfied himself that four of them were 'reasonably supposed and piously believed to be the relics of St Chad'. When St Chad's was consecrated in 1841, a casket designed by Pugin and containing all six bones was placed over the high altar. He wrote at the time: 'I feel great veneration for the relics of this Saxon bishop which have been I may almost say miraculously restored to us.'[82] In 1995 Archbishop Couve de Murville sent the six bones to Oxford for carbon dating and the resulting report confirmed Walsh's supposition: that five of the bones dated from the seventh century and that four of them could well have belonged to one person; the sixth was dated to the next century. The earthly remains of St Chad of Lichfield, long preserved in Catholic Staffordshire, can now be reasonably supposed to rest in the mother church of the diocese to which Staffordshire belongs.[83]

Pugin did not have it all his own way. Charles Hansom was the preferred architect of William Bernard Ullathorne, Walsh's successor as Vicar Apostolic in 1848 and the first Bishop of Birmingham in 1850 – 'Anything that Pugin can do, Mr Hansom can do better.'[84] The Passionist Dominic Barberi employed Hansom to design St Michael's at Aston, built in 1847–9; Hansom had already designed the church at the Passionist mission at Woodchester in Gloucestershire.[85] It was Hansom who designed the church begun at Rugeley in 1849. At Stone Pugin's chapel of St Anne was absorbed into the

The casket containing the relics of St Chad in St Chad's Cathedral, Birmingham. The angel supporters and the canopy with the figure of St Chad were added in 1931 to the design of Gerald Hardman.

grounds of the Dominican convent built from 1852 largely to the design of Hansom and his brother James. Bishop Wiseman was not present at the opening of St Giles's, Cheadle, in 1846, but a few weeks earlier he had sung the Mass for the opening of Hansom's church of Our Blessed Lady and St Alphonsus at Blackmore Park in Worcestershire.[86]

⁂

The passing of Catholic Emancipation in 1829 was not achieved without strong opposition.[87] In Staffordshire meetings were held in villages and towns throughout the county to draw up petitions to Parliament opposing any grant to Catholics of political power in a Protestant nation and signed by Protestant dissenters as well Anglicans. The feeling is summed up in a motion unanimously passed at the Biddulph meeting in January 1829:

> The granting of any further privileges to the Roman Catholics would be to sanction an alien influence already too considerable in the State – to endanger the safety and prosperity of the Empire – and to break the solemn trust committed to every Protestant in the Kingdom for the inviolable preservation of the constitution as preserved by their forefathers at the Revolution of 1688.

The meeting ended with 'nine hearty cheers for "Protestant Ascendancy"'. Over 100 people signed the petition immediately after the meeting, and within a week there were upwards of 460 signatures. It was intended that those who could not write their own name would not be allowed to sign; but when some colliers appeared after the meeting asking to be allowed to make their mark, the rule was waived. At Hanley some 400 signatures were received, at Norton-in-the-Moors over 500, at Stoke-upon-Trent 1,088, at Newcastle-under-Lyme nearly 1,100, at Leek upwards of 3,000, at Wolstanton (which included Tunstall) 2,400, and at Wolverhampton some 9,000. A separate petition from the clergy of the Stafford archdeaconry was 'most numerously signed'.

A new sentiment, however, is to be found, upholding freedom of worship. At the Norton meeting in December 1828 those present 'utterly disclaim being actuated by any animosity or unfriendly feeling against Papists on account of their religion', rejoicing 'that under the mild influence of Protestant ascendancy civil and religious liberty have been extended to and are fully enjoyed by every British subject'; political power, however, was another matter. At Biddulph 'the meeting, duly impressed with feelings of Christian charity as taught by the doctrines of the Church of England, wishes every man to worship his Maker as he pleases'. At Wolstanton the petitioners claimed that under an essentially Protestant government 'the utmost liberty is allowed to every man to worship God in the manner most agreeable to his conscience and that in matters purely spiritual every individual is altogether unrestricted'. They disclaimed 'all wish to obtain interference, in a legislative manner, with the doctrines of the Roman Catholics among themselves or with the peaceful means which they may deem desirable to extend their tenets'.

The Catholic population was not silent. The Eccleshall meeting was attended by two priests from the area. A counter petition at Hanley received nearly 400 signatures, and another was organised at Newcastle. Wolverhampton was 'in quite a ferment', with both sides promoting their views by 'printed papers' and other means.

The protests were, however, mild compared with the storm which, in Staffordshire as elsewhere, greeted Rome's restoration of the Catholic hierarchy in September 1850.[88] It was seen as an act of papal aggression against the Queen, the British constitution and Protestant freedom. Crowded meetings were held throughout the county during the winter to express Anglican and Dissenting outrage and draw up addresses and petitions to the Queen, the Prime Minister and the Bishop of Lichfield. Following the lead of the Prime Minister, Lord John Russell, the opportunity was often taken to deliver a side swipe at the Trojan Horse of romanising tendencies in the Church of England. The meetings were supplemented by sermons, lectures and burnings in effigy.

At Uttoxeter a crowded three-hour meeting convened by the churchwardens was held on 24 November in the assembly room at the Red Lion. It was preceded by an outdoor event on 5 November when the inhabitants, as reported by the *Staffordshire Advertiser*,

> determined to seize upon the occasion to show their loyalty to the Queen, their love for the reformed Protestant religion, and their execration of the unwarrantable and impudent attempt of the Pope of Rome to establish the Roman Catholic religion in this country ... Accordingly a liberal subscription was set on foot, and a figure representing 'His Holiness' in full canonicals, lighted up with pendant fire balls, was paraded through all the streets amidst the hoots and jeers of the inhabitants, a continual discharge of fire arms, and the cries of 'No Popery', 'Down with the Pope' etc. Eventually the effigy was conveyed into the Market Place, where there was a large bonfire, and having been fastened to a long pole which was tied to the stocks, a general fusillade was carried on, whilst the representative of the so-called succession of Saint Peter was burnt to ashes. The concourse of people present was immense, and doubtless so warm and unanimous a display of strong Protestant feeling was never witnessed in Uttoxeter before.

At the meeting in Newcastle town hall, where anti-Tractarian feeling was particularly marked, J. S. Broad, the incumbent of St George's church, rounded off 'a long and eloquent and very powerful speech' with patriotic verses:

> 'Tis said that we again may bend
>   Beneath the yoke of Rome;
> Again may see the idol Mass
>   Rear'd in our sea-girt home.
> But 'tis not so – our English hearts
>   Recoil from e'en the thought;
> We cannot tamely yield the rights
>   Our fathers' lives have bought.

We're sons of those who sent away
      The Stuart in disdain;
And laugh'd to scorn the Gallic sword
      And spurn'd the Roman chain.
Italian priests shall never rule
      Where stands the English throne;
Our sovereign is God's minister.
      No other sway we own.

Besides the meetings in the towns and villages a meeting for the whole county was held in the Shire Hall at Stafford on 28 January 1851. Although the day was a Tuesday and the time noon, the meeting was attended by upwards of a 1,000. It was chaired by the high sheriff, Josiah Spode, and the speakers included the Earl of Harrowby, Viscount Saint Vincent, Earl Talbot and several MPs. It lasted four and a half hours and ended with three cheers for the Queen followed by 'three groans for the Pope, which also were given with a heartiness truly Protestant'.

Once again there was a Catholic response to the outcry. At a densely packed meeting in Stoke town hall in November the local Catholic priest managed with some difficulty to be allowed to speak from the platform. Another packed meeting at Wolverhampton the next week, with a number of Catholics present, was addressed by both Catholic priests of the town. Subjected to considerable barracking, all three priests stressed the spiritual and non-political nature of the episcopal appointments. At Bilston in December a former Catholic archdeacon gave a lecture on 'Popery – its Crimes and Impositions' and 'met with considerable opposition from the Roman Catholics'. He issued a challenge to meet any Catholic priest, and the next day he and the priest from Holy Trinity held a joint meeting. It was a noisy affair, with the police in attendance. At Longton also in December Edward Daniel gave a lecture in St Gregory's, pointing out that the appointment of bishops infringed no law and encroached on no royal privilege, their jurisdiction being entirely spiritual and confined to Catholics. The *Staffordshire Advertiser* found the tone 'tolerably temperate, considering the exciting circumstances of the times'; it reported that 'the chapel was well filled, a great number of Protestants being present, and the lecture was listened to attentively, not the slightest interruption being at any time offered'.

At Hanley there was even a trace of siege mentality. The Board of Ordnance was making a survey of the district in December, and the soldiers involved put up a temporary structure on the tower of Hanley church. The *Advertiser* published a report under the heading 'The Church in Danger':

> Some of the old ladies of the neighbourhood have associated the appearance of the soldiers on the steeple with the papal aggression and have reported it that the Church being in danger in consequence of the papal attack, the soldiers have come to build a barrack on the steeple and intend to occupy it as a guard till the dispute is settled.

⌘

By 1851 there were thirty-four Catholic places of worship in Staffordshire, with a Sunday Mass attendance of some 8,500.[89] A return made by the clergy to the vicar apostolic in 1847 gave the number of Staffordshire Catholics as 17,695; Wolverhampton, Walsall and West Bromwich had congregations of 2,000 each, Bilston 1,694, Longton with Stoke 1,510, Cobridge 1,350 and Brewood 1,200.[90]

John Henry Newman, preaching at Oscott in 1852 to the first synod of the new bishops, hailed the revival of Catholicism in England as a Second Spring.[91] He contrasted the promise of the present with a past where Catholics had been 'a "*gens lucifuga*" – a people who shunned the light of day'; surviving in remote places, they were 'cut off from the populous world around them, and dimly seen, as if through a mist, or in twilight, as ghosts flitting to and fro, by the high Protestants, the lords of the earth'. It is not a picture which fits the facts, least of all in Staffordshire. The Erdeswicks and the Astons were no ghosts. The eighteenth-century Giffards hardly shunned the light, and the Catholic artisans of Wolverhampton were certainly not invisible when it came to compiling lists. The thirteen chapels registered in 1791 do not suggest a low profile, and their number was approaching a threefold increase some years before 1852.

The spring, as Newman foresaw, continued with the uncertainties of an English spring: a time 'of bright promise and budding hopes, yet withal of keen blasts, and cold showers and sudden storms'. It blossomed into a long summer which turned into autumn only in the late twentieth century.

But that is another story – and another book.

Laus Deo Semper

Notes

1 B. Ward, *The Dawn of the Catholic Revival in England 1781-1803*, ii (1909), chapters xxvi and xxvii; L. J. Bird, 'Recusant Epitaphs in the Midlands', *Mid. Cath. Hist.* vi (1998), pp. 12–13.

2 Ward, *Dawn of the Catholic Revival*, ii, chapter xxxii.

3 Anstruther, *Seminary Priests*, iv, pp. 191-2, 288-9; *V.C.H. Staffs.* iii, p. 110; M. N. L. Couve de Murville, *John Milner* (Archdiocese of Birmingham Historical Commission, publication number 2, 1986), pp. 29–30, 32; *Staffs. Cath. Hist.* xiv, pp. 306–7; D. Meara, 'Monuments and Brasses', in P. Atterbury and C. Wainright (eds), *Pugin; A Gothic Passion* (New Haven and London, 1994), p. 194.

4 *Staffs. Cath. Hist.* xx, p. 16; xiv, pp. 309, 382–4; Anstruther, *Seminary Priests*, iv, p. 209.

5 *A History of the Chapel of St Francis of Sales, Woodlane, Yoxall* (1994); *Staffs. Cath. Hist.* xiv, p. 100.

6 For the Lichfield mission see M. W. Greenslade, 'The Popish of Lichfield', *Staffordshire Studies: Essays presented to Denis Stuart*, ed. P. Morgan (Keele, 1987), pp. 133–6. For Tamworth see also *Staffs. Cath. Hist.* xiv, pp. 323–4; ibid.

xvii, p. 43; ibid. xx, pp. 19–20; C. F. Palmer, *The History of the Town and Castle of Tamworth, in the Counties of Stafford and Warwick* (Tamworth, 1848), pp. 321–3; H. C. Mitchell, *Tamworth Tower and Town* (Tamworth, 1936), p. 79; R. Lewis, *Tamworth and District: a Portrait in Old Picture Postcards* (Seaford, 1994), p. 33.

7   M. Fisher, *Pugin-Land* (Stafford, 2002), p. 14.

8   *V.C.H. Staffs.* xiv, p. 176.

9   Ibid., p.155. It then included the Tamworth area: see below.

10 Below, pp. 238–9.

11 *V.C.H. Staffs.* xvii, pp. 240, 258; *Staffs. Cath. Hist.* xiv, pp. 308–12.

12 *V.C.H Staffs.* xvii, p. 61; *Staffs. Cath. Hist.* xiv, pp. 312–13.

13 *Mid. Cath. Hist.* v, p. 41.

14 W. Pitt, *A Topographical History of Staffordshire* (Newcastle-under-Lyme, 1817), p. 232 (which includes the comment on Richmond's difficulties); *V.C.H. Staffs.* viii, pp. 272–3; *Staffs. Cath. Hist.* xiv, pp. 395–6; F. C. Husenbeth, 'Robert, William and Henry Richmond', xix (1980), pp. 14–15.

15 *V.C.H. Staffs.* viii, pp. 54–5, 70; M. J. Bailey, 'Ashley', *Staffs. Cath. Hist.* iv (1963–4), p. 39; ibid., xx, p. 14.

16 Below, p. 225.

17 *V.C.H. Staffs.* vii, p. 140; *A Short History of the Roman Catholic Church in Leek* [1956], pp. 10, 31–2; *Staffs. Cath. Hist.* xiv, p. 664.

18 J. Connelly, 'St Giles', Cheadle: its Priests 1827–1874', *Staffs. Cath. Hist.* xvi (1976), pp. 4–6. For St Giles's see below, pp. 249–52.

19 *Staffs. Cath. Hist.* xiv, p. 661; F. C. Husenbeth, 'The Very Rev. George Morgan, D.D.', ibid., xviii (1978), pp. 25–6; ibid., xx, p. 20; S. Bliss, 'Ecclesiastical Buildings in Staffordshire by A. W. N. Pugin', ibid., xxii (1984), p. 29; below, pp. 243–4, 246.

20 *Staffs. Cath. Hist.* xx, p. 3; W. White, *History, Gazetteer, and Directory of Staffordshire* (Sheffield, 1834), p. 142; G. T. Lawley, *A History of Bilston* (Bilston, 1893), pp. 223–4.

21 *V.C.H. Staffs.* ix, pp. 130–1.

22 Ibid., v, pp. 166-7, 169; *Staffs. Cath. Hist.* xx, p. 16. The spire was added in 1868. For the dedication see below, p. 233.

23 Below, p. 229.

24 For Stone see Sister Dominic Savio, 'Elizabeth Prout,

Foundress of the Sisters of the Cross and Passion', *Staffs. Cath. Hist.* xix, and 'The Churches at Aston and Stone, Monuments to Blessed Dominic Barberi and Father Ignatius Spencer, C.P.', *Mid. Cath. Hist.* v (1996); E. Hamer [Sister Dominic Savio], *Elizabeth Prout 1820–1864* (Downside Abbey, 1994), pp. 26–7; the Dominican Sisters, *Stone and the Catholic Revival* (1949), pp. 37–8; *Our Lady, Mother Margaret and Stone* [*c*. 1960], pp. 5, 12–13; R. O'Donnell, *The Pugins and the Catholic Midlands* (Archdiocese of Birmingham Historical Commission, publication no. 14, 2002), p. 118.

25 Fisher, *Pugin-Land*, chapter 8; P. J. Doyle, 'Catholics of the Cisalpine School: Thomas Giffard 1764–1823 and William Giffard 1789–1861', *Staffs. Cath. Hist.* xii (1972), pp. 37–8; ibid., xix (1980), pp. 14–16, 20–1; P. J. Styche, *Our Lady of Brewood and 'Little Rome'* (1934; copy in W.S.L.), p. 10.

26 *Staffs. Cath. Hist.* viii, p. 29.

27 D. Bellenger, 'Staffordshire and the French Exiled Clergy', *Staffs. Cath. Hist.* xx (1981), p. 26.

28 *Staffs. Cath. Hist.* iv, pp. 33, 36.

29 Ibid., xiv, p. 308.

30 Ibid., iv, pp. 33–6.

31 Ibid., xiv, p. 584; ibid., xx, pp. 16, 27; *V.C.H. Staffs.* v, p. 167 n.; [F. P. Parker], *Some Account of Colton and of the De Wasteney's Family* (Birmingham, 1897), p. 151; above, p. 106. Mary, wife of Sir Walter Blount, inherited Bellamour as coheir of the 5th Lord Aston (d. 1751): [Parker], *Colton*, p. 149.

32 *Staffs. Cath. Hist.* xx, p. 27; *Mid. Cath. Hist.* vi, p. 11.

33 *V.C.H. Staffs.* viii, p. 272; Holmes, 'The Leith Papers', pp. 91 sqq. (for this see above, p. 204, n. 78).

34 *Oulton Abbey* (brochure published by the abbey, n.d.); Pitt, *Staffordshire*, pp. 232–3; *Staffs. Cath. Hist.* xix, p. 14.

35 Fr Thaddeus [Francis Hermans], *The Franciscans in England 1600–1850* (1898), pp. 136–7; *Staffs. Cath. Hist.* xx, pp. 2–3; J. A. May, 'The Mausoleum at Aston Hall near Stone', ibid., xxii (1984), p. 25.

36 R. Eaton, *The Benedictines of Colwich 1829–1929* (1929); *Complete Peerage*, v, p. 338; M. W. Greenslade, 'Staffordshire Catholics in the 1851 Religious Census', *Staffs. Cath. Hist.* viii (1966–7), p. 26.

37 *Staffs. Cath. Hist.* xx, p. 2; xxii, pp. 25–6; *V.C.H. Staffs.* viii,
p. 272; White, *Directory of Staffs.* (1834), p. 702. By 1860,
when the chapel was damp and dilapidated, the pictures 'were
literally in ribbons': *The Roman Catholic Church in Leek*, p.
13.

38 *Staffs. Cath. Hist.* xx, p. 3; *Mid. Cath. Hist.* v, pp. 39 sqq.;
B. Raynor, 'Monsignor Benjamin Hulme', ibid., ix (2003),
pp. 27 sqq.; F. G. Roberts, *The Church and Parish of St
Wilfrid's, Cotton* (no date, post-1956), pp. 14, 16–19. For St
Michael's see below, p. 253.

39 Roberts, *Cotton*, pp. 5 sqq.; Fisher, *Pugin-Land*, chapter 7.

40 B. Penny, *Maryvale* (Archdiocese of Birmingham Historical
Commission, publication no. 1, 1985), pp. 15–19; I. Ker,
John Henry Newman (Oxford, 1988), pp. 319, 332, 337,
340–2, 344, 347; Roberts, *Cotton*, pp. 13–14.

41 A. W. Pugin, *The Present State of Ecclesiastical Architecture
in England* (1843), pp. 103–5 and plate facing p. 102; O'Donnell, *The Pugins and the Catholic Midlands*, pp. 70–2; B.
Doolan, *The Pugins and the Hardmans* (Archdiocese of Birmingham Historical Commission, publication no. 18, 2004), pp.
17–19; M. Belcher (ed.), *The Collected Letters of A. N. Pugin*,
i (Oxford, 2001), p. 142; Penny, *Maryvale*, p. 19; *V.C.H.
Warws.* vii, pp. 405, 408.

42 White, *Directory of Staffs.* (1851), p. 85.

43 *Staffs. Cath. Hist.* xiv, p. 660; P. Bailey, *Painsley: A History
of Cresswell's Roman Catholic Community 1570–2000* (Market
Rasen, 2005), p. 36.

44 Above, pp. 209, 219.

45 M. W. Greenslade, *St Austin's, Stafford* (Archdiocese of Birmingham Historical Commission, publication no. 8, 2004 edn),
pp. 12–13; J. M Robinson, *The Staffords* (Chichester, 2002),
pp. 78 sqq.

46 A. Andrews, 'Burials at Tixall: a Catholic-Anglican Dispute
1832–3', *Mid. Cath. Hist.* viii (2001), pp. 29–30.

47 Below, p. 235.

48 Above, p. 223.

49 *Mid. Cath. Hist.* v, pp. 41, 43.

50 *V.C.H. Staffs.* v, pp. 153, 167; *Staffs. Cath. Hist.* xx, p. 16.

51 *Staffs. Cath. Hist.* xiv, p. 664.

52 M. J. Fisher, *Alton Towers: a Gothic Wonderland* (Stafford,
1999), p. 143.

53 *Staffs. Cath. Hist.* xiv, p. 663.

54 Above, p. 231; below, pp. 241 sqq.

55 Fisher, *Pugin-Land*, pp. 31, 41–2, 153–5.

56 M. Greenslade, *A Brief History of the Catholic Church in Stoke-on-Trent* (1960), pp. 19–20; M. W. Greenslade, 'Staffordshire Catholics in the 1851 Religious Census', *Staffs. Cath. Hist.* viii (1966–7), p. 32.

57 *Staffordshire Studies*, p. 134.

58 Greenslade, *The Catholic Church in Stoke-on-Trent*, pp. 32–4; Sister Mary Cecily O.P. and Sister Mary Barbara O.P., *Mother Margaret Hallahan in Staffordshire* (*Staffs. Cath. Hist.* x, 1968), p. 8.

59 *V.C.H. Staffs.* v, p. 167.

60 *Staffs. Cath. Hist.* viii, p. 32.

61 Ibid., iv, pp. 36 sqq.

62 Above, pp. 190, 211, 219.

63 P. J. Doyle, 'The Giffards of Chillington, a Catholic landed family, 1642–1861' (Durham University M.A. thesis, 1968), pp. 243–5.

64 Above, p. 219.

65 *V.C.H. Staffs.* iii, p. 113.

66 Above, p. 235.

67 Above, p. 220.

68 Above, p. 211.

69 *V.C.H. Staffs.* xvii, pp. 145, 241.

70 For this section see Penny, *Maryvale*, pp. 9–15; Couve de Murville, *Milner*, pp. 20–1; J. F. Champ, *Oscott* (Archdiocese of Birmingham Historical Commission, publication no. 3, 1987), pp. 2–8; J. W. Clarke, 'Devotion, Confraternity and the Social Dimension in Victorian Walsall', *Mid. Cath. Hist.* x (2004), pp. 26–7.

71 E. Norman, *The English Catholic Church in the Nineteenth Century* (Oxford, 1984), pp. 13–14.

72 For this section see Fisher, *Pugin-Land*; O'Donnell, *The Pugins and the Catholic Midlands*; Doolan, *The Pugins and the Hardmans*. For Alton Hospital and the Handsworth convent see also A. W. Pugin, *The Present State of Ecclesiastical Architecture in England* (1843; reprinted in facsimile, Gracewing, Leominster, 2004), pp. 87–90, 103–5.

73 Belcher (ed.), *Letters of Pugin*, i, p. 127.

74 Ibid., p. 137.

75 *V.C.H. Cheshire*, iii, p. 194.

76 Belcher (ed.), *Letters of Pugin*, i, p. 78, n. 1.

77 St Augustine's, Solihull, begun in 1838, was opened in February 1839; St James's, Reading, was begun in 1837 but not finished until 1840.

78 Ibid., i, p. 307.

79 White, *Directory of Staffs.* (1851), p. 766.

80 Above, pp. 223, 229, 231.

81 A. W. Pugin, *Some Remarks on the Articles which have recently appeared in the "Rambler" relative to Ecclesiastical Architecture and Decoration* (1850), p. 9. He was caustic about the painting of the chancel at Brewood by 'a devout amateur' and also the painting of the walls ('it might have been produced by a troop of beetles crawling through a paint pot and then up the plaster'), adding that 'I have no doubt that if the "Rambler" critics saw it, they would exultingly exclaim, "Ah, there's Pugin's taste, that is the way he daubs everything over."': ibid., p. 11.

82 Belcher (ed.), *Letters of Pugin*, i, p. 243.

83 M. W. Greenslade, *Saint Chad of Lichfield and Birmingham* (Archdiocese of Birmingham Historical Commission, publication no. 10, 1996), pp. 16–18, 23, 25–6.

84 Doolan, *The Pugins and the Hardmans*, p. 11.

85 *Mid. Cath. Hist.* v, pp. 41–3.

86 M. Hodgetts, *Blackmore Park 1596–1846–1996* (1996), p. 14. Pugin designed the metalwork: P. Stanton, *Pugin* (1971), p. 206.

87 For this section see M. W. Greenslade, 'Staffordshire and Catholic Emancipation, 1829', *Mid. Cath. Hist.* xi (2005).

88 For this section see M. W. Greenslade, *Staffordshire 'No Popery' 1850–1* (*Staffs. Cath. Hist.* xxi, 1982).

89 *Staffs. Cath. Hist.* viii, pp. 23 sqq. These 1851 Religious Census returns include Abbots Bromley, with no background details, the chapel at Moseley Hall, and the chapel at Sedgley Park school.

90 *V.C.H. Staffs.* iii, p. 113.

91 G. O'Neill (ed.), *Readings from Newman* (1923), pp. 186–7, 195.

INDEX

'Fr' is prefixed to the names of (post-Reformation) regular priests only; secular priests were not so styled in the period covered by this book. English places not identified to a (pre-19th-century) county (except for towns giving their names to counties) were wholly within Staffordshire until the 19th century or later. References in **bold** type are to illustrations and their captions.